# Finding Dahshaa

*Stephanie Irlbacher-Fox*

*Foreword by Bill Erasmus*

# Finding Dahshaa

Self-Government, Social Suffering,
and Aboriginal Policy in Canada

**UBC** Press · Vancouver · Toronto

20   19   18   17   16   15                              5   4

Printed in Canada with vegetable-based inks on FSC-certified ancient-forest-free paper (100% post-consumer recycled) that is processed chlorine- and acid-free.

---

**Library and Archives Canada Cataloguing in Publication**

Irlbacher-Fox, Stephanie, 1971-
    Finding dahshaa : self-government, social suffering, and Aboriginal policy in Canada / Stephanie Irlbacher-Fox.

Includes bibliographical references and index.
ISBN 978-0-7748-1624-3 (bound); 978-0-7748-1625-0 (pbk);
978-0-7748-1626-7 (e-book)

    1. Native peoples – Northwest Territories – Politics and government. 2. Native peoples – Northwest Territories – Government relations. 3. Native peoples – Northwest Territories – Social conditions. I. Title.

E92.I75 2009              323.11970719'3              C2009-900926-9

---

Canadä

UBC Press gratefully acknowledges the financial support for our publishing program of the Government of Canada through the Book Publishing Industry Development Program (BPIDP), and of the Canada Council for the Arts, and the British Columbia Arts Council.

This book has been published with the help of a grant from the Walter and Duncan Gordon Foundation.

**All author's royalties from sales of this book will be donated to the Educational Scholarship Fund of the Délînê Land Corporation (Northwest Territories).**

UBC Press
The University of British Columbia
2029 West Mall
Vancouver, BC V6T 1Z2
604-822-5959 / Fax: 604-822-6083
**www.ubcpress.ca**

When Heaven's servants had made the earth, they took something resembling the hide of a large moose which was soft to the touch, and they spread it over the earth's surface.

Then they lifted it up again and the earth had become more beautiful.

Six times they repeated this process and that was how the world was made so beautiful.

My mother used to tell me that heaven created the earth.

– Dene Nation, *Denendeh: A Dene Celebration*

# Contents

# Illustrations

# Foreword

*Bill Erasmus, Dene National Chief*

This book is an important contribution to the study of the relationship between the Dene and Canada. Dr. Irlbacher-Fox is non-Indigenous, and she has spent most of her life living and working in Denendeh among the Dene, Métis, and Inuvialuit peoples. She has listened to us using both her mind and her heart, which shows in the passion and conviction she conveys in her research and writing. I welcome her contribution to bringing to light aspects of both the strengths and the struggles of the Dene.

In 1973, the Dene won a long-fought victory in the *Paulette* decision, a court decision that shattered the myth that Dene had surrendered their lands and extinguished their Aboriginal rights. In that court case, Fort Smith Chief François Paulette led the Dene to assert their place as stewards of Denendeh in the face of major development. Dene were then, as they are now, a majority of the residents in the Northwest Territories. The *Paulette* decision clearly stated that Treaties 8 and 11 that Dene had entered into with the Crown were not ones of extinguishment. Dene already knew that their ancestors had not given up the land and that the treaties described terms of peace and friendship. Treaty 8, which extends into the northern parts of Saskatchewan, Alberta, and British Columbia, was entered into not only by us but also by our Indigenous neighbours. Therefore, Canada must recognize that all numbered treaties are ones of peace and friendship and then address the articles of the treaties accordingly.

Despite the *Paulette* decision, Canada still maintains that it owns Dene lands, where generations of Dene far into the future will continue to live. Being Dene is to live as part of the land. Dene conceive of "land" not in the capitalist sense as a patch of ground legally surveyed, registered, and paid for. For Dene, the land is not property, which is the way Canada would prefer Dene to see it. The concept of land for Dene is understood as what non-Indigenous people would call the ecosystem or all of the life – animate and inanimate – that makes the world whole: earth, air, water, minerals, insects, animals. The reality that Dene are part of the land will never change. When the Dene are forced to articulate their relationship to the land in Canada's terms, they assert collective ownership, which Canada has great difficulty in understanding because its Constitution is based on individual rather than collective rights. If Canada truly wishes to move forward in its relations with Indigenous peoples, it must accept that Dene and the land are indivisible. As Raymond Taniton is quoted as saying in the Introduction, Dene people cannot change into something else. So to assert that the Crown owns Dene lands is to assert that it has divided Dene from themselves. That makes no sense.

In 2008, Canada offered an apology for what generations of Indigenous peoples were forced to endure at residential schools. That experiment, of forced spiritual and social assimilation through institutionalization, failed not simply because it was executed with such evil brutality and inhumanity. It also failed because, despite everything, Dene and other Indigenous peoples continued to be who they are. Indian residential school survivors are here because they continued to love the land, to care for themselves and for each other. They, their families, and their communities found their strength and themselves in the timeless knowledge and beliefs of their people. Not everyone made it, and many still struggle. Indigenous peoples have come through that suffering and continue to move through and away from it on the strength of being Indigenous, rooted in their lands and ways of life. As part of the Indian residential school settlement, the prime minister of Canada apologized for the Indian residential school tragedy. Canada was required by the settlement to make an official apology. Action must be taken that will make that apology a living sensibility within Canada's Aboriginal policy. That sensibility would strive to understand and work with Indigenous peoples on the basis of who they know they are, not on the basis of what Canada thinks Indigenous peoples might or ought to be. If residential schools have taught Canada anything, it is that any policy based on changing Indigenous peoples, "to kill the Indian," as its first object, will ultimately fail.

Instead, there is a need to focus on the impulse toward reconciliation promised by the Truth and Reconciliation Commission, which began its work in 2008. People need to be able to tell their experiences, be listened to, and witness evidence that they have been heard. Evidence must be found in changes to Canada's approach to addressing the realities of Indigenous peoples. It would include Canada supporting the Declaration on the Rights of Indigenous Peoples, which the Harper government voted against in the United Nations General Assembly during 2007. It would also include Canada moving beyond diagnosing the deplorable conditions in

Indigenous communities and enabling communities to engage in innovative and sustainable measures to improve lives. It would include Canada reviewing all of its policies that are premised on the attitudes that resulted in tragedies such as Indian residential schools and ensuring that there is no continuity between such attitudes and policies and the ones that inform how Canada approaches initiatives with Indigenous peoples today. As this book shows, colonial attitudes are entrenched in the policies under which Canada negotiates today. And, finally, that evidence would include Canada accepting that Indigenous peoples are who they say they are and making social and political space for Indigenous peoples to exist as Indigenous peoples, in the spirit of the original treaties of peace and friendship that we continue to honour as the basis of our relations with Canada.

# Acknowledgments

I am grateful for the opportunity to share the experience and knowledge in this book. Many people provided support and encouragement along the way. Among these, my first debt of both love and thanks is to my husband, Andrew, who is the rock on which my life is built, and to our sons, Everett and Simon.

For a non-Indigenous researcher, this sort of work demands constant personal decolonization. The love and stability provided by my family are critical in steadying me through that continuing journey. So too are the encouragement and intellectual validation offered by friends and colleagues. In particular, I thank Taiaiake Alfred, whose insights have been invaluable and whose own writing is so inspiring.

Early development of this work at Cambridge University was guided with great patience by Barbara Bodenhorn of the Department of Social Anthropology. Subsequent versions of the manuscript benefited from comments provided by Nigel De Souza and Elana Wilson; I thank Scott Duke for excellent editorial suggestions. At various points throughout research and writing, ideas were shaped by advice and encouragement from Piers Vitebsky, Michael Bravo, James Tully, Joyce Green, Colin Samson, Frances Abele, Michael Asch, Graham White, and the late Vine Deloria, Jr.

At home in the Northwest Territories, friends took time from their own commitments and responsibilities to aid me in my research. In particular, Dene National Chief Bill Erasmus gave generously of his time to teach me about Dene peoples, ways of life, and struggles, and I continue to learn much from him. Mahsi cho and quyanini to Bob Simpson and Vince Teddy for their friendship and collegiality. I want to thank Danny Gaudet for convincing me five years ago to work on Délînê negotiations for just three months and allowing me to experience that very special place, Délînê. I thank

Albert Lafferty and the Fort Providence Métis Council for the opportunity to research Dehcho Métis political history, a rich and rewarding experience working with council members and learning much about the place of the Métis peoples in the NWT. During fieldwork research, a number of government officials and negotiators from both the territorial and the federal governments participated in interviews, and although for reasons of confidentiality I cannot name them here I wish to thank them for their time and generosity, without which this book would not be possible. I would also like to acknowledge a debt of gratitude to the late John Bayly and the late Elder Albertine Rodh, who each gave generously of their time during the course of my research.

I have had the privilege of working for the community of Délînê on its self-government negotiation process for the past five years and continue to benefit from the generosity and wisdom of my many friends and colleagues there. Mahsi to Danny and Gloria Gaudet, Elders Alfred Taniton and Leon Modeste, Morris Neyelle, Jane Modeste, Patricia Modeste, Fred Kenny, A.J. Kenny, Raymond Tutcho, Raymond Taniton, Leroy Andre, Peter Menacho, and Les Baton. For the past several years, I have had the opportunity to work with incredible women committed to tanning moosehides; I thank them for their friendship and acknowledge their awesome strength: Denise Kurszewski, Diane Baxter, Ruth Wright, and Elaine Alexie. Mary Barnaby, Judy Lafferty, Margaret Kelly, and Mary Louise Drygeese, mashi for your patience and kindness, and for such generosity in sharing your knowledge. I would also like to thank friends whose wit and wisdom have sustained me during the life of this project: Candy Hardy, Kim Thompson, Ginger Gibson, Shannon Ward, Wynet Smith, Jackie Price, Julie Jackson, and Elder Bertha Francis.

I wish to express my gratitude for the efforts of several individuals in the production of this book. To Brandy Wilson, thank you for your friendship, artistic soul, and inspiration. And to the editorial staff at UBC Press, Jean Wilson, Darcy Cullen, Anna Eberhard-Friedlander, Holly Keller, and Laraine Coates, I am sincerely grateful for your dedication and commitment to seeing this project through.

Several institutions provided funding that allowed pursuing the research on which this book is based. For providing both funding and such a convivial and magical intellectual home during my years at Cambridge, I wish to warmly acknowledge Master Duncan Robinson and Fellows of Magdalene College, particularly Dr. Mark Billinge; the Donner Foundation; the Cambridge Commonwealth Trust; Director Julian Dowdeswell and the staff of the Scott Polar Research Institute; and the Social Sciences and Humanities

Research Council of Canada. The Walter and Duncan Gordon Foundation provided a generous grant to cover publication costs of this book; for that and for all of their wonderful work supporting research and community development projects throughout Northern Canada, I wish to thank the Board of Directors and James Stauch, manager of the foundation's Northern Program.

# Pronunciation Guide

| | |
|---|---|
| Délînê | Day-lee-nay |
| Délînê Got'ine | Day-lee-nay Go-tee-nay |
| Gwich'in | Gwit'-chin |
| Inuvialuit | Ee-noo-vee-a'-loo-eet |
| Liidlii Kue | Leed'-lee Kweh |
| Tłîchô | Klee-chon |
| *dahshaa* | Daa-sha' |
| Dene | Deh-neh |
| Inuvik | Ee-noo'-vik |

# Finding Dahshaa

# Introduction

Canada comes up with new programs and policies for Native people all the time. Self-government is one of those. It's like Canada is on this long journey, where bit by bit they are able to understand rights of People [Dene]; they are just at the beginning stage. And sure, we will sit with them and take those programs, that's for our People. What they haven't understood yet is that we are Dene, and nothing will change that. No policies or money or agreements or whatever. We are Bear Lake People, we have always lived here. We are not like the Mountain Dene, for instance. They live over there and have their ways, their area. We have our ways. That lake we depend on. And yet we get along with the Mountain People, even when we are different. It has always been like that. It will be like that a thousand years from now too. We are Dene, and that will never change.

> – Former Délînê Land Corporation president
> Raymond Taniton (interview, 2005)

This book is among the first of many analyses of self-government negotiations. It seeks in part to understand and deconstruct assumptions and premises of Aboriginal policy in Canada. The quotation above gives voice to an experience of a consistent message of Aboriginal policy in Canada: Indigenous peoples must change, and government can provide the tools, programs, and funds necessary to change. Change has many dimensions and is to various ends: more sophisticated governance tools; greater control; healthier communities; better educational attainment; modernizing practices and ways; achieving certainty of rights and lands and resources ownership. It seems that circumstances require change of Indigenous peoples, an adaptation necessary to achieve living conditions, life chances, and lives similar to those of other Canadians. It seems there is much to change about Indigenous communities, governance practices, cultures, and values.

Is it Indigenous peoples who need to change? Or might something else need to change?

This book presents a different perspective on change and Indigenous peoples, namely that Aboriginal policy itself should change to provide a far more effective route to improving the lives and life chances of Indigenous peoples.[1] This refocusing would result in changing oppressive circumstances rather than requiring people to change to better cope with oppressive circumstances. Change would substantively (rather than symbolically) redress injustice and accommodate indigeneity instead of requiring change of Indigenous peoples in terms of their cultures, lifeways, and rights.

By examining self-government negotiations in the Northwest Territories (NWT), we can see how Canada promotes Indigenous change as a way to accommodate and normalize ongoing injustice as the basis of relations between the state and Indigenous peoples. Through positioning both Indigenous peoples and the injustices they suffer as non-modern and historical, and itself as a source of social, political, and material redemption, the state manages to legitimize both injustice and its ongoing colonial-based interventions into the lives of Indigenous peoples. This positioning is explored in the context of self-government negotiations through a combination of discourse analysis, narrative evidence of both Indigenous peoples and government negotiators, and ethnographic description of Dene moosehide tanning that functions as a Dene cultural referent for understanding Indigenous perspectives and interactions that take place during negotiations. To begin, this introduction overviews key conceptual and theoretical insights grounding the analysis in subsequent chapters.

## Self-Government and Land Claims

This book is based on research into self-government negotiations in the Northwest Territories, Canada. It is not about land claims or co-management – although land claim negotiations and agreements are closely related to those of self-government. Land claims and self-government rights and authorities as understood by the Canadian state are distinct and until the 1995 Inherent Right Policy were dealt with separately. Despite this, land claim authorities are sometimes described as elements of self-government. However, in this book, the self-government rights and authorities being referenced are those under discussion in self-government negotiations proper.

Although there is an extensive literature on land claim and co-management arrangements in Canada based on experiences during and after their implementation (Berkes 1999; Berkes and Henley 1997; Feit 1998; Nadasdy 2003; Scott 2001; Spaeder and Feit 2005; Usher 2003), a parallel literature on self-government simply does not exist. A few self-government arrangements have been negotiated under the Inherent Right Policy, but there is very little scholarship on either the negotiation or implementation of self-government agreements, with the significant exception of contributions being made respecting the British Columbia Treaty Process (Penikett 2006; Woolford 2005). Instead, most scholarship tends to focus on legal and theoretical aspects of self-government or program-based examples of local control of programs or services (Belanger 2008; Hylton 1999; see also Newhouse and Belanger 2001). This is largely due to the fact that few self-government arrangements have been negotiated and implemented.

## Ongoing Injustice

Injustice toward Indigenous peoples in Canada is not only historical. It is also on-going. Historical injustices are discrete, specific events experienced by communities and individuals. For example, dispossessing a First Nation of lands without consent or the Indian Act's outlawing cultural and spiritual practices. In contrast, ongoing injustice is the complex of existing policies, state institutions and governing arrangements, and fraudulent land and resource transactions that continue to be imposed on Indigenous peoples. These range from the existence of the Indian Act itself to Canada's assertion of ownership over lands and resources never relinquished by Indigenous peoples. Ongoing injustice includes the persistent colonial relationship between the Canadian state and Indigenous peoples. The legal relationship structured by statutes such as the Indian Act is evidence of this,[2] as are Third World living conditions plaguing Indigenous communities.

The content of the state's Aboriginal policy is based on both its legal obligations to Indigenous peoples and what the governor general of Canada in 2004 called the "shameful conditions" that many Indigenous communities suffer.[3] Yet it does so from a vantage point where shameful conditions are seen as a combination of legacies of "historical" injustice and the clash between modernity and indigeneity. So the only option is to work for a better future. This is because circumstances resulting in present conditions are characterized as unchangeable: past wrongs that stand as lessons to be learned from rather than injustices to undo. In that view it is only the nature of indigeneity that can change, specifically its perceived temporal quality of pastness. And so Aboriginal policy focuses on "present suffering" as though that suffering were unrelated to injustice and instead primarily the result of poor lifestyle choices and the non-modern nature of indigeneity itself.

This approach says that to assert that injustices matter is to live in the past and that chances for a better life emerge only if the past is left behind, because circumstances created "in the past" will not change. It requires that Indigenous peoples themselves must change – that is, from being Indigenous to being Indigenous in a way that reconciles Indigenous rights, interests, and being with what conforms to the norms of the Canadian Constitution, democracy, and dominant culture. Self-government (not self-determination) is designed to achieve this.

Conventional wisdom on solving the "Indian problem" (or, alternatively, the colonizer problem) suggests change of either the state or Indigenous peoples. It takes the form of proposing indigenization of the state and its agencies, various models of Indigenous assimilation, or power-sharing proposals that maintain the continuity of the institutional status quo. These suggestions seek to better accommodate difference and so restore Indigenous peoples to wellness by changing Indigenous cultural norms to better operate within those social and political structures that have been oppressive to Indigenous peoples. Such change among Indigenous and non-Indigenous peoples and institutions will mean that finally Aboriginal rights are meaningfully reconciled with Canadian sovereignty.

Recent writings of scholars such as Glen Coulthard (2007), Paul Nadasdy (2003), Colin Samson (2003), and Dale Turner (2004) have shown that solutions emerging from the indigenization/assimilation paradigm such as land claims, self-government, and co-management have failed expectations. For those of us who live and work in predominantly Indigenous communities or within the Indian rights industry, this is no surprise.

Fortunately, a new paradigm advocating Indigenous resurgence has begun to be advanced by Indigenous scholars, a paradigm responding not only to the evident policy failure but also to the de-spiriting of the people that results from that failure. Developed through activist Indigenous scholarship advocating strategies for social and political change through personal rejection of colonization and regeneration of culture (Alfred 2005), writers have applied these concepts to personal and collective resumption of Indigenous ways to a range of diverse topics such as governance (Wilson and Yellow Bird 2005), pregnancy and birthing (Simpson 2006), and diet and exercise (Mihesuah 2003). As developed in the work of Taiaiake Alfred (2005), the paradigm rejects addressing Indigenous social suffering through redemptive programs of the state and instead proposes un-doing the causes of suffering through Indigenous resurgence as determined by Indigenous peoples, drawing on Indigenous philosophical and cultural ways. It calls for a rejection of colonized mindsets, among both Indigenous peoples and settlers, and, instead, a regeneration of Indigenous cultures through freedom in thought and action from a colonial relation between Indigenous peoples and the settler state. Resurgence, by opting for Indigenous connection to lands, resources, and cultures in peaceful ways outside the colonizer's sanction, presents a far greater challenge to the Canadian state than any legal reconciliation of Aboriginal rights with Canadian sovereignty. It poses a challenge to the key component of all Aboriginal policy that says Indigenous peoples must change (specifically "modernize") as the only route to (Western notions of) wellness and prosperity. The resurgence paradigm proposes ending suffering through self-decolonization and self-determination of individuals and collectives: Indigenous peoples being true to their Indigenous ways.

A fundamental element of this radical notion, that Indigenous peoples can find peace through being culturally, spiritually, intellectually, and physically themselves, drawing on all the tradition and change that entails, requires acknowledging the nature of injustice not simply as dispossessions, ongoing structures of injustice, and banal indignities imposed by a colonial state. It requires rejecting the notion that the state cannot undo injustice and that injustice and present suffering are disconnected. If the mounting evidence of massive policy failure is considered, Indigenous resurgence presents the only viable path toward replacing Indigenous assimilation and social suffering with Indigenous being and well-being as the basis for Aboriginal-state relations.

This book takes up from the resurgence paradigm, partly by adding to the literature documenting shortcomings of Aboriginal rights-reconciliation approaches taken over the past thirty years in Canada (see Ladner 2001; Green 2003, 2008; Nadasdy 2003; Penikett 2006; Samson 2001; Woolford 2005). It shows that self-government negotiations marginalize and exclude Indigenous peoples' experiences and aspirations, to the point that agreements reached do not represent a form of self-determination but rather another iteration of colonization and forced dependence. This is shown partly by offering a theory of Aboriginal policy accounting for the role of what may be seen as often well-meant but ultimately misdirected actions perpetuating rather than alleviating social suffering among Indigenous peoples.

Canadian Aboriginal policy does not take responsibility for present suffering or for ongoing injustice. Its emphasis on both injustice and things Indigenous being historical restricts state actions to symbolic reparations and programs addressing present suffering, as though present suffering was not related to injustice. Meanwhile, injustice becomes embedded and normalized as the basis of the relationship between Indigenous peoples and the state. Self-government negotiations offer a window into understanding how this policy approach is expressed in concrete terms. The following chapters contain examples of how Canada, through its policies' temporal characterizations of injustice toward Indigenous peoples, denies and obscures the true sources of Indigenous peoples' suffering, namely the dispossession of lands, resources, and self-determination, which are only symbolically instead of substantively redressed through processes such as land claims and self-government.

Before discussing the differences between self-determination and self-government, it is important to explain why land claims can be viewed as symbolic rather than substantive reparations. Generally, land claims are evaluated at face value: if the government gave anyone millions of dollars, ownership of lands, and rights to resources, it would be a substantive settlement in the capitalist sense of having a cash or market value. News stories emphasize such values of land claim settlements, making much of market values of lands and resources, trilling about millions of dollars for small populations of individuals.

The fact that Canada does not live up to its legal obligations under land claim settlements is discussed in a later chapter. Implementation problems aside, it is important to understand that lands returned to Indigenous people under settlements usually represent small percentages of the original Indigenous territories. Rights to depleted resources are recognized but simultaneously curtailed by participation in and adherence to land and resource management regimes and regulations that consider settlers' and settler governments' interests, not just those of Indigenous peoples. Cash components of land claim settlements equal a small fraction of the market value of lands given up and do not provide "back-rent" or compensation for depletion or use of resources and lands since they were illegally dispossessed. The lands that are returned are subject to expropriation by the state, and most do not include sub-surface rights; agreements also ensure that access across returned lands by government or third parties is not impeded. As for the millions of dollars? Generally in the NWT, land claim organizations have placed most cash received from agreements into a combination of trusts and investments, since cash provided under final agreements is itself final. Since after the settlement is finalized most Indigenous lands and resources are no longer theirs, and the cash payment is the only one Indigenous peoples will receive, it must last for future generations. Payouts to individuals, if any, are usually from the proceeds of investment interest, amounting to several hundred dollars per adult per year. Individual access to funds may take the form of employment in Indigenous-owned companies, which also employ significant numbers of non-Indigenous people (see, for example, Aarviunaa 2004), and access to funding for education or cultural pursuits. Notably, some land claim governments have used income from investments to fund healing programs dedicated to cultural and social cohesion, to address the types of social suffering specific to a collective colonial experience.

Taken at face value, land claim agreements do lead to significant political recognition and rights recognition, including access to resources and land ownership. However, what is exchanged for the settlement is also significant: lands alone that Indigenous peoples must relinquish rights and title to are worth many, many times the market value of lands restored to Indigenous peoples. The spiritual and psychological values of the lands are often inestimable. Although some authority and participation in decision making are recognized, what is recognized does not nearly approximate the freedom Indigenous peoples enjoyed prior to the settler government asserting sovereignty. This is why land claims can be viewed as symbolic: they are settlements that return small fractions of lands, resources, and authorities to Indigenous peoples, and in that sense the settlements to a great extent cement rather than change the fundamental dominant-subordinate relationship between the state and Indigenous peoples.

## Self-Government and Self-Determination

Self-government should not be confused with the concept of self-determination. Self-government is a term denoting the extent to which Canada is willing to recognize Indigenous peoples' authorities in a range of areas, from education to natural resource management. Self-government (as the term is used throughout this book) refers to the various authorities available for negotiation as determined by the Canadian state, deriving from within the Canadian legal and constitutional framework. On that view, self-government is something that exists because Canada exists, circumscribed by Canadian law. Self-government is therefore not viewed as an aspect of self-determination that can exist apart from or outside of the Canadian constitutional framework. During 1995, Canada first officially recognized Indigenous peoples' inherent right to self-government within its Inherent Right Policy. The policy describes in detail Canada's view of the scope, nature, and extent of self-government, prescribing a limited framework for negotiations.[4] Canada's approach has been ostensibly to reach "practical arrangements" on how the right will be implemented rather than defining the right in an abstract sense. The series of events leading up to the establishment of the Inherent Right Policy included national consultations with Indigenous peoples and the failed Meech Lake (1990) and Charlottetown (1992) Constitutional Accords. These accords, negotiated between federal-provincial-Indigenous leaders, were meant primarily to address Quebec's concerns over the Canadian constitution and issues about the federal-provincial division of powers. In addition to recognizing Quebec as a distinct society, the 1992 accord recognized the Aboriginal right of self-government. These events, combined with first ministers-Indigenous leaders conferences during the 1980s about the nature and extent of Aboriginal rights, established broad-based consensus among Canadian government leaders that self-government is an existing right that should be implemented.

Self-government agreements are meant to describe the practical implementation of the right of self-government without extinguishing rights, but this has not been the case in practice. Certainty clauses have resulted in the agreements providing de facto definitions of the scope and extent of the right. Imposed by the federal government, certainty clauses require Indigenous peoples to express their inherent right to self-government only as described in the self-government agreement. Although the agreement may provide that aspects of the inherent right not dealt with in the agreement may be negotiated at a later date, certainty clauses essentially extinguish those un-negotiated aspects. For example, in section 2.6 of the Tłîchô Agreement (2003), detailed certainty clauses include "cede, release, and surrender" language in reference to future rights conflicting with those described in the Tłîchô Agreement. Although many Indigenous negotiators are inclined to negotiate agreements establishing stability in their community's governance institutions, certainty is seen as a double-edged sword, providing stability while jeopardizing future negotiation of self-government rights that are not currently recognized in federal policy.

At negotiating tables, federal mandates are shaped by the content of completed self-government agreements (such as the 2003 Tłîchô Agreement), which are precedents used for comparison in other negotiations. Governments also emphasize the importance of harmonizing programs and services delivered by different governments, including program standards. Although often viewed as reasonable goals by all parties, compatibility and harmonization requirements may occasion burdensome administrative arrangements between governments or may prevent self-governments delivering services in a culturally appropriate manner. In addition, authorities may be fragmented between governments where Canada's view is that the inherent right extends only to specific aspects of a subject area. For example, a First Nation may have authority to pass laws yet will be denied the ability to establish a court system, resulting in First Nation law being prosecuted and enforced by non-Indigenous courts or enforcement officers. Essentially, self-government agreements are about the sharing of authority between different governments. However, in the NWT, often authorities secured in a self-government agreement may not extend beyond authorities available under current federal and territorial policy. For example, Canada's First Nations Policing Policy allows for establishing First Nations police forces, which are not uncommon in the provinces. However, establishing First Nations police forces is not possible through self-government agreements negotiated in the NWT simply because the territorial government has not yet passed a policing law. Legally, until the territorial government occupies that field of jurisdiction delegated to it by Canada under the NWT Act, that jurisdiction cannot be shared (see Irlbacher-Fox 2008).

That self-government and self-determination are two distinct concepts is borne out by the way communities view self-government agreements in relation to their circumstances and futures. In the NWT, I have not encountered an Indigenous community or people that has defined in precise detail a static conceptualization of self-determination or self-government. Even where Indigenous negotiators have detailed mandates ensuring accountability to their communities, the negotiations environment is bounded by the Inherent Right Policy and government mandates and is in that sense driven largely by government rather than Indigenous mandates. Indigenous peoples' concepts of self-government do not necessarily describe specific institutional arrangements or the nature of authorities sought. Instead, these concepts provide general policy directions to Indigenous negotiators, providing flexibility to develop innovative mechanisms consistent with the fundamental values, goals, and aspirations expressed through their communities' visions of self-determination.

Visions of self-determination among Indigenous peoples I have worked with far exceed the limitations of self-government. Indigenous visions encompass natural resource management and economic capacities gained through land claims; seek sectoral or other agreements with governments and private industry; and have social, political, psychological, and spiritual dimensions resulting from the importance placed upon fostering Indigenous cultural identity, rights, and practices. Indigenous peoples therefore combine what requires change, namely the interference and control of government, and the negative consequences of that, with a collective sense of self-realization originating in Indigenous culture. And every Indigenous people has distinct senses of how that might shape practical arrangements negotiated through self-government and the various other agreements negotiated with the federal and territorial governments, industry, et cetera. One element all visions have in common is acknowledging the importance of flexibility in self-governing arrangements. This is because legal and policy environments change and evolve. As Indigenous institutions develop they can expect to engage with forces that are local, national, and global in scope and with changes encompassing social, political, spiritual, cultural, and environmental dimensions.

Self-government agreements are not viewed as the answer to all social and economic ills of Indigenous communities or as some final stage in a continued effort toward decolonization or reaching a mutually respectful partnership with Canada. Indigenous negotiators and elders have explained to me that agreements are viewed as one tool available among the many possibilities that may assist communities to achieve self-determination. They recognize that self-government agreements are imperfect, and often disappointing for communities, but the utility of an agreement is measured with a view to how it fits within the bigger picture and over the long term.

Often the utility and efficacy of self-government agreements are subject to how they are implemented. Frustration over land claim implementation has resulted in the establishment of the twenty-one-member Land Claim Agreement Coalition (LCAC), a group consisting of all comprehensive land claim governments in Canada, established to lobby Canada about common implementation concerns.[5] The LCAC has held two conferences to discuss common issues and concerns, with the goals of initiating a federal implementation policy and improving federal land claim implementation practices. Its credibility has been significantly enhanced by audits by the Canadian auditor general calling for greater consistency and accountability and a more realistic approach to implementing federal land claim obligations (see, e.g., Government of Canada, Auditor General of Canada 2003). Land claim implementation flaws have subsequently led to scrupulous attention and significant resources being expended on implementation planning and readiness activities in advance of self-government agreements. As I have noted elsewhere (Irlbacher-Fox 2008), unless conditions creating an enabling environment exist, agreements and the rights they purport to implement may be rendered meaningless in practice.

## Structure of the Book

The book explores how Aboriginal policy is expressed through self-government negotiations in the NWT, based on three case studies drawn from negotiations between Canada and the Inuvialuit and Gwich'in, the community of Délîne, and the Dehcho First Nations. They provide a sense of the diversity of circumstances, peoples, and potential of self-government negotiations in the NWT. The core of the analysis focuses on the relationship between ongoing injustices experienced by Indigenous peoples, the resulting social suffering, and self-government, prompted by the following three questions: How are injustice and social suffering relevant to the parties to self-government negotiations? How do government negotiators interpret and engage with injustice and suffering narratives during negotiations? Can self-government agreements address injustice and the resulting social suffering of Indigenous communities?

The case studies give a sense of how negotiations over different law-making authorities are shaped by both social suffering and the ways in which the state denies its role in perpetuating ongoing suffering. The case study drawn from the Dehcho process focuses on resource revenue sharing as an element of self-governments' financial independence from other governments which is an important element of the Dehcho vision of self-determination. Similarly, discussion of jurisdiction over Child and Family Services in Délîne allows a glimpse into how areas of jurisdiction may speak directly to the spiritual, social, and cultural resurgence at the heart of First Nations' motivations to negotiate. The example drawn from the Inuvialuit and Gwich'in negotiations over heritage, culture, and language reveals ways in which events viewed as "historical," even by Indigenous peoples themselves, continue to breathe and flex within peoples' lives and may in a sense be deepened when their relevance is denied recognition.

The contours of suffering, and how suffering is expressed and received within negotiations contexts, are drawn out largely through analytical tools borrowed from Iris Marion Young's (2000) theory of democratic decision making as applied to discourse within negotiations and sociological analyses of social suffering after Veena Das (1995). Young's theoretical insights are discussed in the context of the Dehcho case study, used to highlight the way that communicative norms of the state and those of Indigenous peoples can learn from or alternatively talk past one another. These are themes built on through subsequent examples. Das's concept of a state "theodicy" is applied to the settler-state's colonial-induced suffering, suffering remade as inherent Indigenous dysfunction, used to simultaneously distance the state's causal role in suffering and present that suffering as a rationale for ongoing state intervention. This argument is developed primarily in Chapter 4 by examining the negotiations of Délįnę's authorities over Child and Family Services. The final case study provides an example where both incommensurate communicative norms and the theodicy's denial of state responsibility for suffering are brought to bear on an Inuvialuit negotiator's experience of residential school, a phenomenon that is a root cause of social suffering throughout Indigenous communities in Canada. Through this analysis, ways in which state policy and its orientations narrow and often predetermine negotiating outcomes are elucidated in terms of the types of self-government authorities discussed in negotiations. The final chapter takes up from the insights provided through examining the negotiating process, turning to discuss how agreements based on current policies will continue to promote suffering. It includes consideration of how Indigenous peoples' governments are forced to both compromise and strategize to obtain the tools they require to realize Indigenous visions of self-determination.

Ethnographic descriptions of Dene moosehide tanning provide a sense of the cultural context grounding self-government negotiations. Drawn from the author's experiences working with Sahtu elders and Gwich'in and Inuvialuit women tanning several moosehides over successive summers, tanning descriptions provide a Dene cultural referent for understanding the self-government process. The purpose is to relate social dynamics resulting from a cultural enterprise based on a collective animation of Dene values and ways and so function as an ethnographic contrast to the dynamics of the negotiations process. Moosehide tanning and its purpose are introduced fully in Chapter 2. One obvious distinction between negotiations and moosehide tanning is that, although negotiations are largely a male-dominated activity, moosehide tanning is the realm of Dene women. These contrasting activities themselves provide a gendered element to this study.

My perspective as a non-Indigenous practitioner and academic is tempered by over a decade of working exclusively for Indigenous peoples' organizations on self-government and related community development and territorial political development processes in the Northwest Territories. This included four years working as a full-time assistant negotiator and then a further three years as a consultant to the joint Inuvialuit and Gwich'in self-government negotiations (from 1996 to 2003), and for six years (from 2002 to the present) as a political advisor on the Délînê First Nation and Land Corporation's self-government negotiation team, and in support of their participation in NWT Devolution and Resource Revenue Sharing negotiations. In addition, I conducted six months of fieldwork in the Dehcho region during 2001 and then worked for four years (from 2003 to 2007) as a political advisor and researcher for the Fort Providence Métis Council, a member of the Dehcho First Nations.

This experience informs the perspective from which this book is written and I believe has opened up a unique way of seeing self-government negotiations. Although I was raised in Inuvik, NWT, my professional experience has meant travelling extensively throughout northern Canada to witness different negotiations and different cultures and peoples throughout. Despite the differences, in all places where I have worked, a critical motivation of Indigenous peoples for negotiating self-government seems always to be about achieving better lives and life chances. This book was written to provide insight into why self-government negotiations are so important and into the disconnection between the way Indigenous peoples and the state view self-government's purpose, a disconnection that has a profound effect on negotiation outcomes. My hope is that this book contributes to the identification of issues, problems, and challenges in both the negotiating processes and the policies shaping those processes. And that policy makers, scholars, and activists might make use of its insights to bring us closer to finding a way toward a just relationship between the state and Indigenous peoples in Canada.

# 1

# Context and Concepts

## Self-Government Negotiations in the NWT

Negotiations over lands, resources, and governance between Canada and Indigenous peoples in the Northwest Territories have been ongoing for the past thirty years, processes analyzed to different degrees in works on northern political development (Cameron and White 1995; Dacks 1990; Dickerson 1992; Kulchyski 2005). Canada first began negotiations with Dene peoples in 1899 and 1921, entering into Treaties 8 and 11 respectively, in order to exploit northern mineral potential. "Half-breed" (Métis) Scrip Commissions accompanied the Treaty Commissions, seeking release of Métis Aboriginal rights. The Inuvialuit, approached about taking treaty in 1929, refused (Fumoleau 1976, 274). This chapter provides an overview of political development in the Northwest Territories with respect to Indigenous peoples' organizations and their struggle for rights recognition and assertion. It describes the self-government negotiations process in a generic sense, as background to the case studies in subsequent chapters. That description is followed by a discussion of main theoretical concepts fleshed out through the case studies, namely the concepts of social suffering and the dysfunction theodicy at the heart of the state's Aboriginal policy.

## The NWT Context

Inuvialuit territories in the far northwest corner of the NWT, extending into the Beaufort Sea, are bordered inland by the delta and mountains of the Gwich'in (Dene). Their territories are rich in natural gas and mineral deposits respectively. Southeast of the Gwich'in are the Sahtu Dene, North Slavey peoples who include the Mountain, Bear Lake, and Hare, whose mixture of boreal forest and tundra lands anchored by the pristine freshwater Great Bear Lake includes significant oil reserves and is being increasingly staked for minerals such as uranium and silver. Their neighbours to the southeast are the Tłîchô Dene. The barrenlands, forests, and freshwater

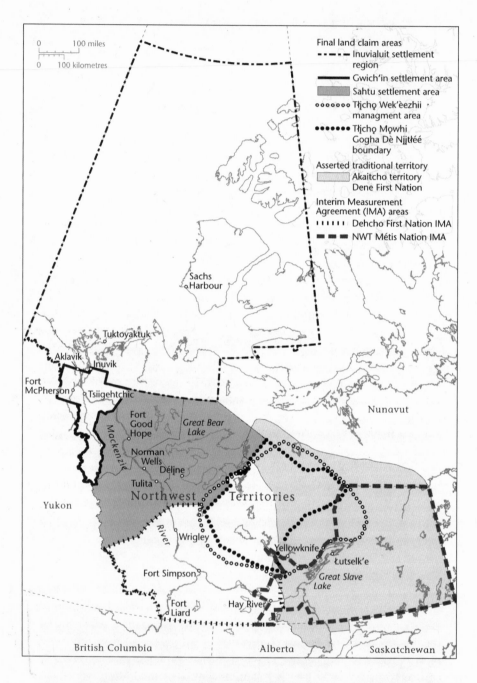

*Map 1*  Settlement areas and asserted territories within the NWT.
*Source:* Government of the Northwest Territories, Department of Aboriginal Affairs and
Intergovernmental Relations.

lakes in Tłîchô territory, bordering their Inuit neighbours to the north and Akaitcho (Chipewyan) Dene to the south, have become home to Canada's first four diamond mines since the 1990s. Southwest of the Akaitcho are the Dehcho (South Slavey) Dene, whose resolve to refuse development of significant oil, natural gas, and mineral potential in their traditional territories without adequate land protection and Dehcho involvement in decision making has resulted in unstable and protracted negotiations with Canada over lands, resources, and governance since the early 1990s. Different  ent Métis peoples share these homelands with the Dene, most notably the Northwest Territory Métis Nation in the southern part of the Akaitcho area, the Sahtu Métis peoples, and the several Métis locals accepted as Dehcho First Nations. Formerly united through the now defunct Métis Association of the NWT, each Métis people now represents itself politically. ⟵

Although Dene entered into treaties with Canada in the early part of the twentieth century, their incomplete implementation and significant differences between Canada and Dene about their interpretation resulted in additional agreements being sought through the comprehensive land claim negotiations process. The Dene/Métis comprehensive land claim process was initiated in part as a result of a court case known as the *Paulette* case.[1] Fort⟵ Smith Chief Francois Paulette, along with sixteen NWT chiefs, attempted to register a caveat on the Mackenzie Valley lands in part to stop the construction of the Mackenzie Gas Pipeline. In 1973 Justice Morrow of the NWT Supreme Court found that there was substantial evidence that the Dene did not believe that Treaty 11 had extinguished their Aboriginal rights to the area and that treaties were unfulfilled. Although the ability to register a caveat was overturned by Canada's Supreme Court, the findings with respect to Aboriginal rights were not overturned. Within months of that decision, the Supreme Court of Canada decided the *Calder* case.[2] In *Calder*, the court determined that Aboriginal title of the Nisgaa' in British Columbia existed in common law. However, the court was split as to whether Aboriginal title had been extinguished. Three judges believed that it had not been extinguished by statute or treaty and three that it had been extinguished prior to British Columbia entering Confederation. The chief justice decided the case against the Nisgaa' but without ruling on whether Aboriginal title existed. Although specific to the Nisgaa', it was widely believed that the case had implications for Aboriginal title in other parts of the country. Canada was prompted by the findings of the *Paulette* and *Calder* rulings to hold public hearings on the pipeline (hearings that became known as the Berger Inquiry, see Berger 1977) and subsequently enter into negotiations with Dene and Métis (Chambers  1996; Dene Nation 1984; Watkins 1977).

Initially, Dene, represented by the Indian Brotherhood of the NWT (now

Dene Nation), worked together and in partnership with the now disbanded Métis Association of the NWT to negotiate an "umbrella" claim, similar to that of the Yukon First Nations. The coalition was tenuous, both among Dene regions and between the Dene and Métis. The Inuvialuit, who had originally begun negotiating an agreement in partnership with other Canadian Inuit peoples, decided during the mid-1970s to negotiate a separate agreement due in part to the increasing oil and gas exploration in Inuvialuit territories at the time.

Land claim processes heralded the emergence of Dene, Métis, and Inuvialuit peoples as leaders and decision makers challenging Ottawa's colonial control of the NWT, exploitative practices of multinational business interests, and dominance of resident white politicians and administrators. An energetic cadre of Indigenous activists, young men and women in their early twenties who after forming social networks at residential schools, and through their education in elite high school programs and university, were inspired by human rights and Indian rights movements sweeping North America to challenge the oppressive treatment that wrought poverty and misery in their communities. With the support of leaders and elders, they were in a position to analyze their situation and articulate Indigenous views in ways that could be neither ignored nor refuted by colonial administrators. The Indian Brotherhood of the NWT emerged after several years of increasing activism by Dene leaders during the late 1960s, supported by a strong Dene culture and spirituality. The Dene Nation (1984) describes various social movements among the Dene taking place in the 1960s and 1970s, such as the establishment of co-operatives, friendship centres, Dene language school instruction for children, the recognition of prophets, and increasing ties with other Indigenous peoples and leaders supporting the Dene cause. At a meeting convened by Indian Affairs officials in Yellowknife during 1968, chiefs and band representatives repeatedly dismissed government officials from their presence when discussing ideas about forming an association to resolve treaty issues. The following year a decision to establish a national park in the Lutselk'e Dene territory was met with local resistance, prompting a delegation of twenty-one government officials to meet with the chief and community to pressure for their consent. Affronted, Chief Pierre Catholique convened a meeting of chiefs in Yellowknife soon after, inspiring commitment among leaders to support one another. According to Chief Catholique, "never again will one chief sit down with many government people. From now on, if 21 government people come to a meeting, 21 Indian leaders must come and sit across the table from them. From now on, we the chiefs, must talk with the government only when we are all together" (Dene Nation 1984, 24). Dene activism of the 1970s culminated in the Dene Declaration, passed unanimously in 1975 at Liidlii Kue (Fort Simpson). Issued on the heels of the *Paulette* and *Calder* decisions resulting in Canada instituting a formal land claim policy, it articulated a Dene vision of self-determination within Canada. Specifically, it identified both Canada and the Government of the Northwest Territories as illegitimate governments, imposed on the Dene without consent, and called for recognition of Dene self-determination.

The Dene/Métis negotiations, which were ongoing during the same time period as the Berger Inquiry hearings, were a time of intensive research by Dene on their culture and history and political relations with Canada. Similarly, the Métis Association of the NWT conducted its own extensive oral history and cultural research, including research on the Scrip Commissions that had accompanied the Treaty Commissions. Together, the Dene and Métis conducted extensive land use and occupancy research and mapping.

The Dene/Métis claim negotiations lasted until 1990, when an agreement was reached with Canada. Throughout the two decades of its negotiations, the Dene and Métis relationship, and relations between different Dene regions, were at times tumultuous. Questions about the recognition of rights and identity of Métis peoples in relation to the Dene and the different economic pressures on the various Dene regions resulted in the coalition's increasing instability as the negotiations progressed. In 1990, Dene negotiators recommended an agreement to their people that included an extinguishment clause. The clause would have extinguished Dene/Métis Aboriginal rights in Denendeh in exchange for the rights as recognized in the agreement. Agreeing to the extinguishment contradicted the consistent instructions of elders that maintaining ownership and control of the land, and the ability to live on the land, were more important than money; the land was not for sale. At the Dene assembly in the summer of 1990 convened for the purpose of ratifying the agreement, instead of ratification approval, negotiators received extensive instructions for renegotiating the agreement. Canada subsequently refused to continue negotiations with the Dene Nation.

Instead, on November 12, 1990, Canada announced it would negotiate individual land claim agreements with Dene regions wishing to enter talks on the basis of the unaltered 1990 agreement. The Gwich'in, facing considerable development pressures and seeing land claim benefits accruing to their Inuvialuit neighbours, were the first to enter talks, reaching an agreement in 1992. The Sahtu Dene and Métis settled during 1993. Having reached agreements before the inherent right of self-government was recognized, the Gwich'in, Sahtu, and Inuvialuit are currently involved in self-government negotiations. The Tlîchô Dene reached an agreement during

2003, the first combined comprehensive land claim and self-government agreement in the NWT. North Slave Métis, headquartered in Yellowknife, have yet to achieve a process, and the Fort Smith-based Northwest Territory Métis Nation have reached an agreement in principle on a lands and governance agreement. Treaty land entitlement talks with Akaitcho Dene and the Dehcho process negotiations are ongoing.

### The Negotiations Environment

Self-government negotiations in the NWT are the result of Canada's legal obligations described in land claim agreements and federal policy. The Gwich'in and Sahtu land claim agreements include provisions where Canada commits to negotiating self-government, detailed in Chapter 5 and Appendix B of each agreement. The Inuvialuit agreement, signed in 1984 prior to political consensus being reached among federal and provincial leaders that an Aboriginal right to self-government existed, contains a "trigger" provision, 4.3, whereby the Inuvialuit are entitled to engage in talks about reshaping the regional public government alongside any other Native group who may engage in such a process. Consequently, the Gwich'in Agreement's guarantee of self-government negotiations triggers section 4.3 of the Inuvialuit Agreement. The federal 1995 Inherent Right Policy describes the scope and extent of self-government rights to be addressed in self-government negotiations. Taken together, land claim agreement provisions and federal policy provide a clear description of the types of power that can be negotiated under self-government. These documents also recognize that the form of self-government will differ between regions and possibly even between communities within the same region. In addition, they reflect the federal preference that in the NWT self-government be combined with public government – municipalities and regional government – responsibilities, a preference particularly suited to smaller communities where the vast majority of people are Indigenous.

Negotiations are a bureaucratic construct, based on policies, procedures, and practices developed by governments. Negotiations are initiated by Indigenous peoples' governments, who may seek a process based on a land claim agreement obligation, within the context of negotiating a comprehensive claim, or a stand-alone process. Indigenous peoples' negotiators participate but often have little success in changing or significantly shaping the formal procedures that structure the conduct of negotiations. Every negotiation is governed by a process and schedule agreement describing which subjects are to be negotiated, a time frame to achieve an agreement, and "ground rules" guiding the process: recognition of each party's representatives, frequency of meetings, et cetera.

Governments possess seemingly unlimited personnel and expertise and have access to funding and resources far outstripping those of Indigenous negotiators. They also set the limits on what can be negotiated by establishing "bottom lines" (positions from which they will not waver) in mandate documents, which must be consistent with their various internal policies, jurisdictional and legal frameworks, and political interests. In contrast, Indigenous peoples' negotiating teams receive funding according to their adversaries' funding policies once negotiations start. They are required to submit reports on expenditures, sometimes including the products of their research and consultations, to Indian and Northern Affairs Canada (INAC), with whom they are negotiating. Often funding levels are determined according to criteria unrelated to the nature and amount of work required to negotiate, criteria conforming exclusively to INAC's or the Canadian Treasury Board's own administrative logic. Indigenous negotiators may also have mandates, usually determined based on consultations with both leaders and community members.

As elaborated in the following chapters, the frequency and format of negotiations vary depending on the circumstances and policies shaping them. As a rule, NWT negotiations are conducted in English, with Indigenous language translators present depending on demand and the ability of Indigenous organizations to pay for the service out of their yearly funding. Negotiating sessions are usually held for three to five days each month and usually in the communities that will be affected by the agreement. Held in meeting rooms ranging from corporate board rooms to community halls, the public sessions' atmosphere varies depending on the level of contentiousness or comfort generated by the issues under discussion and individuals in attendance. Meetings usually take place during business hours, beginning at 9 a.m., breaking for lunch, then continuing until 5 p.m. each day. Position papers, generated by individual teams based on their internal research (or, in the case of Indigenous teams, also through community consultation), are tabled by the parties at sessions or prior to sessions and are public documents, with the occasional exception of government positions which may be marked as confidential to the table and its participants. Confidentiality may apply when governments are tabling positions or information that may prejudice or misinform discussions at other negotiations to which they are party.

Community-based meetings are marked by a casualness of dress and demeanour among the parties often absent in the more formal meetings held in major centres where officials of various government departments are often present in addition to their negotiating teams. For community sessions, negotiators may wear jeans and casual shirts, suitable for travel by small aircraft or several hours' drive on ice roads to meetings in small communities, often in temperatures falling below -30° Celsius during the winter months. Accommodations in communities range from comfortable to rustic, with arrangements occasionally complicated by unexpectedly being "weathered in," usually when small aircraft are unable to fly due to storms or fog.

Indigenous peoples' negotiators are usually Indigenous individuals having extensive knowledge of community, territorial, and federal institutions as well as fluency in the culture and/or language of their people; they may or may not have a university education. In contrast, the usually university-educated government negotiators are generally non-Indigenous, having little background or experience of Indigenous communities or issues. However, particularly for federal government teams, it is not unusual for one or more of the Ottawa-based team members to be Indigenous. As well, Canada's chief negotiators are hired on contract by the minister of INAC and may have close personal or political ties to that minister.

Although non-Indigenous negotiators' lack of knowledge of Indigenous peoples can significantly slow the pace of negotiations in some respects, it also provides an opportunity for Indigenous peoples' negotiators to educate government negotiators in an attempt to increase the likelihood of government negotiators taking a more sympathetic approach to negotiations. This is the Indigenous negotiator's double burden: to educate government negotiators away from erroneous assumptions, or plain ignorance, toward an Indigenous understanding of the negotiating context. Government negotiators have discretion to control the pace of progression through their mandates and may sometimes use that discretion strategically. According to one government negotiator, "I have seen colleagues power-trip at negotiations; there are situations where they have pulled things off the table or refused to give on something that is well within their mandates. Sometimes it's strategic; sometimes it's just to bring the First Nation negotiator under control, or it's about their own ego, where they want to get back at a First Nation negotiator who made them angry" (Federal negotiator, interview, 2002c). Generally, boardrooms are favoured as negotiating sites over hunting or fishing camps, although the latter are sometimes sites of negotiation. For example, the Délînê negotiating team has had "on-the-land" negotiating sessions; one in particular was used specifically to have the federal negotiator educated by the elders. Elders spent several days at the camp relating oral traditions about the Prophet Ayah and discussing how oral traditions influence the community's vision of self-determination. It was also an opportunity to teach the federal negotiator and the other government representatives about the lands, fish, and animals near Délînê that the people rely upon for their spiritual, material, and cultural existence. For at least one government negotiator, a similar initiation and ongoing education and experience in the community changed him in what he regards as profound and personal ways. A former federal negotiator on another file also reported being profoundly affected by learning through individual interaction:

> Negotiating has had an effect on my perspective on Aboriginal rights and on me as a person. When I started negotiating, from an academic perspective I believed in Aboriginal rights, and my views were supportive, and I felt I had a good understanding academically. You can't understand what is being lost, what people are fighting for, until you see it for real. There is a real lack of understanding [by the public] of the human side. For example, when people say Aboriginal people are just there for handouts; then you go and see an elder in a community when it's minus forty degrees outside, with plastic bags on her feet because her slippers are worn out. Or when you represent the thing [the government] that has devastated their culture and then they invite you in for tea ... I'm a different person now. Nothing is black and white – I look for the grey; there is so much to learn from people ... It has humanized the academic understanding I had; I am more willing to push boundaries [inside government] as a result." (Federal negotiator, interview, 2002c)

However, despite the efforts of Indigenous negotiators, there are some government negotiators who simply refuse to see self-government issues informed by an Indigenous experience. One government negotiator I spoke with saw no reason why it might be necessary to be sympathetic to the Indigenous position. According to the negotiator, each party comes to negotiations with specific goals and is responsible for achieving those goals to the best of his or her ability. He believed there was no requirement of him to push boundaries to assist Indigenous negotiators; for him, all parties were aware of the mandates and legal frameworks within which a deal would be negotiated. For another government negotiator, "feeling" was not a factor. When pressed on how it felt personally when the First Nation he was negotiating with refused to recognize the Government of the Northwest Territories (GNWT) at negotiations (which he represented), he responded, "you don't take it personally. It's just another factor you deal with at negotiations. At other tables there are other issues that arise. You just deal with those, and eventually when it gets down to the details people realize that we are the government that has the experience and has to be dealt with. It's just another factor in the negotiating environment that has to be waited out" (Territorial negotiator, interview, 2002a).

Among Indigenous peoples' self-government negotiators, strategies at the table are often reflected in their interpersonal relations with government negotiators. The observation of the federal negotiator grappling with the irony of being invited to tea by the people whose lives the government had destroyed crystallizes a constant tension within self-government negotiations. One observer's remark to me revealed a sense of futility, frustration, and distrust that many Indigenous negotiators have gained through personal experience: "How do you negotiate with people who hate you?" Often, awareness of this tension complicates personal interactions and negotiations strategy. This generates its own type and level of stress when negotiators work together intensively for one or two weeks each month, over a period of years.

Different Indigenous peoples' negotiators manage personal interactions differently. At some tables, such as the Dehcho First Nations during 2000, a non-Dene negotiator and advisors viewed government negotiators simply as the enemy – with suspicion and distrust – and often treated them with rudeness and derision. It was a surprising contrast with the strong yet respectful and dignified approach of the Dehcho leaders themselves. Coupled with the non-Dene negotiator's tendency to release his reactions to government negotiating positions through the media rather than at the negotiating table, the atmosphere of the negotiations was one of tension and distrust. In contrast, the community of Délînê, represented by Délînê elders and a Métis negotiator selected by leaders and elders, built strong personal and professional relationships with Canada's negotiator, in order to educate the negotiator on the aspirations and circumstances of the community. The result was a highly participatory atmosphere fostering open discussion. The Inuvialuit and Gwich'in, represented by Inuvialuit, Gwich'in, and non-Indigenous negotiators, conducted their negotiations in a cordial yet reserved manner with Canada's representatives. Although those negotiations were sometimes heated, individuals often exchanged pleasantries, shared meals, and ended each session on a genial note. According to one former federal negotiator,

> We are all here to solve the same problem, stuck with each other for at least a week every month – the least we can do is try to be civil to one another. We're all in this thing together after all. For God's sake, sometimes it's like I've got Stockholm syndrome – I actually miss it! I think we are lucky to be here that way ... I have heard that this is one of the best negotiations files in the country to have, because we see each other as people, and that many other negotiations can get acrimonious. I think that spending energy and time disliking each other would not be a very

productive way to approach this file; things get done more quickly if you create an open and co-operative atmosphere rather than a difficult one. Overall, doing this job is not easy, but I think all the teams have very good people on this file, and it shows in our progress. (Federal negotiator, interview, 2002b)

Negotiations are an intense and demanding pursuit; for all participants they involve weeks away from home for negotiations and related meetings; mentally and emotionally demanding days are spent in stuffy boardrooms, punctuated by meetings and shared meals with team members discussing and debriefing the day's events and issues. For Indigenous peoples' negotiators serving more than one community, additional requirements include travel to provide information and consult at community and leaders' meetings. Between sessions, all parties have the task of generating technical analyses and responses to negotiating proposals, informing and receiving instructions from their respective leaders, and for Indigenous negotiators planning and doing regular community consultations.

It is not unusual for government negotiators to be invited to community events or for the Indigenous team to sponsor a community feast and meeting where residents have the opportunity to talk with negotiators and ask questions about the agreement and issues being negotiated. In addition, government negotiators may be invited to community workshops and meetings on specific issues relevant to negotiations, to immerse them in the local culture, including exposure to experiences and issues which Indigenous negotiators are asked to have resolved through the negotiations. Holding negotiations in Indigenous peoples' communities is another way to provide an overall sense of the people and place the agreement will affect, their day-to-day living conditions, and local issues. In this way, government officials can experience to some extent how policies developed without reference to context interact with communities' realities. However, it is up to individual negotiators to integrate what they learn with their role within the bureaucracy and at negotiations.

### Recipes for Explosions
A striking characteristic of self-government negotiations in the NWT is that few chief negotiators are women. On this issue, one of the few female chief negotiators had this to say:

I'm not sure why there are no women negotiators. It's not a very fun job. It used to be, but now it's a grind. It just keeps going on and on and just gets frustrating. The other thing is that women have two jobs to do – raise their kids and do the wage labour, and negotiations involve lots of travelling and high stress. There was a survey on negotiators in INAC a couple years ago, and it found that the divorce level is three times as high among negotiators. It's a stressful job – you go away for a week where everyone craps on you, and you get home, and you are drained. There is nothing left to give. To me it's all about boundaries – you have to set them.

And that is particularly true with Aboriginal rights negotiations. It's a very emotionally charged atmosphere. You are dealing with a population that is suffering and living with the consequences of colonization. Those wounds are very fresh and very alive – the negotiations often conjure up those fresh experiences.

As a government, you see right there that you have destroyed a people. They are dysfunctional, their communities are suffering, and it is very personal. So you have to set boundaries on a personal level as a way to facilitate getting through that. And then when you get non-Native negotiators who go in there and don't have the cultural awareness or know the history behind that – it's just a recipe for an explosion. (Territorial negotiator, interview, 2002b)

Although her answer and the rest of our conversation assisted me in analyzing the participation of women in negotiations, what was striking was the way it also revealed the nature of the relationship between other characteristics of negotiations: the prevalence of individual and community suffering narratives in negotiations and the inability of government negotiators to engage with suffering at both personal and policy levels. The conversation I had with her that day provided a critical insight about self-government negotiations: the negotiations and their outcomes are about defining governmental authorities in a way that neither validates nor addresses the experience or resolution of social suffering endemic to Indigenous communities.

For many, particularly government negotiators, such a disconnection seems reasonable. One familiar refrain heard from many government negotiators in response to suffering narratives arising during negotiation discussions is "I'm not here to change the past. I am here to negotiate self-government." And the primary reason communities negotiate is not to change the past; rather, it is to limit to the greatest extent possible the continuing interference and control of governments and outsiders. This is in part because the past has certainly taught valuable lessons: governmental and non-Indigenous control that has wrought incomprehensible Indigenous destruction, from the first waves of disease and dispossession to the present continuing control under the Indian Act. It is present suffering, such as poverty, disease, social pathologies, and addictions, that can be traced both to past injustices and to ongoing injustices and policy ineptitude that provide a major impetus for negotiating. Canada's first attempt at adjudicating claims and providing monetary compensation to Indian residential school survivors is one such example of ongoing injustice. It was abandoned when a government audit found that 90 percent of initiative funding was spent on the bureaucracy rather than being paid to claimants. An all-party parliamentary Standing Committee on Indian and Northern Affairs found that

> The Committee is drawn to the inescapable conclusion that the Alternative Dispute Resolution (ADR) process is an excessively costly and inappropriately applied failure, for which the Minister and her officials are unable to raise a convincing defense. Specifically the ADR process is a failure because:
>
> 1 It is strikingly disconnected from the so-called pilot projects that preceded it.
> 2 The consultative mechanisms that informed its development did not include a sufficiently broad range of participation by former residential school students and other relevant professionals – legal, cultural, psychological and healing.
> 3 It is failing to provide impartial and even-handed due process.
> 4 It is not attracting former students to apply in credible numbers.
> 5 It is structured to compensate too narrow a population of former students.
> 6 It provides grossly inadequate compensation when, grudgingly, it does so.
> 7 It excludes too many of the some 87,000 remaining former students from eligibility.
> 8 It is proceeding too slowly, allowing too many former students to die uncompensated.
> 9 It is using a model of dispute resolution that is disrespectful, humiliating and unfeeling and re-victimizes former students, who are now elderly and vulnerable.
> 10 It is an arbitrary administrative solution that is vulnerable to political whim.
> 11 Its high structural costs are fixed and will always be disproportionate to the size of compensation granted.
> 12 Its so-called verification process imposes an egregious burden of proof on the applicants that programs failure into the resolutions process, requires irrelevant data and imposes a cost on the applicant that can exceed the size of an award.
> 13 Former students do not trust the process.[3]

When Indigenous negotiators seek control of a jurisdiction, for example education, they have not only the argument that the inherent right of self-government requires the government to recognize Indigenous control. They also have numerous stories of residential school survivors, of public school curriculum deficiencies, of inadequate facilities and low graduation rates in communities to back up their arguments. Those are the types of arguments repeatedly given to Indigenous negotiators by community members at community consultations on negotiations. A clear message from communities, applicable to all government authorities being negotiated, is that there is a profound lack of trust in the government. This is based on wide-ranging experience of all generations, over the long term, which informs peoples' expectations of government action in the future.

However, government negotiators view their task as far more focused. Committed career bureaucrats are given a mandate to represent their governments' interests in reaching agreement on how to share powers over government services with Aboriginal governments that are perceived as having little relevant experience and huge capacity deficits. In its task, the government is to protect the rights of all people and to ensure that programs and services are delivered to a consistent standard within and between territories and provinces. In this sense, knowledge and experience that do not directly relate to discharging jurisdictional or administrative authorities are irrelevant. The governmental focus on determining power-sharing arrangements in accordance with its own political interests and without regard to community aspirations and experiences often results in the silencing of suffering narratives and Indigenous peoples' negative experiences of government control.[4] Yet perhaps this silencing does not occur intentionally, for the government position often is "The experiences you describe are regrettable. We are talking about legal jurisdiction over health care/education/et cetera, which is very costly to deliver, is highly technical, and in which you have no experience, and which must conform to uniform standards throughout the territory." Suffering wrought by external control is not a valid rationale in a negotiations context that focuses on addressing Indigenous peoples' legal rights. Valid rationales for increased Indigenous control are ones that prove a legal claim to authority or satisfy practical concerns about program delivery.

It is this last requirement that captures the irony that suffering is both silenced and used as a rationale by government to deny aspects of self-government. For it is the suffering, the social pathologies, the "capacity deficits" created through ongoing colonization that are a concern both in discussions of jurisdictional authority and in its implementation. The government's paradoxical treatment of suffering is brought into stark relief in later chapters: suffering is not acceptable as a rationale for greater Indigenous control yet is a standard rationale for ongoing state intervention in and exercise of discretion over Indigenous authorities contained in self-government agreements.

## Social Suffering

Descriptions of negotiations provided in this chapter would be incomplete without understanding what is meant by the term "social suffering" and its significance to Indigenous peoples' motivations for negotiating. Later chapters give diverse descriptions of the nature and effect of social suffering experienced in different communities and how suffering experiences inform Indigenous negotiating mandates. This section details the concept of social suffering. I begin from the understanding that the complex of colonialism in Canada – discrete historical events; ongoing injustices; and legal, social, and institutional structures and norms – induce social pathologies among Indigenous peoples. Throughout the book, descriptions of suffering and its significance are not intended to appropriate voices or reinscribe the pain and suffering of Indigenous peoples. Concern about reinscribing pain by scholars who write about suffering is prevalent throughout the social suffering literature (Wilkinson 2005). However, like scholars who write of the suffering of peoples in many places, the purpose here is to include suffering as an analytical category that otherwise would escape the conceptual bounds of academic disciplines unfamiliar with or unwilling to engage with suffering as a relevant component of the experience of social or political phenomena. Indeed, one of the motivations for choosing to analyze self-government through the lens of its implications for social suffering, and vice versa, is to illuminate the relationship between the two that has been silenced in both scholarship and the negotiations processes. However, this focus is intended neither to sensationalize nor trivialize suffering, nor to replace with academic understandings the voices and experiences of individuals who bear suffering in their daily lives. Rather, focusing on suffering as a category of analysis is meant to scaffold a "politics of hope" (Wilkinson 2005): to generate awareness of the many forms in which Indigenous peoples' social suffering is both caused and exists and how these forms have relevance for self-government negotiations. It is also meant to recognize the social and political importance that witnessing suffering has to contributing to social and societal change. As E.V. Daniel, a writer who examines social suffering wrought by the violence among Tamil peoples in Sri Lanka, states, "one may avoid [such] problems by doing nothing" (1996, 5). I have chosen to witness an important and much unanalyzed reality that is overwhelmingly present yet

unspoken, in both self-government scholarship and self-government negotiations in Canada. In doing so, the purpose is also partly to correct a
widely held confusion of suffering with dysfunction, a terminological distinction elaborated below.

The term "social suffering" is used in part to expand understandings of
the consequences of inequality, injustice, and oppression within social and
political norms and institutions. Conceptualizing social pathologies that
result from injustice as a category known as social suffering allows us, in
part, to "devise sociological and anthropological scripts for bearing witness to the lived experiences of suffering" (Wilkinson 2006, 1). Writing
on the human experience of suffering is not new: philosophers since the
1800s have been concerned with the nature of suffering and its implications for humanity. However, in recent years, as is noted by Wilkinson
(2005), scholars have turned to exploring lived experiences of suffering in
terms of its impact on sufferers, its meaning for social life, and its gene-
sis within social, political, and economic structures. Within scholarship
in Canada on Indigenous peoples and colonization, indigenous-state relations, and related literature, social pathologies in Indigenous communities
are acknowledged as being primary motivators for political change (Adams
1999; Alfred 1999; Asch 1985; Cook and Lindau 2000; Hylton 1999; Warry
1998). However, only recently have Indigenous-specific social pathologies
been conceptualized variously as historical trauma or social suffering.
Naomi Adelson's (2001) work was among the first to conceptualize
pathologies common to Indigenous communities in Canada specifically
as social suffering resulting from colonization, and the concept of social
suffering has increasingly been applied to the situation of Indigenous peoples in Canada (see Samson 2008 and other contributors to Kirmayer and
Valaskakis 2008). And the historical trauma paradigm theorized by Maria
Yellow Horse Brave Heart and Lemyra DeBruyn (1998) has increasingly
gained currency among academics concerned with identifying the social
impacts of colonization among Indigenous peoples in Canada (Kirmayer and
Valaskakis 2008; Wesley-Esquimaux 2007).

Generally, social suffering research is ethnographically grounded, in part
to put a human face on the "everyday miseries" encountered by marginalized groups of people (Bourdieu et al. 1999). Since the 1990s the concept
of social suffering has grown in terms of disciplinary reach and situational
diversity both in Europe and in North America, including in medical anthropology; anthropology of politics, war, and conflict; and sociology (Bourdieu
et al. 1999; Daniel 1996; Das 1995, 2001; Farmer 1997; Frank 2001; Kleinman 1988; Kleinman and Kleinman 1991; Morris 1991; Scheper-Hughes
1992, 1998; Wilkinson 2005, 2006). Researchers' work concerned with

social suffering, and most notably the activist work of Paul Farmer (1997, 2005), who has contributed significantly to raising the political profile of suffering resulting from political and economic inequalities, finds commonality in its purpose as part of a politics seeking humanitarian resolutions to the various crises giving rise to suffering. Another common thread throughout the literature on social suffering is researchers' sense of being unable to adequately witness or give voice to suffering that is inherently unspeakable (Frank 2001), issuing as it does from physical, social, and psychic pain caught in a wilderness of inexpressibility far from the bounds of social norms and discourse. Related to this, within the literature there is a sustained interest in how individuals, communities, and peoples can move beyond suffering experiences, usually through culturally based frameworks of revisionist interpretation (Das and Kleinman 2001; Kleinman 1988; Scheper-Hughes 1998). Much of the Indigenous resurgence literature may be read partly as a praxis of reflexive recovery: suffering is acknowledged as issuing from colonial sources correctly identified through the embodied knowledge and experience of Indigenous peoples themselves. The articulation of suffering experiences by Indigenous scholars (such as colonization's complex of dispossession, disease, ongoing injustice, and their constructs) informs resurgence philosophy and action toward overcoming suffering and achieving spiritual, psychological, and cultural wellness.

Social suffering can generally be understood as the various social pathologies afflicting Indigenous communities in Canada, a complex of disease and unwellness, poverty, and social issues often referred to as "Third World conditions" common in Indigenous communities. Simplistic analyses of these conditions often champion the idea that Indigenous peoples are solely responsible for this situation, for example through unhealthy lifestyle choices, and that injustice is restricted to past events, which have no relation to the social ills evident in communities. In this way, Indigenous peoples suffering colonial pathologies are often characterized as "dysfunctional," a label that adheres suffering's causes to the sufferers. However, the argument advanced throughout this book is that these Third World conditions are actually the expected outcomes of colonization and injustice that are ongoing, an argument supported by evidence and insight within the work of a range of scholars, researchers, and medical experts familiar with the situation of Indigenous peoples in Canada and internationally.[5] In the words of one participant at a community workshop, "if it's all in the past, why does it hurt so much now?"

That question brought our small group discussion to a standstill. It was February 1998, and more than sixty people were separated into small groups throughout the cavernous meeting room at the Recreation Complex in

Inuvik. As a member of the Inuvialuit and Gwich'in negotiating team, I was responsible for facilitating small group discussions among community members during a two-day consultation meeting about our team's negotiating mandate. Seated in a semi-circle around a flip chart in a corner of the room, for several hours our group of about ten adults, elders, and youth discussed experiences of government services such as health, education, and justice. As expected, much of the discussion centred on painful residential school experiences, eventually turning to talk about how things should be done differently under self-government, with general statements being made about "the past." However, the question posed made us realize that participants were not talking about the past. What was being referenced by that question was how the many disconnections between ways and values of the mainstream society and those of the Inuvialuit and Gwich'in played out in government policy. Discussion centred on the ongoing experiences of injustice that extended across generations and into the future. The question raised a sentiment common among the group's participants: negative past experiences remain vital and in a sense are compounded by recent and similarly difficult experiences. Injustice still hurts now because discrete past events are the basis of ongoing unjust systems, policies, and practices – and resulting suffering. This larger complex of unrestituted wrongs and suffering shapes the lives of people in the present.

At the same meeting, discussion in another group led one prominent leader to declare she was "tired of all this wallowing in despair." Such was the extent that discussion of government programs and services resulted in sharing of suffering narratives.

Throughout this book the concept of dysfunction has been replaced by the concept of social suffering. Although the notion of dysfunction implies that people are responsible for their choices leading to unwellness, or can change the circumstances they are in, in order to become "functional," the term "social suffering" understands unwellness as symptoms of ongoing injustice, circumstances created and imposed by external agents. This term recognizes that the social pathologies endemic to Indigenous peoples are the reasonably expected result of ongoing injustice and are not a dimension of indigeneity. Recognizing the pathologies plaguing Indigenous communities and individuals as the expected outcomes of ongoing oppression is explored in Bonnie and Eduardo Duran's *Native American Postcolonial Psychology* (1995) and again specifically with respect to historical trauma by Maria Yellow Horse Brave Heart and Lemyra DeBruyn (1998). These works indicate that suffering is not simply about lifestyle choices made by the sufferers. In Canada, the nature and scale of social suffering within Indigenous communities coincide with ongoing injustices suffered by Indigenous peoples as subjects of the Canadian state's Aboriginal policy. Below the concept of the state's dysfunction theodicy is introduced, elaborated throughout the three case studies in subsequent chapters.

## The Dysfunction Theodicy

The focus on determining whether self-government agreements might address social suffering resulted in identification of what I assert as the state's "dysfunction theodicy." A theological concept, a theodicy is a rationale for the existence of evil despite God's existence. In times of suffering and pain, individuals often seek spiritual reassurance in the form of a reason for suffering. Religions provide such rationales through concepts such as karma, retribution for sin, or God's plan. Such reassurance provides those suffering with hope, comfort, or the basis for personal or spiritual action to ameliorate or prevent further suffering. Transferring this concept to political and social suffering, and specifically to the situation of Indigenous peoples in Canada, Canadian Aboriginal policy provides a rationale to Indigenous peoples for their suffering while simultaneously positioning the state as a source of redemption and healing. This positioning functions as the state's theodicy, characterizing Indigenous peoples as unmodern and dysfunctional, caused respectively by cultural difference and poor lifestyle choices. Injustice, being in the past and therefore neither a credible source of suffering nor a candidate for restitution, is substantively irrelevant. Unable to cope with modernity either culturally or morally, Indigenous peoples are encouraged to turn to the state as the source of redemption through programs and services that will assist both their modernization and their development of necessary knowledge and techniques to overcome self-imposed dysfunction. In this way the state can acknowledge that it may have made "mistakes" in dealing with Indigenous peoples in the past, mistakes whose role in current relations is primarily as lessons for the state's learning, rather than injustices inducing suffering and requiring substantive redress. In this view, Indigenous peoples who see the state as responsible for suffering simply misunderstand or are in denial of their situation, often accused of "living in the past" when they raise injustices as a rationale for increased autonomy or substantive redress.

The dysfunction theodicy is elaborated in the chapters that follow through analysis of discourse and outcomes of different self-government negotiations; however, this section looks at Aboriginal policies underlying dysfunction theodicy assumptions. A decade of participating in self-government negotiations, combined with an analysis of Canada's Statement on Indian Policy, better known as the White Paper (1969), Inherent Right Policy (1995), and Gathering Strength Policy (1998), led to identifying two key policy assumptions of Canada that narrows the scope of both possible restitution for past injustices and the potential scope of policy choices shaping the future. Each of these policies marks an important turning point in state-Indigenous relations in Canada. The White Paper gained its notoriety for proposing to do away with recognition of Aboriginal rights and associated protections and programs, reviled so completely and effectively by Indigenous peoples that it was never fully implemented. The White Paper proposed as a key principle shifting responsibility for Indians and associated programs and benefits to provinces. Although this shift was not implemented in the provinces, in the NWT this is what has occurred to a large extent. Many Dene peoples believe the GNWT has usurped federal authority over Indigenous peoples to the extent that, for example, money for health and education for Treaty 8 and 11 peoples goes into the general revenues of the territorial government and is not separately accounted for, which has proven problematic for costing program and service implementation responsibilities when planning for self-government.

The 1998 Gathering Strength Policy, released in response to the 440 recommendations of the Royal Commission on Aboriginal Peoples (RCAP), established priorities in the Department of Indian and Northern Affairs, focusing mainly on governance renewal and capacity building initiatives. The 1995 Inherent Right Policy describes the broad scope and extent of authorities available under self-government. The following chapters examine exchanges between negotiators during negotiating sessions, where similar to the approach of the written policies government negotiators tend to characterize injustices as specific, unchangeable events. "Historical" and similar temporal terms signal that the current government is neither responsible for nor in a position to substantively address injustice as a cause of present suffering.

For example, at the outset of the White Paper (1969, 7), injustices, legal bases of Indigenous rights, and governmental actions and obligations are conflated by the term "history": "The weight of history affects us all, but it presses most heavily on the Indian people. Because of history, Indians today are the subject of legal discrimination; they have grievances because of past undertakings that have been broken or misunderstood; they do not have full control of their lands; and a higher proportion of Indians than other Canadians suffer poverty in all its debilitating forms. Because of history too, Indians look to a special department of the Federal Government for many of the services that other Canadians get from provincial or local governments."

Decades later, the Canadian government maintains a less strident yet similarly rhetorical reliance on temporal terms to characterize Indigenous experiences. Laying the groundwork for policy priorities within INAC since 1998, the Gathering Strength Policy's opening remarks are eerily reminiscent of the temporal characterizations used to conflate injustice with history in the White Paper:

> As Aboriginal and non-Aboriginal Canadians seek to move forward together in a process of renewal, it is essential that we deal with the legacies of the past affecting the Aboriginal peoples of Canada, including the First Nations, Inuit, and Métis. Our purpose is not to rewrite history but, rather, learn from our past and to find ways to deal with the negative impacts that certain historical decisions continue to have in our society today. (Government of Canada, Department of Indian Affairs 1997, 4)

> The federal government is living up to its commitment, made in *Creating Opportunity – The Liberal Plan for Canada*, to build a new partnership with Aboriginal peoples and strengthen Aboriginal communities by enabling them to govern themselves. Our goal is to implement a process that will allow practical progress to be made, to restore dignity to Aboriginal peoples and empower them to become self-reliant. Aboriginal governments need to be able to govern in a manner that is responsive to the needs and interests of their people. Implementation of the inherent right of self-government will provide Aboriginal groups with the necessary tools to achieve this objective. (Government of Canada 1995, 1)

Although an in-depth analysis of government policy is not provided here, the above paragraphs are representative of the first of the two key assumptions within government policy: that injustice is historical. The result is that, by conflating specific unjust events, policies, and laws with "history," what is unjust becomes temporally separate from the present, unchangeable. This narrows options for restitution: we cannot change the past. The pursuit instead turns to justice "in our time," which instead of focusing on substantive restitution focuses on symbolic restitution such as land claims that return minuscule portions of Indigenous lands and resources or social programs that address social suffering. That suffering, such as poverty or unemployment, is actually the symptom of unrestituted deeper injustices, such as dispossession. Therefore, the result is that injustices, substantively unrestituted, can reasonably be expected to produce ongoing suffering. Aboriginal policy, then, and its associated mechanisms focus on symptoms of injustice rather than on substantively addressing injustice.

One result of the assumption that injustice cannot be changed is that what can and must change are Indigenous peoples themselves. This is clear, for example, in the quotation provided above from the Gathering Strength Policy. It echoes another era, when assimilation of Indigenous (and indeed of all non-European) peoples was viewed as the answer to erasing inconvenient cultural, social, and economic difference. This orientation is echoed in the Inherent Right Policy, which emphasizes the need for Indigenous peoples to "modernize": "Many First Nations have expressed a strong desire to control their own affairs and communities, and deliver programs and services better tailored to their own values and cultures. They want to replace the outdated provisions of the Indian Act with a modern partnership which preserves their special historic relationship with the federal government."[6] In fact, an accurate description of the Indian Act would be colonial, not "outdated"; thus, the repair required is not so much modernization of a colonial relationship as decolonization. To simply modernize an unjust relationship creates a disabling environment, where no Indigenous people can reasonably be expected to become self-determining in the face of ongoing control and exercise of discretion by the state with respect to key governmental authorities.

The preoccupation with historicizing injustice extends to historicizing indigeneity itself. This phenomenon is not new and has been identified by Indigenous scholars as "Indian as past" (Deloria 2004; Fixico 2003; Jojola 2004; King 2003; Mihesuah 2003). This notion adheres particularly to culturally based practices and knowledge: for example, moosehide tanning done yesterday, which requires extensive familiarity with knowledge of moose, bush survival, and tanning techniques, is viewed as "traditional" knowledge rather than simply as Dene knowledge or contemporary moosehide-tanning knowledge.[7] Aboriginal policy casts the government as a benevolent helper, eager to minister to an encountered dysfunction that is unmodern and not of the government's making. Governmental help will result in a modernity of happiness, wellness, and assimilated "normalcy." At the same time, aspects of indigeneity will be preserved in ways compatible with this version of modernity. This merely requires profound change on the part of Indigenous people, since, according to the dysfunction theodicy, Indigenous dysfunction stems from a non-modern indigeneity.

the ability to hunt or having a partner who hunts, and a social or kin net-work for the provision of hides, caribou or moose brains, and other equip-ment and assistance, are also necessary.

Moosehide-tanning tools and techniques may vary between communi-ties and regions; however, the sequencing of the different steps involved tends to be consistent. For example, some women use scrapers made out of sharpened moose leg bones; others use ulus whose blades have been flat-tened and so changed from their original curved shape. In the archives of the Prince of Wales Northern Heritage Museum in Yellowknife, June Helm's original fieldnotes disclose that during the 1950s she witnessed women at Jean Marie River using flattened and sharpened tin cans as scrapers. Through experience, each tanner tends to develop her own preferences for equipment suitable to her own style and techniques: some prefer the ten-inch Old Hickory knife for fleshing the hair side and the twelve-inch version for cutting away the meat of the flesh side of the hide. Others may opt for long-handled scrapers or homemade versions of the ulu-style scraper, and some may even use pumice stones to scrape the thinnest parts of their hides. Gifts of tools among tanners are common, scrapers and knives carrying the thoughtfulness of the giver, and accompanied by advice and information on the manufacture of the tool and its correct usage, knowl-edge passed among generations of women.

According to Dene knowledge, the newly created Earth was made beau-tiful by a moosehide. In the NWT, ceremonial, special occasion, and every-day uses of moosehide continue to make the world beautiful. Moosehide clothing is a signifier of Dene cultural knowledge, artistic ability, and arti-sanal skill. Tanning, sewing, or beading moosehide items requires intense skill and attention that few people possess. Tanning hides requires tan-ners to be close to the land. This is in the sense that the tanning process is most easily learned and understood in a bush camp setting, since so many of the materials and functional requirements are easily gathered and/or met there. It also requires, at least until basic competence levels have been achieved, that a person work with more experienced tanners, apprenticing through the creation of several hides before striking out on one's own.

On a corridor wall of the Délînê Land Corporation hangs a moosehide adorned with an artist's drawing of Great Bear Lake and the signatures of most community members, a memento of the signing of Délînê's Self-Government Agreement-in-Principle during 2003. The hide provides a physical representation and celebration of the Dene way of life that con-tinues to sustain Délînê Got'înê (Délînê Dene) through and despite an ever-changing relationship with the state. At events and ceremonies in the NWT, such moosehide artifacts and clothing are markers of formality and respect. At land claim and self-government signing ceremonies, moosehide vests, jackets, and slippers adorned with colourful beaded flowers or geometric designs are worn proudly. The clothing and beadwork are produced predominantly by women and are sold for a fraction of their true value. Moosehide is not easy to obtain, since hand-tanning hide is not widely practised. It requires the co-ordinated efforts of many people, and the tanning process itself is physically and mentally demanding. Skills and knowledge are passed down from grandmothers and mothers and shared among friends. Some men do practise tanning, but it is generally seen as skilled women's work.

Tanning hides is often perceived and described as a tradition, part of Dene history. It is a valuable connection with "the old days." Producing hand-tanned hide is time consuming, physically and mentally challenging, and economically undervalued. At the same time, there is a great demand for tanned hides and a universal respect for the women who produce them, who are recognized as holders and practitioners of important cultural knowledge. However, what often goes unnoticed is the effort required of many family and community members to make tanning a reality. Caring for hides is a constant, active occupation requiring the focus and attention of tanners, almost to the exclusion of all else. So women must rely on their families to take care of the many domestic tasks that would otherwise occupy their time. They must also rely on relatives and community members to supply hides, assist in setting up and maintaining the camp, and help with tool making and maintenance.

The intense, participatory, and profoundly family- and community-oriented nature of tanning makes it a fitting cultural analogy for analyzing self-government negotiations. And at the same time, characterizations of hide tanning also echo characterizations of Indigenous peoples used by governments in negotiations discourse. Through negotiations, Indigenous peoples' rights, identities, and experiences of injustice are effectively undermined by being made over into historical rather than ongoing events. Similarly, to view tanning as a "dying tradition" is to disconnect it from the vitality, energy, and creativity that it signifies to those familiar with its demands. Tanning is probably one of the most empowering and positive things a person can do – not only because it is a tradition or results in a "product." Tanning is about collective co-operation, responsibility, tenacity, self-reliance, commitment, and accomplishment requiring multiple and specifically Dene knowledges. In many respects, it is about configuring personal strength and individual initiative to the benefit of the collective. Rather than a dying tradition or a quaint expression of historical Dene culture, it functions as a community-centred cultural practice, developing and transmitting cultural knowledge and values. It is an example of an enterprise predicated on and suffused with Dene values and worldview and successful because of that. In that sense it functions as both analogy and example of self-determination.

The tendency toward erroneously historicizing things Indigenous is not exclusive to expressions of Indigenous culture. This phenomenon has important implications for self-government negotiations. Self-government negotiations discourse conflates injustices with the past, in a way similar to how Indigenous practices and ways are read as things historical. References to Indigenous peoples and the injustices attached specifically to being Indigenous are inevitably structured by references to time. Temporal characterizations, framed in terms such as "traditional," weave perceptual webs that silence Indigenous realities refusing to self-historicize. In this way, terms of respect such as "traditional" are subverted, incorporated into the discourse of dispossession. As a result they become indices of difference: for example, "traditional," a word intended to establish the legitimacy of a practice through its aspect of historical continuity, is instead read as an indicator of historicity. As a result, knowledge or practices are understood as memory rather than as reality, as traditional rather than as Indigenous, bound exclusively to dead ancestors rather than the living. And so Indigenous people in the present are separated from things explicitly Indigenous. Things Indigenous and things contemporary are structured as opposites: historical tradition versus the modern present. Instead of being recognized simply as Indigenous, indigeneity is both reified and problematized as reconciling tradition with modernity.

Beginning with an individual's desire and commitment to create something, tanning is transformative in terms of the material, spiritual, cultural, and social processes it entails. Tanners often give freely of their expertise to a less experienced learner, passing on a combination of technical knowledge, individual technique, work ethic, and cultural knowledge. Community members sharing in the effort are free to observe and appreciate how their contribution animates progress and influences the sequencing of tasks. The hundred individual actions of an entire community give the tanner's purpose its expression. Beauty and utility result from the commitment of one person that inspires and marshals the expertise, participation, and constant support and input of many. The long, intense hours of not only physical work but also mental focus, patience, and stillness require physical, mental, and spiritual strength. For many, the complex of demands and interactions both draw on and replenish internal resources, providing the predominantly women tanners with time for quiet reflection and respite from their many domestic and work responsibilities.

Descriptions throughout this book sketch the contours of the moose-hide-tanning process. They pick up on themes and issues in self-government negotiations, providing a tactile, practical contrast with the abstractions dominating negotiation discourse. Describing tanning, and positioning it as an example of a Dene enterprise, provide in part a framework for think-ing about the relevance of Dene values for self-government and so the disingenuousness of characterizations of Indigenous cultures as temporally distant. It is appropriate to caution here that tanning descriptions are both reflected through the experience and understanding of a non-Dene observer and are not meant to capture the entirety, depth, or cultural significance of the process. However, their inclusion in part provides insight into the importance of sequence and experience as measures of progress rather than the passage of time. Too often a basis of conflict between dominant and Indigenous perceptions stems from senses of time, both in the sense of Western perceptions of indigeneity's position within it, and in terms of West-ern perceptions of Indigenous cultural values not being shaped by a West-ern notion that time is unilinear. Western society adheres to clock-run scheduling, whereas Indigenous cultures often place primacy on sequencing of events, events which should not be impoverished of quality or content to move along within a process (Deloria 2004; Waters 2004). Here we are put in mind of jokes about "Indian time" made when meetings in communities start later than scheduled or when people tease someone young about "acting like an elder" if he or she speaks at a meeting for a longer than anticipated length of time. In contrast, Western culture uses time periods as a short-hand indicator of quality: years of experience stand in for quality or content of experience, for example. With respect to tem-porality, moosehide-tanning descriptions challenge the notions that (1) things Indigenous, relevant both materially and socially to modernity, are "traditional" in the sense of being historical rather than continuous with and a contemporary expression of an enduring culture, and (2) clock time is a relevant or reliable indicator for the content or quality of an experience.

Challenging these two notions is important for challenging perceptions informing self-government negotiations and other expressions of Aboriginal policy. For the purposes of self-government negotiations, it is important to understand that differences between indigeneity and the mainstream society stem primarily from culture rather than temporal positioning. And appreci-ating an Indigenous cultural emphasis on sequencing of events over their duration allows for better understanding of Indigenous worldviews inform-ing negotiating positions and ideas of self-government generally. The benefit of these insights allows for conceptualizing the inclusion of cultural knowl-edge in approaches to self-government not as the preservation of tradition but as the strengthening of culture. In a practical sense, this means simply remaking administrative norms relevant to clients. It also allows for reconceiving approaches to community enterprises, such as community consultation, not as seemingly endless and lengthy processes but as events shaped by cultural norms emphasizing qualitative experience and appropriate sequencing.

## Tanning against History

**From Field Notes, Tanning Camps during July 2001 and July 2003**
The early morning sun was bright as the two elders, Jane and Marie, walked into the woods beyond the clearing with their axes and canvas bags, leaving the radio blaring country music. They had gone to collect spruce boughs to place beneath the smoking stages and fleshing poles where the moosehides would be placed during the day. The boughs, placed in a woven pattern on the ground to create a solid, soil-resistant surface, would help to protect the hides should they touch the ground. Ella, a young Inuvialuit woman, had already started the fire, coffee steaming as she dialled her husband on her cell phone to remind him to pick her up later that day with their boat. We stood inside history together that morning, watching the brain water solution warm on the fire as the eternal sun rose above us.

Visitors came and went, friends and acquaintances of the ten women and men who had gathered to learn tanning, curious about the tanning process and the motivation for learning it. People spoke about tanning as a dying art, a dying tradition, a dying site of cultural knowledge. An anachronism. Yet our very real arms and backs ached from carrying pails of water from the river to the clearing where we would pour them into the large plastic tubs where our hides lay to rinse in between their being smoked and scraped. And by evening the day's work of twisting and fleshing hides meant flexing our fingers was incredibly painful. Clearly, all this hard work was real and current.

Participating in that first tanning camp created both a desire and an opportunity for several of us to continue to work together each summer to develop our knowledge of tanning. The following summer Janice and I agreed to spend time at her camp on the river near Inuvik working on hides, each of us scheduling ten days away from our work and families. Our plans were frustrated every day for a solid week. With a graduate degree in education and diverse experience as a teacher and school principal behind her, my friend Janice's wisdom and thoughtfulness attracted a steady stream of Gwich'in leaders and respected elders to her side. We wanted to get out to her camp but found only reasons to stay. Some people came to talk policy and politics, others to just visit over tea, telling stories and asking questions as we scraped our hides on tarps in the mud room at the front of her house. Everyone was fascinated with the process. Occasionally, we took breaks to visit people in town who might be able to assist us in finding the materials we required, so we were able to scavenge poles for our smoking stage and caribou heads for the brains we needed. One day caribou brains arrived for Janice from a lady in Aklavik who had heard we needed some. People stopped by regularly to check on our progress. Two more caribou heads unexpectedly surfaced from Jen's freezer, another fledgling tanner who had worked with us the previous year.

Finally, we got out on the river. We had to rely on Ron to take us to the camp each day in his boat, but we would sometimes first stop at John and Sara's cabin. Visits were full of laughing and stories and the elders challenging us to scrape and fillet fish in exchange for their expertise in skinning the caribou heads. On one visit, Sara showed us a cache of dahshaa she had saved, telling us she wanted us to take it.

*Dahshaa* is a Gwich'in word for the rotted, dried spruce wood used to impart the distinctive bronze colour to hand-tanned moosehide. Equipped with axes, work gloves, and canvas sacks, tanners gather it in the summer, mainly from hillsides, during hot, dry weather. It is distinctive for its colour and light, almost crumbly texture, marked in part by a complete absence of spruce gum or moisture. It is found in quantities usually measuring no more than a few handfuls at best. It is this rare combination of qualities that makes it so elusive, qualities developing naturally over many years of exposure to the elements. It takes the sharp eye of an experienced tanner to locate it, someone who knows the patterns of forest growth and decay, local land formations, and a sense of place necessary to determine promising locations. Once found, packing it out of the bush in the square canvas packs with shoulder and head straps takes physical strength and agility. Knowing all this, Sara's gift was accepted with a mixture of awe and relief, but we knew it would not last. It reminded me that I had to continue to seek the knowledge and discipline necessary to find *dahshaa* one day on my own.

Sara wanted us to take the dahshaa she had found; she said she didn't tan hide, but she said that when she found it she told her boy to leave it where it was because she knew it was for tanning. The dahshaa, rotted and dried to a golden bronze colour over many seasons of exposure to the elements, was a rare find. We stuffed the light, brittle pieces of it into a canvas sack, overjoyed. She talked about her memories of her grandmother tanning as we worked. Smiling and laughing, she told us how happy she was to give that dahshaa away, finally, because now someone was tanning.

We became connected. The moosehide took charge of people, creating attachments, calling forth the specific manner and force of our respect: for each other, for it, for the values we share, the values that separated us. A young woman visited the house after checking on her son nearby and stayed to sharpen our knives for two hours, talking and keeping us company. Elders stayed for tea and told stories of tanning. Others simply watched.

The first time I learned to tan, one of the elders who taught us gathered us together in a circle beside the freshly smoked hides hanging all around us, golden on the racks of grey spruce poles. We had just finished. We were tired, having just spent three weeks outside in sun and rain, doing the hard physical work of not just tanning but contributing to keeping a camp going. All of us were anxious to get back to our homes and lives. I never wanted to see another moosehide again. She told us that we had now been given knowledge that is a responsibility. We had to keep doing this. It wasn't mystical, though it spoke to our spiritual and moral senses – we were given knowledge, and she challenged us to integrate that with who we were. Our knowledge – though we didn't realize it at the time – bound us to each other. We needed each other to continue improving our techniques, to support each other, to share. We needed the men who hunted and the ones who found the poles and built our smoking stages. And the women who sent us the caribou heads, and the people along the river and in the town who were drawn to the hides, or to the smoke of our fires, and then stayed to tell their stories of moose and tanning and grandmothers and make too-casual mentions of their wishing for new moosehide slippers and vests. The hides were the magic that wove us all together and bound us back to the sense we had of ourselves and our place within the mix.

For the anthropologist, tanning can be viewed as a complex gift exchange network evolving beyond kin groups; power relations and hierarchies abound; and tanning itself might be perceived as a political act, a form of resistance, or a form of social control. The hides that focused our concentration and brought us together in our enterprise animated the meaning of the activity in ways that revealed how the values underpinning tanning practices echoed those underpinning other community-centred processes. It revealed how an entire community's meaningful engagement in a project could similarly temper and pace that project, as a result of practising the same values essential to successful tanning, but within a different context, such as self-government negotiations. However, instead of analyzing the tanning process as a way to elaborate non-Indigenous views of indigeneity, descriptions of the tanning process present an opportunity to take advantage of a Dene cultural framework for understanding self-government negotiations, particularly the clashes that arise out of encounters between differing worldviews.

To be engaged in a vital, enjoyable, and transformative process and to be told that it is a dying tradition comprises the paradox of tanning. This is continuous with a view that remakes indigeneity as historical rather than real, constantly interpreted as a reaction rather than a reality. Too often being Indigenous is viewed as forms of resistance – against the state, mainstream society, Western values. Too seldom indigeneity is viewed as people being – culturally, entirely, being themselves, whether engaging in ceremonies, seeking recognition of their existence, or asserting their rights. In this sense tanning embodies the principles of Indigenous resurgence: people simply being culturally themselves toward a positive outcome, without reference to the state or any negative forces.

## Getting Ready to Tan

### From Field Notes, Tanning Camp, July 2002

We arrived at the bush camp in the early afternoon. We were at Martha's bush camp, about twenty minutes from town by boat, and anxious to begin. The boat ride from Inuvik had been cold and windy, but our spirits were lifted by the golden eagles that soared overhead. Jane and Marie dropped their knapsacks at the main cabin, walking quickly to Martha's small smoke house at the edge of the clearing of the camp to check on the unprocessed moosehides and determine the preparations they would need to ready them for tanning. The hides had been frozen since winter in the local Department of Renewable Resources walk-in freezer at Inuvik (the only freezer big enough to store eight hides) and had been taken from there to the camp two days before. The hides, still partially frozen, lay in the shadows of the plywood-covered structure. Four piles of eight- to ten-foot lengths of dead spruce poles lay at intervals in a large grassy area, just behind the small log cabins where we would sleep.

The camp had a main cabin at the centre of a large cleared area, an area surrounded by the willow and stunted spruce and pine characteristic of the Mackenzie Delta near the tree line. The main cabin contained a kitchen with a woodstove for heat and cooking, an eating area, and two small sleeping areas. The meals were prepared here, a wide variety of both store-bought and country foods, everything from hot dogs to fresh fish netted in the river to roasted moose nose. Two smaller log cabins used for sleeping sat to the left of the main cabin, connected by a well-worn pathway. To the right and behind the cabin were the smoke house, and then farther away, nearer the edge of the clearing, was the outhouse. Two canvas tents measuring eight by twelve feet, complete with small woodstoves, had been set up to the right of the cabins, at the far edge of the clearing. The tents would be used for working on hides if needed, to shield the tanners from rain, excessive heat, or wind, any of which were possible during the month of July in the Arctic.

That first day of tanning was warm and sunny with a light breeze, about eighteen degrees Celsius, and wasting no time Marie and Jane began to drag the moosehides out into the sun, placing them flesh side up on tarps, pulling apart the frozen folds of skin, and pouring water into the stiff depressions of flesh to thaw them more quickly. We were told to handle the hides with respect; one should never step on or over a hide, make disparaging remarks, swear, or smoke cigarettes in their presence. Placing a hide on a tarp, I dragged it to a grassy bit of clearing near the tents, taking directions from Jane and Marie about how to pour water onto it, then wait for a few minutes to pull apart the thawing folds, then repeat the process until the hide lay flat on the tarp.

The tanning camp was being run by the local college as an open course, and altogether there were ten students taking part. Two elders had been hired from Fort Good Hope to spend three weeks with us at the bush camp of an Inuvialuit elder on the Mackenzie River near Inuvik, instructing us in tanning hides. We had been told to prepare to stay at the camp during the week, expect long hours from early morning to late evening, and this developed into our schedule, with occasional nights spent in town. Most of our time was spent tanning, but at some points that work was paused to gather spruce boughs, or the rotted wood needed for smoking the hides, or sometimes dahshaa. The elders would bring back canvas sacks full of wood from these forays, emptying them onto clean tarps once they reached camp, where the wood was then separated into piles. Inevitably, these became large, loose piles of wood spilling across half the tarp, beside which would be a small bucket or bag, half full of perfectly dried bronze pieces of dahshaa. As we walked through the bush gathering the wood, I asked questions to determine the distinct characteristics of dahshaa in relation to regular rotted wood. It seemed impossible to differentiate. I was consistently told, "if you keep looking long enough, you will know it when you see it; it takes patience." Once, when at a tanning camp several years after first learning to tan, I was talking with Jane as she smoked a hide at a fire located near a pile of wood Marie had previously sorted through. I thought I spied a piece of dahshaa in the pile, picked it up to examine it, then held it out for Jane to look at. "Isn't this dahshaa?" I asked. "No." She shook her head. I put it back and took up another desiccated, crumbling bit of wood. "Jane," I said, "I think Marie must have missed this one, look, it's dahshaa." She glanced at it, then gave me a quizzical look. "No." I surveyed the pile again, sure that some of it was dahshaa, and gave it one last try. "How about this?" I held up a powdery, beautiful, golden bit of wood for her to inspect, certain I had found some dahshaa. She ignored it and looked at me thoughtfully and said, "Mom sorted through all that wood. It's no good for final smoking." Then she turned away to tend to her hide.

At the first tanning camp, all the tanners were Inuvialuit and Gwich'in (except for me, as a non-Indigenous participant), and primarily women, from Inuvik and the surrounding communities. We ranged between the ages of twenty and sixtyish and were paired together randomly, each pair responsible for a shared hide. While the hides thawed, we set to work on setting up the camp. The first task was to set up fleshing poles; the hides would be placed on one or two poles about four feet high that had been staked in the ground. Jane and Marie walked the clearing to find appropriate places for the poles, directing the camp helpers as they hammered them into the grass with sledge-hammers. We would cut the flesh from the hides once they were draped over these poles, grasping the edge with one hand and with the other use an upward motion to slide a knife blade between the thin membrane separating the meat from the skin. Smoking stages also had to be built. This was a more involved task, and as we set to work fleshing, the two young men hired as camp helpers began to construct two large smoking racks near the far edge of the clearing opposite the tents. They used the dead spruce poles, set side by side at intervals of half a foot apart to create a platform about five feet by six feet, approximately four feet off the ground. The poles were secured together by rope, as the stages would be taken down after the camp and the poles used again. Once fleshed, the hides would be laid flat on the stages to be smoked by a fire of rotten spruce burning underneath. Wind and rain would be kept at bay by tarps set up to shield both the fire and the hide itself, secured to nearby trees and the spruce poles of the smoking structure. Later the hides would be smoked on rounded miniature hut-like structures made of young willows. Ah', or spruce boughs, had to be collected and placed on the ground around both the fleshing poles and the smoking stages to ensure a clean surface to protect the hides in case they touched the ground.

After a few hours of setting up, Jane set us to work on the hides that had thawed, taking the hair off. Few of us knew each other, but conversation developed as we began to work on the hides. I sat down in front of the hide I had tended, held my knife at an angle to the surface beneath the hair, and began to slide it under the coarse brown fur at its roots. It was sharp and slid easily at the surface of the skin, the hair rising up and falling to the side as it was shorn, revealing fine downy hair on the grey-brown skin underneath. I looked across at a young Gwich'in man who took up a knife and began working on the same hide opposite from me. He did a double take. "I never thought I'd work on hides with a white woman! Why are you here?," he exclaimed.

We talked briefly. His name was Joe, and we soon fell to silence, absorbed with the work. It was difficult to cut off the hair at the roots, revealing the downy skin, without cutting the hide. Removing the skin would come later; to cut it now would create dry patches on the hide and render its thickness uneven.

After a while I sat back from the hide and surveyed our work. "Hey," I said to my new friend with surprise, "the moose's skin is brown underneath all this hair – look at it!"

He looked at me, momentarily puzzled, then smiled widely. "Of course it's brown. What, you thought that moose would be white, just like you?" He sat back and began laughing, and after a minute I began laughing with him, embarrassed.

I hadn't thought about it that way.

# Moosehide Tanning

Denise Kurszewski of Inuvik removes the hair from a thawed hide, Inuvik, 2002. Photo:
author.

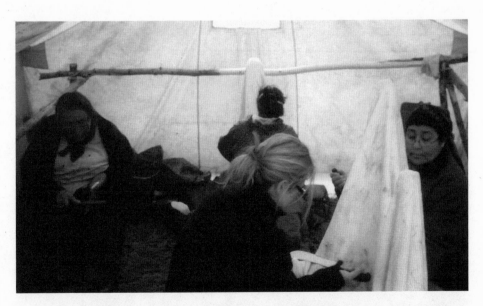

Clockwise from left to right: Inside a canvas tent at Inuvik, 2002, Elder Mary Barnaby of Fort
Good Hope sharpens a knife; Lillian Wright of Inuvik (background) fleshes the hair side;
Gladys Alexie from Fort McPherson and the author flesh a hide by separating membrane from
the moose skin with upward movement of fleshing knives. The tent floor is covered in spruce
boughs woven together.

Denise Kurszewski scrapes the hair (outer) side of a moosehide, Inuvik, June 2006. Photo: author.

A moosehide is flat smoked just after scraping is finished, Inuvik, 2007. Holes in the hide have not yet been sewn. Initially, the hide appears raw when smoked. Photo: author.

Elder Judy Lafferty flat smokes a hide, Inuvik, 2007. Photo: author.

As the hide is smoked, its appearance begins to resemble light-coloured leather. Photo: author.

Denise Kurszewski twists a hide, Inuvik, June 2007. Photo: Amanda Clarke.

A smoked hide hangs to cool; another is affixed to a wringing (twisting) post, Inuvik, June 2007. Photo: author.

The author tends a hide being smoked on a round smoker, Inuvik, June 2006. Round smoking is done after several flat smokings of the hide; round smoking intensifies penetration of both heat and smoke.

A moosehide twisted and left to dry between smoking, Inuvik, June 2006. Photo: author.

A chunk of *dahshaa*, the rotted, petrified wood used in the final smoking of moosehides. Dettah, September 2007. Photo: author.

A tanned moosehide, September 2007. Photo: author.

# 3
# Dehcho Resource Revenue Sharing

KAKISA, NWT – The federal government is considering breaking off talks with the Dehcho First Nations.

Métis in the region are asking the courts to order the federal government to provide them with the same core funding that First Nations get.

And for months, Dehcho leaders have been threatening court action on another front. They say they were not properly consulted when a plan for reviewing a Mackenzie Valley [gas] pipeline was developed [by governments].

Robin Aitken represents the federal government in the Dehcho negotiation. Yesterday he addressed delegates at the Dehcho assembly in Kakisa.

"We don't negotiate and litigate at the same time," he says. "If you want to go to court, that's fine. We'll see you in court. And it won't be me, it will be paper copies of Treaty 8 and Treaty 11 versus the Dehcho version of what happened or what didn't happen. That's high stakes. No one wants to go that route."

Aitken says that despite the differences a final agreement is within grasp.

He urged delegates to focus on the future rather than the present or the past.

> – "No Past or Present, It's Make or Break for
> Dehcho Deal," CBC Radio, NWT, June 30,
> 2004

Indigenous peoples in Canada often have had to rely on civil disobedience to draw government and public attention and action to the resolution of outstanding disputes over lands, rights, and participation in decision making. The above news report demonstrates that, in cases where Indigenous peoples access legal remedies for injustice, even those actions may be construed as unreasonable. The Mackenzie Gas Pipeline referenced in the previous news item is a revived proposal of the original gas pipeline project rejected during the 1970s; 40 percent of the pipeline route runs through Dehcho territory. The settlement reached out of court between the Dehcho and Canada over Dehcho concerns regarding their exclusion from pipeline environmental review consultations included funding related to Dehcho capacity building, project funding, and participation in Mackenzie Gas Project consultations in the amount of $31.5 million, land withdrawals, and related provisions.

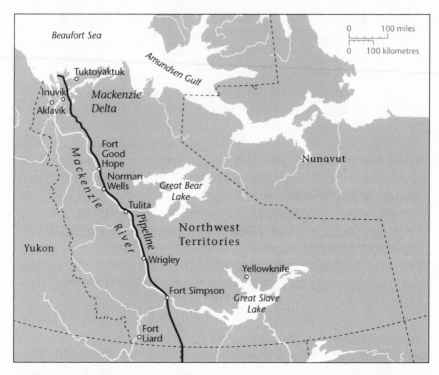

*Map 2*   Proposed Mackenzie Gas Pipeline route. The pipeline route runs the length of the NWT.
*Source:* Mackenzie Gas Project website, www.mackenziegasproject.com/theProject/index.html#.

The news story also highlights the temporal positioning of reality favoured in Aboriginal policy: forget the past and present injustices and suffering – have faith the government will do the right thing in the future. Yet such positioning prompts the question: What reasonable person would make major decisions about a constitutionally protected treaty without taking into account experiences of Canada's policies toward Indigenous people? Ultimately, the Dehcho First Nations (DFN) settled out of court with Canada on the dispute over Mackenzie Gas Project consultations.[1]

The DFN and Canada have engaged in fitful negotiations over lands, resources, and governance since 1990 in what is known as the "Dehcho process." This term was adopted in part as an indication of the Dehcho's reluctance to label the negotiations as seeking a comprehensive land claim in the sense that land claims are understood by Canada. What distinguishes the Dehcho negotiations from those of other regions is in part Dehcho resistance to using the Dene/Métis Agreement of 1990 as a basis for its negotiations. Canada, seeking to maintain parity with agreements reached in the NWT, has proposed using the 1990 Dene/Métis Agreement, including a Mackenzie Valley-wide resource management and resource royalty-sharing regime, as the basis for negotiations. In contrast, the vision of the DFN includes Dehcho control of all lands and resources in the region, without resorting to what is viewed as "land sales" where cash is provided in return for giving up Aboriginal rights and interests in vast swaths of traditional territories. The Dehcho alternative proposes establishing a Crown in right of the Dehcho, acting through public government institutions with authority over lands, resources, and government services. The public government would include majority representation of the Dehcho First Nations in decision making and have own-source revenues from resource royalties. Own-source revenues are outside the control of Canada or other governments. Usually, the majority of self-government financing comes directly from Canada or through the territorial government and is tied to specific policies, programs, and standards determined largely by the funding government. As the vision statement on their website – "Strong, proud, happy people through self-government and sustainable economic development while maintaining the integrity of the land and Dene/Métis traditions" – indicates, the Dehcho vision of a lands and governance agreement includes mechanisms to ensure financial independence from Canada as a key component of self-determination.

The NWT's wealth lies largely in its non-renewable resources, such as oil, gas, diamond, and mineral deposits. Currently, Canada receives all resource royalties and then returns tiny percentages of those royalties to Indigenous governments with which it has agreements. It is also negotiating additional Indigenous and GNWT shares of royalties through devolution talks.[2] Canada and the NWT, and since the early 1990s Indigenous governments, have engaged in discussing the devolution of ownership and powers over lands and resources from Canada to NWT governments. Any deal is likely to include a resource revenue sharing agreement, since Canada's current ownership and control of lands and resources means it also receives all resource royalties, save for shares provided to Indigenous governments through land claim agreements. This chapter focuses on negotiations between the Dehcho First Nations and Canada over resource revenue shares (oil, gas, and mineral royalties) during negotiating sessions held in November 2001 and January 2002. To better understand negotiators' exchanges within the broader context of Canada's Aboriginal policy goals, the next section overviews both negotiations terminology and analytical tools used to deconstruct the discussion.

### Terms of Art in the Negotiating Process

Terms specific to self-government negotiations are used throughout this book. "The parties" refer to organizations participating in a negotiation, such as the Canadian government, the Government of the Northwest Territories, and the Indigenous government (for example, Dehcho First Nation, the

Gwich'in Tribal Council). The substance of negotiations focuses on "subject matters," which are jurisdictional areas such as health, education, or social services. Discussions are led by chief negotiators for each party who are supported by technical people, such as lawyers and researchers. Negotiations take place at "main table" sessions, which are the formal discussions attended by all negotiating team members and where the chief negotiators attempt to reach agreement. Detailed discussions on legal wording or information sharing between parties may take place within "working groups" away from the main table and composed of supporting members of the different negotiating teams. For example, a Legal and Technical Working Group would involve all parties' lawyers developing legal language giving effect to how an idea or policy position might be worded within the agreement, a detail-oriented and time-consuming task requiring specialized knowledge. Working groups meet independently in between main table sessions, then jointly present recommendations to chief negotiators for discussion. Each party provides their "interests" or "positions" to the other parties at main table sessions, which then become the basis for discussions. Interests generally are principles, values, or objectives of each party relating to a specific subject matter and are usually presented in discussion paper format. Positions in contrast reflect a party's view on a specific jurisdictional or administrative arrangement and are more usually presented as a series of clauses drafted by legal counsel. Usually, initial discussions on a subject matter focus on the different parties' interests; then parties may move to tabling their positions for further discussion.

For both governments and Indigenous organizations, the chief negotiator is responsible for the overall management of his or her team, the pace of negotiations, and liaising with political leaders. Chief negotiators do most of the talking at negotiations and usually have extensive experience in program and service management if they work for government; Indigenous peoples' chief negotiators usually have knowledge of both government systems and community organizations and issues. Assistant negotiators and researchers do the bulk of research, undertake analysis and writing, network with other Indigenous negotiation teams and organizations, keep records of negotiations, and organize the team's work. Lawyers are heavily involved in both research and legal drafting of the agreements. Governments may also draw subject area experts from their line departments, a resource unavailable to Indigenous teams. If provided with additional funding by INAC, Indigenous teams are occasionally able to hire subject area experts such as accountants, economists, or land use planners to conduct specific research, but this is rare. In addition, Indigenous teams spend significant parts of their budgets on constant communications and consultations with their community members, elder and First Nation advisors, and translators for both negotiating sessions and communication materials. Since budget amounts are always uncertain, and revealed to Indigenous teams usually in June or July of fiscal years beginning in April, it is extremely difficult for Indigenous teams to hire full-time community-based staff, since positions cannot be guaranteed beyond the fiscal year. The yearly funding cycle, resulting from a combination of Treasury Board and INAC funding policies, has an extremely destabilizing effect both on building capacity and on conducting negotiations. At self-government negotiations in the NWT, it is unusual for Indigenous peoples' teams to have their core negotiations team as full-time staff based in the community. Although the chief negotiators and communications staff are almost always community based, it is unusual for lawyers or research staff to be based there also. Funding is structured in a way that only allows hiring on a year-to-year basis and at a less than full-time salary for the level of skill and knowledge required. This makes capacity building extremely difficult within communities, a major concern where the community has little opportunity to build either corporate or technical knowledge that will be important for implementing the self-government agreement.

Throughout, participants are referred to as "Canada," "the Government of the Northwest Territories," or, for example, "the Gwich'in," "Délînê." This allows difficult discussions to ensue without necessarily personalizing or attributing difficult and sometimes offensive positions to the representatives at the table, who sometimes have little influence over the position being taken. These terms are ones used by negotiators themselves when putting forward their positions and arguments. This terminology also links specific discussions to the wider collective interests and responsibilities of representatives. It functions as a reminder of the political and constitutional positioning of each of the participants in relation to one another.

## Colonization

The arguments in this book rest in part on the fact that Indigenous peoples were and continue to be the colonial subjects of the settler governments (federal, provincial, and territorial) which have authority over various aspects of their lives. Generally, scholars writing on relations between the state and Indigenous peoples acknowledge the colonial roots of that relationship, and most acknowledge that the colonial relationship is ongoing, as evidenced by various state structures, including the Constitution, Aboriginal policy, bureaucratic institutions such as the Department of Indian and Northern Affairs, and the Indian Act (Alfred 1999; Green 2008; Miller 2003; Tully 1995; Turner 2006).

Colonization occurs when settlers establish institutions premised on dominating the geographic, material, economic, cultural, psychological, and spiritual existences of the original inhabitants of a place. Colonialism has moved from visceral expressions of asserted European cultural and economic superiority through actions such as slavery, forced removal, or slaughter of Indigenous peoples, to more legalistic and bureaucratized forms of domination. In Canada, for example, colonization has moved from practices of enforced assimilation and destruction of Indigenous cultures in the 1800s to current practices, including the persistence of colonial control of Indigenous lives through the Indian Act and Aboriginal policy maintaining and perpetuating structures facilitating the continued dispossession and alienation of Indigenous peoples from their own lands and resources and without substantive recompense. The psychological implications of colonization of Indigenous peoples have been explored in classic works by Frantz Fanon and Albert Memmi, more recently with reference to the North American context specifically by Duran and Duran (1995), and, as mentioned previously, in a growing body of work on historical trauma, an analytical paradigm developed by Maria Yellow Horse Brave Heart and Lemyra DeBruyn (1998).

It is often said that, given the immensity of the effort on so many fronts to eradicate Indigenous peoples over the past 500 years, it is a testament to the strength of Indigenous peoples and their faith in themselves and their cultures that they continue to exist at all. For some, self-government appears to be an opportunity for Indigenous peoples to begin to come to terms with, and begin to move beyond, a present painful colonized existence. However, government negotiators seem to view self-government as a process of meeting legal obligations to power sharing. In other words, for Indigenous peoples, it seems self-government may hold hope for change toward overcoming a specific reality of colonization, whereas for government it amounts to a bureaucratic restructuring.

## Communicative Democracy

Indigenous peoples have Aboriginal rights and interests in lands and resources that must be addressed by Canada before those lands and resources can be developed or sold. Once recognized, Aboriginal and treaty rights are protected through sections 25 and 35 of the Constitution Act, 1982. Canadian courts have over the past several decades defined principles about aspects of rights and interests that must be addressed, with respect to the consultation and consent of Indigenous peoples in decision making.[3] In rulings, it is not unusual for courts to encourage Canada and Indigenous peoples to negotiate either a resolution to the issue being litigated or the form of its implementation.[4] However, courts generally make no recommendations as to principles ensuring equality among negotiating parties in resolving such issues. As pointed out by the Canadian auditor general,[5] and well known by Indigenous negotiators, Indigenous peoples enter into negotiations often at a distinct disadvantage compared to governments in terms of money, staff and infrastructure resources, and power. In the self-government negotiations context, for example, Canada controls the "rules of the game" – what may be negotiated, according to the Inherent Right Policy; the allowable expenditures for funding provided to Indigenous parties, according to Canada's own criteria rather than demonstrated need; and, through its imposition of "bottom lines" or final positions in negotiations, limits on the outcomes of negotiation, according to its own policies (which may change as legal decisions or political leaders change). Several anthropologists and sociologists in recent years have examined similar discourse power imbalances associated with co-management and resource management decision-making forums among Indigenous peoples and the state in Canada and Alaska.[6] As several of these studies indicate, one of the ways that unequal power relations play out is in negotiations discourse, revealed through analysis of the way people speak about and to each other in negotiations, shaped in part by shifting power relations among them.[7]

This chapter engages with Iris Marion Young's (2000) work, political theory concerned with the way in which democratic decision making requires inclusion of a diversity of peoples in her theory of communicative democracy. Her analysis asserts that often cultural and interest diversity results in a multiplicity of communicative styles that do not necessarily "translate" effectively and are thus in danger of marginalization, non-understanding, and silencing by dominant communicative norms. Moreover, Young argues that different communicative styles and different social knowledges that the styles contain and embody contribute to a "total social knowledge" beyond the form and substance of a dominant group's knowledge. Three communicative components are examined: greeting, rhetoric, and narrative. According to Young, unmaking such exclusion requires recognition and respect of a plurality of communicative approaches within democratic decision making:

> Though formally included in a forum or process, people may find that their claims are not taken seriously, and may believe they are not treated with equal respect. The dominant mood may find their ideas or modes of expression silly or simple, and not worthy of consideration. They may find that their experiences as relevant to the issues under discussion are so different from others ... that their views are discounted. I call these

familiar experiences *internal* exclusion, because they concern ways that people lack effective opportunity to influence the thinking of others even when they have access to *fora* and procedures of decision-making. (55)

In her analysis of modes of inclusive communication, Young begins by examining uses of recognition and greeting. Actions such as handshakes and polite exchanges at a meeting's outset are essential for establishing what Young calls discursive equality among participants. Her analysis calls to mind standard Dene communicative practices at meetings, including negotiations. People shake hands with and greet all present within the room before the meeting commences; latecomers may exchange discreet handshakes or nods of recognition. Meetings are also usually opened by an elder saying a prayer in his or her language and/or English or by a political leader giving a short welcome in which the presence of visiting officials is recognized and appreciated. These practices help build relationships and trust among participants. And communicative comfort levels are tested. Introductions establish contextual information and simultaneously both signal and acknowledge the authority and legitimacy of individuals participating and acknowledge their right not only to speak but also to be listened to. Dene people I have spoken with about this relate such behaviours to the maintenance of positive social and political relations, emphasizing that greeting rituals are ongoing throughout meetings and decision processes.

Young (2000) argues that generally the type of discourse established as the institutional norm in such decision forums may be presented as neutral or scientific where it is in fact embedded within cultural values and perspectives of the mainstream society, to the disadvantage of marginalized peoples. Young draws from Habermas in arguing that rational speech is communicative and based upon reason, whereas rhetorical speech is emotional. Although the dominant discourse may include both types of communicative approaches, at the same time it may be presented and accepted as neutral and universal. She argues that "what such privileging takes to be neutral, universal, and dispassionate expression actually carries the rhetorical nuances of particular situated social positions and relations, which social conventions do not mark as rhetorical and particular in the same way that they notice others" (63). Rhetorical elements include the illocutionary force of statements; the emotional tone of the content of speech; the use of figures of speech; attitudes produced by using those specific figures; forms of making a point that do not involve speech; and how claims are structured to play on the assumptions, history, and particular idioms familiar to a specific audience. In this chapter we learn how the federal negotiator and later the Dehcho grand chief use rhetoric. Take, for example, the assertion on the part of Canada that potential resource revenues in the amount of $2 million per year are extremely generous by saying the purpose of negotiations is not to make anyone "rich." Classifying this amount as excessive wealth is accomplished by decontextualizing the dollar amount from its uses, the number of governments sharing it, or indeed the fact that Canada would receive a far larger amount as its share of the revenues. Grand Chief Nadli's speech, on the other hand, situates his remarks within an unspoken and presumed knowledge by the audience: of Dehcho people's experiences resulting both from not being treated fairly by Canada (e.g., Treaty 11 not being honoured) and by insisting that Dehcho rights should not be extinguished.

Discourse analysis requires accounting for both things spoken and unspoken. In negotiations, silence is employed as much as language in denying the continuity of injustice into the present, thereby refuting that injustice experienced at some previous date continues to shape Indigenous interests in negotiations. The news report provided at the outset of the chapter provides an illustration of this: a federal negotiator silences galling realities by referring to injustices and suffering as "the past" and "the present." Hard realities captured within the ambiguous temporal labels are effectively erased and made benign and irrelevant as considerations for making decisions about "the future." By refusing to acknowledge suffering, the issue is relegated to a place outside the discourse.

Finally, Young (2000) argues that the use of narrative, stories containing situated social knowledge, is critical to creating a shared social knowledge among groups having different experiences, values, and perspectives. The creation of shared social knowledge is necessary to reach understandings based on shared premises. In situations in which different groups of people bring different social knowledges, the experience of one group of people usually dominates that of another group. Telling stories may be used if no normative language is available for effectively expressing experiences of injustice. In that sense the marginalized language of experience is beyond or apart from the acceptable discourse. According to Young, "stories are told not to entertain or reveal oneself, but to make a point" (72). Discursive reflection through the telling of stories creates a normative language promoting effective communication.

Insights provided through relating experiences may assist in correcting erroneous non-understandings of non-dominant actions. Young (2000) argues that the significant benefit of narrative in communicative practice is the inclusion of many voices necessary to create a "total social knowledge" unavailable through a dominant perspective.[8] Through this, individuals may learn more about themselves and others. The potential for normative functions of narrative according to Young consists in teaching and learning.

Negotiators representing Indigenous peoples often relate suffering experiences to support rationales for increased control of authority. Although such stories are employed as context or rationale for decreased government involvement in service delivery, they are also stories of collective identification through struggle. Stories also convey profound differences in social and cultural practices and understandings between Indigenous and non-Indigenous peoples. Often Indigenous negotiators find it necessary to give examples of why government ways do not work in communities to persuade government officials of the difficulties arising through a lack of local control.

Communicative democracy theory provides tools for understanding the role of discourse in making and unmaking the significance of injustice to negotiations. Young's theoretical insights illuminate the injustice-as-history conflation as a basis for the federal negotiator's stance on royalty sharing to the disadvantage of the Dehcho First Nations. Since a key component of the federal position is to ensure DFN parity with other regions where resource revenue deals have been reached, the discussions examined here in many ways can be taken to echo similar talks at other NWT self-government negotiations.

## We Cannot Extinguish Ourselves

The DFN position in negotiations with Canada has been consistent with a philosophy expressed by Dene representatives in the *Paulette* case (1973), at the hearings of the Mackenzie Valley Pipeline Inquiry of the early 1970s, and in arguments rejecting the 1990 Dene/Métis Agreement. The DFN's official position is that the land (conceived broadly as an ecosystem of which Dene are integral) cannot be bought or sold. As people who have lived there for millennia, the Dene must oversee its responsible stewardship. It is impossible for the Dehcho to agree to extinguishment, because the responsibilities of stewardship are a central part of being Dehcho Dene.[9] The DFN argue that Dehcho Dene laws and ways are the basis of stewardship of lands, resources, and human coexistence. In this view, the GNWT is an illegitimate government, usurping Dene authorities. For the DFN, an increase of GNWT responsibilities proposed through the negotiations is inappropriate because Dene governments, not the GNWT, are the only legitimate institutions with authority over Dene. It is this philosophical stance, echoed within the Indigenous resurgence paradigm, that earned the Dehcho First Nations notoriety as political "radicals," refusing to renounce their own truth in the face of constant pressure from Canada and even other Indigenous leaders to settle a land claim quickly and thus reap the material benefits that would ensue.

Throughout the 1990s, Dehcho representatives held intermittent talks with Canada, attempting to negotiate an agreement on lands, resources, and governance. A special envoy, University of Toronto Professor Peter Russell, an expert in national constitutional reform efforts, travelled throughout the Dehcho communities, conducting consultations on terms of negotiation. Together with Dehcho representatives, he developed a document describing twenty-one common ground principles between Canada and the Dehcho First Nations (Dehcho First Nations 2000) on which negotiations between the DFN and Canada would move forward. The document notes areas of disagreement, namely on ownership, sovereignty, and jurisdiction. However, and importantly for the DFN, the document establishes the principle that "the Dehcho First Nations and Canada intend their relationship to be based on mutual recognition and sharing and to achieve this mutual recognition and sharing by agreeing on rights, rather than by extinguishing rights."

The departure from the extinguishment policy was seen as major progress toward the DFN embarking on developing a new relationship with Canada. However, it is unclear whether this is a matter of semantics. As evidenced by the Tłîchô agreement finalized during 2003, extinguishment has now been replaced by the word *certainty*, which is regarded by Indigenous negotiators generally as *de facto* extinguishment. In addition to the non-extinguishment principle, the "21 Principles" document provides comfort to the DFN in that Canada will commit to a good faith negotiations process; that financial issues will be included in an agreement; and that the future Dehcho government will be public, based on Dene and Canadian laws and customs.

The "21 Principles" document and DFN insistence that the negotiating process be referred to as a "Dehcho process" rather than a comprehensive claim process do little to distinguish the Dehcho negotiations from other land claim and self-government negotiations for Canada. Although the DFN insist that their process is not a comprehensive claim process, comments at the negotiating table by the federal negotiator have made clear that this distinction, reflecting the perspective of the DFN and not Canada, can be presented as either more or less important depending on the audience. Although the process may not be a comprehensive claim, the federal negotiating mandate falls within the comprehensive claim policy (see, e.g., Russell 2002). However, it is true that specific initiatives unavailable in other negotiations have been available to the Dehcho (and Akaitcho), such as interim measures agreements over resource management and revenues, agreements which take effect prior to the beginning of substantive final agreement negotiations. Prefacing discussions toward final agreements by reaching interim agreements allows all parties to agree that the process negotiations are, in that respect, unique.[10]

The 1998 *Dehcho Proposal* document articulates the Dehcho vision of self-government, seeking co-stewardship of lands with Canada, for example by establishing a Crown in right of the Dehcho. It will either own all lands in Dehcho territory or with Canada will co-conveyance full title to lands. In this way, the parties can finesse the important legal distinction of establishing land ownership versus title. Ownership vests with the Crown in accordance with legal doctrine relating to land ownership. "Title" is a legal mechanism recognizing that, while the DFN may possess and use lands, underlying ownership rests with the Crown, not the DFN. As a result, DFN ownership and establishing a Crown in right of the Dehcho are not proposals Canada is likely to entertain as a final agreement option. Canada has consistently rejected the "Crown in right of the Dehcho" model as being tantamount to provincial recognition. For Canada, agreeing to co-convey lands to the Dehcho government would provide the Dehcho government with underlying title to the land which constitutionally has only been extended to provinces. By agreeing to co-conveyancing, Canada would be moving in a direction treating the Dehcho government as "province-like," affording the potential to open up a variety of legal and political advantages to the Dehcho which are jealously guarded by provincial governments. Based on negotiating position documents posted on the Dehcho process website, Canada sees the Dehcho agreement containing provisions similar to other comprehensive claim agreements in the NWT – where the DFN have surface and subsurface title to a percentage of lands in their traditional territory and may participate in land and resource management. According to a report by Peter Russell on the results of a governance workshop held at the Dehcho community of Trout Lake in the spring of 2002,

> The government of Canada's preference is to treat land issues in a similar manner to that used in "comprehensive [land claim] agreements." If this approach were followed, full Dehcho control and ownership would only apply to "community lands," while the remaining parts of Dehcho territory would be Crown lands on which Dehcho jurisdiction is devolved by the federal government and resource management is shared with the federal and territorial governments. The government of Canada recognizes that this is different from the approach favoured by the Dehcho which calls for Dehcho ownership and jurisdiction of and over the whole Dehcho territory. (2002, 1)

To its credit, Canada is also contemplating that a regional public government may manage aspects of Crown ownership of lands, a scenario that was contemplated for all regional and Indigenous governments at NWT devolution negotiations that took place between 2001 and 2006. I attended several public Dehcho negotiations during 2000-01, and at that point in discussions few details of governance and land ownership and management had been discussed since the focus was on interim measures. At that time, optimism among stakeholders was high that the Dehcho process would result in a final agreement significantly different from other NWT land claim agreements. As the government responds to concrete positions, and details of mechanisms for actualizing principles are fleshed out, it is apparent that the DFN are likely to achieve an agreement similar to other NWT comprehensive land claim agreements. However, the Dehcho are enjoying the advantages of small improvements in government policies, such as interim measures agreements regarding lands and resources, and Canada's willingness to devolve authorities to a regional government, resulting in part from a constantly evolving legal and policy environment.

The next section of this chapter recounts differences in positions between Canada and the DFN, illustrating ways that Aboriginal policy's injustice-as-history conflation has a specific and detrimental bearing on calculating resource royalties the DFN will receive. The government's separation of injustice from present suffering undercuts DFN arguments for receiving a greater share of royalties. From this we move to a speech by the grand chief at a negotiating session that exemplifies the difference of the DFN approach to negotiations from Canada's approach. The DFN view is rooted in history, experience, and the continuity of both with the present and the future. This view contrasts with that of Canada, which asserts positions narrow in scope, devoid of history, and contextualized within the future, as outlined in the news report at the beginning of this chapter.

### Greed and the Future

We are not here to make anyone rich.
We are here to rebalance the situation.

– Chief negotiator for Canada, Dehcho process
negotiations, November 2001

Dehcho Dene along with their Akaitcho Dene neighbours to the southeast are the last of the five Dene peoples in the NWT to negotiate with Canada over rights to lands, resources, and governance. The Dehcho negotiations began during 2000, initially focusing on interim measures ensuring DFN participation in land and resource management while simultaneously negotiating a land and governance agreement. One key element of interim measures includes the DFN receiving a share of resource royalties from resource extraction in the Mackenzie Valley. This was favoured by the DFN, consistent with the belief that Dene should enjoy benefits of resources in Dehcho territory prior to finalizing an agreement with Canada.

During discussions ultimately resulting in two interim measures agreements – the Interim Resource Development Agreement (2001) and the Interim Measures Agreement (2001) – the DFN proposed that successful resource exploration applications on DFN traditional territories should be determined by the amount of royalty payments developers would be willing to make directly to the DFN, beyond what was required by Canada (Dehcho First Nations 2002a). The DFN reasoned, in part, that billions of dollars of resource royalties made from unceded Dene lands have flowed to Canada since treaties were signed in 1900 and 1921. Given that the NWT has the lowest royalty rate in Canada, the DFN were confident additional royalty sharing, essentially private agreements between developers with the Dehcho, would not deter resource developers.[11]

Revenue sharing agreements included in the Gwich'in and Sahtu land claim agreements amount at most to a few hundred thousand dollars a year.[12] Indigenous governments' shares are based on a formula anticipating eventual equitable shares of royalties from resources in the Mackenzie Valley to all Indigenous governments in the NWT. The position of First Nations and Métis councils of the Dehcho, negotiating as a collective, is that a few hundred thousand dollars a year to share between all Dehcho governments do not reflect their collective fair share of the value of the resources being taken from their lands, compared with the profits to developers and royalties flowing to Canada at current market value.

The next section recounts an exchange between Canada and the Dehcho during revenue sharing negotiations. It captures issues at the core of the disagreement over financing between the DFN and Canada. Critical to Canada's arguments is the implicit characterization of the DFN as becoming wealthy as a result of their revenue sharing proposals, particularly compared to other Dene peoples in the NWT. This sentiment resonates with widely held mainstream perceptions that such agreements are "handouts" rather than long-overdue economic rent for Indigenous-owned resources. Canada's remarks include constant reminders that the land and resources in question are owned by Canada. This latter assertion can accurately be described as fantasy, given the genealogy of the Dehcho process, with its origin partly in the findings of *Re: Paulette* (1973), a court judgment that found Dene had not surrendered their lands.

### November 2001 Negotiations

These negotiations, like so many others, were held in a large boardroom at the DFN offices in Liidlii Kue (Fort Simpson) over three days during November 2001. Rectangular folding tables were set up in a large square, around which representatives of each negotiating party sat facing each other. Dress was casual, with government and Indigenous teams alike sporting casual jeans and shirts; that of the audience was punctuated with the occasional moosehide jacket, mittens, or vest. Government teams included negotiators, lawyers, and resource people. DFN representatives at the table included a chief negotiator/lawyer based in Toronto, negotiator Herb Norwegian, the DFN's executive director, and several elders, chiefs, and band councillors. Band council chiefs, elders, and band councillors attending intermittently sat in the audience, occasionally congregating briefly at the coffee maker near the entrance at the back of the room, along with members of the public and the DFN's communications team. Also at the back of the room sat two translators taking turns translating proceedings from English to Slavey and Slavey to English as required, which the audiences availed themselves of through small plastic headsets that had been provided at the meeting's start. Audio recordings were made for transcription and the DFN's permanent records.

Negotiations generally are tedious affairs, meetings held in airless boardrooms in places like Ottawa or Yellowknife or in cavernous meeting halls in small communities. Often meetings take place in the affected community/ies, but the presence of large numbers of technical officials or the need to meet with southern-based lawyers and consultants sometimes makes meetings in larger centres more economical. To their credit, often Canada's Ottawa-based negotiators travel long distances from home for extended periods to negotiate in communities. Similarly, Indigenous negotiators are required to travel frequently to attend to negotiations-related business with various government officials based in larger centres, meet with southern-based team members, or speak at conferences or meetings. Although to some this lifestyle may seem glamorous, a more apt description was captured by the government negotiator in the first chapter, who cited a study that found divorce rates among negotiators extremely high. Negotiating is not all dinners out and high-level decision making. On the contrary, several years of constant travel can be physically and psychologically wearing, and most negotiating teams undergo several changes of leadership and technical advisors during the lifespan of a negotiation. The negotiations themselves are usually detailed discussions of technical aspects of programs, services, and legislation, often described by one negotiator I worked with as "about as interesting as watching paint dry." Separated frequently from family, unable to maintain consistent participation in community activities, and often having to forgo social lives due to work commitments, negotiators hold a job requiring significant personal sacrifice.

The personal demands of the negotiating lifestyle often affect the attitudes and negotiating styles of those involved. Southern-based participants are often openly anxious to finish sessions and return home to their families, changing travel plans during breaks if they believe a session will finish early, or asking their colleagues to take stock of progress throughout a session, indicating that their travel plans will change if they can leave early. Sometimes this may affect their willingness to engage in substantive discussions of items that may take more time than anticipated. Tensions between teams and the difficulties of being away from domestic responsibilities, coupled with negotiating's inherently stressful nature, can often make for tense and heated discussions.

The exchange below took place between the chief negotiators of Canada and the DFN respectively. The manner of the DFN chief negotiator at that time was often caustic, resulting in the atmosphere remaining at a high level of tension throughout discussions. Similarly, Canada's negotiator adopted an offense-oriented hard-line attitude. Their respective attitudes were conveyed through both tone of voice and choice of words as well as off-hand remarks and body language such as crossed arms or frustrated shuffling of papers or impassive staring as negotiators explained their positions. The overall result was for discussions to become heated quickly, negatively affecting the potential for mutual problem solving. The discussion focuses on a proposal from Canada that the Dehcho would receive 12.5 percent of resource revenues generated in the Mackenzie Valley on a yearly basis. Canada was offering an amount larger than that contained in similar agreements with the Gwich'in and Sahtu Dene.

> Canada (C): The purpose of these negotiations is not to make people rich, it's to rebalance the situation.
>
> Canada would do things like look at caps on revenues that the Dehcho was slated to receive under a royalty sharing agreement. So there are drawbacks in this just as there are in territorial funding formulas [which allow the federal government to claw back revenues once a certain revenue threshold has been reached]. The Dehcho will be a public government with a strong Aboriginal component, so essentially the Dehcho government would be paid for by revenue generated in Dehcho territory with Dehcho resources.

We are getting at financing really early on in the game here. The big issue to come will be regional versus community sharing – who will get what? Canada is looking at a small scale revenue agreement where seed money would go to communities for them to operate. They could then open up small areas of their territory for development and build up capacity so that if large scale development occurs, then we know people will be able to take advantage of it.

Dehcho (D): The Dehcho has yet to discuss how any funds would be shared among its member governments. The more we can show funds flowing from the development of their territories to Dehcho member governments, the more we can look at opening things up for development. The discussion to date has been about opening up 1 or 2 areas for development, negotiating Impact Benefit Agreements, then looking at how that would be shared.

C: Canada is dealing with the DFN (Dehcho First Nations). If you've got internal deals to make, make them ... Until we know what community governments are responsible for and how that is funded, Canada reserves its position. How you internally want to share your wealth is up to you.

D: All that is being offered here on revenue sharing is a [standard] comprehensive claim revenue formula. The Dehcho wants something different. We want a market based revenue share.

C: We think the formula on the table right now is fine. In addition to that you also want a land bonus! [A "land bonus" is money over and above the revenue share, a market-value-based fee paid by developers for the opportunity to develop the land.]

D: We want an arrangement that generates new money. Our proposal would tell us if the market would bear that. It doesn't touch the existing royalty regime. As long as the royalties are being pooled for the Mackenzie Valley we expect that the Dehcho would get some share of that, we just want to see if we can generate some extra money ... We recognize that it ties into which [oil and gas development] exploration parcels [of land] to open up – the parcels have to be the right size to get mid and large size [oil and gas exploration] companies interested. That would give the Dehcho incentive to open up larger parcels, rather than keeping it to small parcels.

C:  Canada's position is that the Dehcho does not own the land [therefore the Dehcho is not in a position to charge extra fees to companies wanting to exploit resources on lands not owned by the Dehcho]. If this [proposal] was to fly, there would be reluctance to paying out over and above what was put on the table [in the final agreement]. Canada says it will take a governance approach: if you are going to get money, what are you doing with the money? You would have to pay for governance with the money you would get. (Dehcho negotiation sessions 2001)

The above exchange illustrates fundamental differences between Canada and the DFN. Canada asserts land ownership. However, this assertion directly contradicts its own rationale for entering into the Dehcho process, with which the Dehcho agrees: land claim agreements in the NWT are necessary because, as determined in the *Paulette* case of 1973, provisions of Treaties 8 and 11 were unfulfilled, rendering invalid the land rights extinguishment provisions of those treaties.

Canada does not see resource revenues as monies being provided to the DFN in recognition of ownership, as compensation for revenues on resources extracted from their traditional territories and resources. Instead, Canada's position is future-focused, dwelling on neither past nor present, taking into account neither injustice nor suffering: a governance approach. Funds provided through resource revenue provisions of the agreement should be used to pay for the costs of governance according to the agreement. It is not meant as compensation for injustice that the Dehcho may use according to their own priorities or as recognition of Dehcho ownership. Governance costs are those for which Canada would otherwise be responsible.

It seemed Canada had carefully considered how money and financing provisions should be understood by the DFN and how funding should be separated from notions of injustice, land ownership, and past and current experiences of Dehcho people in terms of governance, poverty, and future aspirations. Canada's arguments, in part, attempt to marginalize the narrative offered by the DFN by insisting that the same financing principles applied to other Dene should apply to the Dehcho. At the outset of discussions, the criteria of the dominant party determine the funding rationale: governance costs of authorities recognized in the agreement, according to its own criteria. When the Dehcho raises the issue of their concerns that amounts will be shared among member governments, Canada's response is essentially that it is not Canada's problem if the money is shared or not: "If you've got internal deals to make, make them." Dehcho perceptions, concerns, plans for determining their own future seem to be irrelevant.

Not only does Canada determine that resource revenues should only be used for governance purposes, but as we see below at the outset of "negotiations" Canada proposes what appears to be a final offer, while simultaneously admitting the content of a final agreement – and therefore the costs of governance – are unknown.

## Predetermined Negotiation Outcomes:
## The January 2002 Negotiations

The following exchange is taken from resource revenue sharing discussions during a negotiating session in January 2002. Again, the session took place over a period of three days, at the DFN boardroom in Liidlii Kue. It was a particularly cold week, with temperatures hovering around -45° Celsius. I had driven to Fort Simpson from Yellowknife for the session, delaying my return trip on the advice of various people that my truck, a reliable sport utility vehicle, might not make the eight-hour trip back to Yellowknife in such extreme cold.

The meeting room for the session was located just off the front entrance of the DFN offices. When the door to the meeting room was not closed, a chill would sweep through the room when the nearby exterior door opened. It was cold enough that most people kept their jackets at their seats to ward off the frequent shocks of cold air. Despite the frigid temperatures, the negotiations commenced on time at 9 a.m. The negotiating teams were dressed in casual sweaters and jackets, several sitting on coats for warmth against the cold plastic of their chairs. They sat together around a series of about twenty inexpensive folding tables arranged in a wide rectangle so that negotiating teams could face each other. The two translators, along with about twenty observers from the community, sat near the back of the room, closer to the door. As though a testament to the meagre resources provided to the Dehcho First Nations for their operations, the meeting room was a large multi-purpose space, starkly lit by overhead fluorescent lights and sparsely decorated with a few posters tacked to the walls. Plastic stacking chairs were arranged in rows facing the negotiating table, on a chipped and well-worn floor of linoleum tile. A small table set up in the back of the room held an industrial model Bunn-O-Matic coffee maker sporting two half-full carafes. Beside it was a worn white plastic kettle to boil water for tea, along with packets of store-bought cookies that would appear intermittently throughout the meeting. The décor and food were in stark contrast to the warm and well-appointed boardrooms with large wooden meeting tables surrounded by padded ergonomic chairs for both participants and observers and catered snacks of baked goods and fresh fruit that characterized surroundings of government meeting rooms in Yellowknife and larger centres.

C: We are putting ... resource revenue sharing on the table early in the game. That is unprecedented ... You would not believe the nervousness in Ottawa regarding the possibility of no land selection. Of course we must take into account [what is happening at] other tables. The Canadian public [interest] demands it. Ever since the Peter Russell approach [a ministerial envoy appointed to initiate discussions with the Dehcho] we have gone a different way [than the comprehensive claims approach taken with other Indigenous peoples in the NWT]. Lots of outside issues and pressures have begun to affect this table in a negative way ...

So we are negotiating governance and resources at the same time here. I need to know what's happening here, what you want your model to be. If it does not include land selection then that's fine – it is definitely an interest of Canada to look at new models. (Dehcho negotiation sessions 2002)

And later on during the same session,

C: The issue for us here is equitable sharing across the NWT. The oil and gas play around Fort Liard has been critical for allowing us to do things differently at this table – it shows the potential of the Dehcho ... The [royalty sharing] formula proposed in the federal draft would be acceptable in a Final Agreement.

D: That formula gives us nothing!

C: Your support is required ... Canada won't go ahead without it. And Canada is prepared to wait. (Dehcho negotiation sessions 2002)

Young's (2000) theory of communicative democracy does not anticipate decision processes where outcomes are predetermined through mandates of the state. By any standard, the comments of Canada in this exchange cannot be received as good faith negotiation. Rather, it is internal exclusion of the worst kind – blatant coercion. Instead of considering the DFN position in relation to need, or seeking clarification as to why Canada should be convinced to alter its policy, the negotiator simply asserts its superior resources – Canada is able and willing to wait out the DFN, which, having been completely dispossessed of lands and resources, and carefully controlled through the federal Indian Act, is left without independent sources of revenue or income. It is expected by Canada that the DFN, eventually, will come to heel, when they have been exhausted by the mounting pressures that prompted the Dene to regional claims in the early

1990s: resource extraction enriching private interests and other governments, creating opportunities for Indigenous peoples with land claim agreements, and denying similar opportunities to those without an agreement. Sadly, these negotiating tactics are not specific to the Dehcho negotiations. At some point during all other negotiations in the NWT that I have attended, I have witnessed this type of coercion, without exception.

The September 1998 *Auditor General's Report* underscored the significance of the disparity in relative power and resources between Canada and Indigenous peoples at land claim negotiations (Government of Canada, Auditor General of Canada 1998). It noted that negotiations are weighted in favour of Canada, which determines the criteria for accepting claims, the policy parameters restricting subjects for discussion, and the participation funding available to Indigenous people. In light of these realities, it is easy to feel, as a representative of Indigenous governments, so outresourced and overpowered that any attempt at negotiating what communities really want is futile. Instead, it feels as though negotiations are really a forum for governments to consult on and develop mechanisms that will merely offload programs to Indigenous communities in a way that does not inconvenience the bureaucratic systems of governments.

The above exchange highlights the ability of governments to control process outcomes. The threat of passive coercion, such as the indication given that Canada will simply do nothing and instead wait for an agreement, is one in a range of tactics used by government negotiators that amounts to discounting Indigenous rationales and arguments. Marginalizing approaches also include silence: refusing to respond to negotiation positions for months at a time. Continuous, minute wording changes of specific clauses in agreements over a period of years may be pursued until an intended objective is achieved, and the language preferred by Indigenous negotiators is argued out of the text on the advice of Ottawa-based legal and policy advisors whose place of residence and life experiences lie far from the people and the daily impacts of the agreement. In this case, while Canada's representative pressures the DFN to submit a governance proposal justifying its revenue demands, his position on revenue sharing appears final – Canada is prepared to wait out the Dehcho's initial refusal. If this is merely a negotiating tactic, the message is clear that a change in the current resource revenue proposal will come at a cost to the Dehcho, which will have to compromise its position on some other element of the negotiations to secure a better resource revenue share.

The next day at the same negotiating session the discussion continued. The tone of the federal negotiator remained consistent, a harsh insistence punctuated by occasionally leaning forward in his seat to emphasize a point. A neatly dressed Aboriginal man in his mid-thirties, his demeanour was confident, arms folded as he leaned back in his chair, conveying his sense of confidence and authority of Canada's positions:

> C: This agreement has to be comparable with other agreements, taking the different circumstances into account: population, lands, the value of the lands ... The Dehcho thinks there should be a Crown in right of the Dehcho, and that it should be more than symbolic. For us, this will depend on how the other issues in this agreement are resolved. We are looking at options such as the co-conveyance of land [where Canada and the Dehcho would convey full title of Dehcho traditional territory lands to each other] – both sides [Canada and Dehcho] disagree on title and so under that model, both sides would wind up with title. This certainly may be a way to finalize the land title issue.

> D: Earlier you made the comment on comparability of this agreement with others and that the value of our agreement must be compatible with other ones. We are not sure what that means. The Dehcho wants own source financing other than self government specific financing, and the Dehcho wants control of lands. The core issues are for us not so much about money, as about control over pace of development and environmental management, and a secure [and independent] source of revenue. Making sure that we are not dependent on the two other governments [Canada and the GNWT] is more the focus of what we are saying. (Dehcho negotiation sessions 2002)

The notion of comparability with other agreements raises the potential of the DFN having to make an agreement with Canada based on extinguishment. Canada's insistence on comparability with other agreements is perceived as dismissing essential DFN concerns.

### Getting Rich? Costs of Colonization

There are thirteen First Nations and Métis Locals represented in negotiations; it is expected the Dehcho agreement will recognize all of these and a regional government with ten communities to administer, with approximately 4,500 Indigenous people represented,[13] 2,879 resident in the Dehcho region of the NWT.[14] Under the 12.5 percent royalty sharing proposal, all of these governments would share $2 million a year – under favourable market conditions.[15] No one bothered to point this out to Canada's negotiator. Furthermore, as Canada indicated, the money would most likely be considered "own-source revenue" of the Dehcho government.

Therefore, it could be taken into account when determining overall funding to the Dehcho government recognized by an agreement. Since finance agreements are usually negotiated separately from the agreement itself, that status at the time was uncertain. Under financing agreements, Canada usually reduces its contribution by a percentage of what self-governments take in own-source revenue, for example fifty to eighty cents on the dollar (or more). So, for example, a $2 million revenue payment to a Dehcho government would mean Canada could reduce its self-government financing funding by $1 million to $1.6 million. Clearly, the federal negotiator's insistence that the Dehcho would have to use any revenues for governance indicates that Canada would expect to reduce its funding to the Dehcho in direct proportion to the revenues generated.

The federal negotiator's arguments implied that royalties would mean abundant wealth beyond DFN needs: there would be caps on revenues, he said, and these royalties would have a bearing on the amount of funding that would be provided to operate the Dehcho government. The implication was that basic operations and their capacities would be controlled according to what Canada thought the Dehcho required.

The future reality of wealth projected by Canada onto potential DFN gains resulting from a volatile market-driven frontier oil and gas industry that had failed in the past, as evidenced by the "bust" cycle experienced by the Mackenzie Delta in the 1980s, was met with silence from the DFN negotiator. Like so many other everyday insults and disingenuous government posturing, the accusation of greed was too ridiculous to register as an argument worth comment. Perhaps protesting Canada's tactics would have distracted from DFN arguments directed toward the overarching goal: minimizing DFN risk and vulnerability vis-à-vis the government, instead creating a future marked by independence from Canada's control of DFN lands, resources, and lives. Out-resourced, denied recognition of experienced injustice, and forced to prove a need for resources consistent with Canada's ideas of how funding would be used, the DFN could do nothing but reiterate its position and wait for the chance to reiterate its position again in the context of the subject matter next on the agenda for that day's discussion.

The DFN represent approximately 24.5 percent or just over 4,000 of a total of 19,000 Dene people in the NWT and approximately 300 Métis.[16] Theirs is a story typical of Indigenous peoples in the NWT in terms of unemployment, where rates range from 11 percent in Fort Simpson to 38 percent in Wrigley,[17] with an overall unemployment rate for Indigenous people being approximately 20 percent, as compared to an overall rate of 10 percent in the NWT[18] and 6.3 percent in Canada as a whole.[19] In the

Dehcho region, Dehcho culture and the Slavey language are relatively strong compared with the culture and language of other regions, as are subsistence pursuits such as frequent hunting and fishing.[20]

In many ways, the situation of the Dehcho peoples is similar to that of Dene throughout the NWT. Where I lived during fieldwork for a time in Liidli Kue (Fort Simpson), generally well kept older stick-built and log houses lined dirt roads. Smokehouses and storage freezers stand in many yards and porches. People share wild meat and fish and other country foods, which remain a dietary and social mainstay for many residents. As in many other Dene communities, the Dehcho struggles with both experiences of past and continuous colonial intervention, combatted through efforts toward sobriety and healing. For example, a residential school survivors group was established through the efforts of a Fort Providence resident in 2002, and in casual conversation testimonies of overcoming personal struggles with unwellness are closely linked to narratives of culture and tradition as a source of strength and purpose. The Dehcho process figures prominently in narratives of healing, recovery, and increased educational and training opportunities despite the circumstances of colonization: the process promises a chance at prosperity. This prosperity is conceived of as primarily cultural and spiritual and to a lesser degree material. A critical aspect of prosperity is a state of non-chaotic, stable existence, predicated on Dene values and practices, unmediated by the social pathologies of colonization. This vision of what in part constitutes wealth is in stark contrast with the worries of Canada expressed at negotiations that the DFN's resource revenue sharing proposals would make the Dehcho rich. Although money and economic concerns are certainly a basis upon which social suffering could be addressed, addressing suffering requires not only material aid but also attention to spiritual, psychological, and cultural resources. Having control of revenues independent of federal or territorial governments would allow the DFN freedom to create its vision of prosperity on its own terms.

### Being Dehcho Dene: An Indigenous Refusal of Colonization

For the DFN, virtually all other initiatives – from devolution negotiations to involvement in territorial resource management initiatives to approving a Mackenzie Valley pipeline – are assessed in terms of their relationship with and effects on the Dehcho process. At leadership meetings held three or four times each year at alternating locations in the region, in addition to an annual assembly open to all members usually held at Kakisa in June, chiefs and elected representatives gather to discuss strategies and issues relating to economic development, lands, and hunting, fishing, and trapping issues, as well as cultural and social concerns. INAC and territorial government initiatives are discussed. The Dehcho process is always a major agenda item, and woven throughout the diverse array of topics on meeting agendas are constant references to the source of strength of the Dehcho First Nations: the vitality of Dehcho language and culture.

Most leaders speak Slavey, and simultaneous translation is provided at leadership meetings, as at negotiation sessions. Leaders as a rule pride themselves on prioritizing Dene knowledge and principles in their dealings with government. At the January 2002 negotiating session, this consistent pattern of commitment to Dene principles and beliefs was established by several leaders speaking to the experience of being Dene. Functioning as a combination of greeting and narrative, the opening words of Grand Chief Mike Nadli to the negotiators and audience emphasized the consistent commitment to Dene ways through the history of negotiations in the NWT and as a central tenet of ongoing discussions between Canada and the DFN. The way he spoke and the content of his remarks provided an example of Dene-specific (rather than negotiations) discourse as an integral part of Dene narrative being used to educate negotiators of the Dehcho views and indicated that their negotiators speak with the full authority and support of the leaders.

**From Field Notes, Dehcho Process Negotiations, Liidlii Kue, January 22, 2002**
Grand Chief Mike Nadli gave the opening prayer, praying to the Creator, and to the Prophet who lived among the people at the time of the Treaty 11 signing, who was a source of great leadership. A pair of beautifully beaded moosehide gloves lie on the table in front of him, as he has just come into the meeting from the cold. His manner is calm, authoritative, and sincere, and he speaks in a low tone, though his voice carries to the back of the room. During the prayer he continues that the elders remind us that we should still pray to the Creator. He mentions the people who have committed themselves to this process, seeking blessing both for them and for their families back home and especially their children. Chief Nadli's prayer was followed by welcomes from the Liidlii Kue chief Rita Cli and Métis elder Albertine Rodh. Chief Nadli acknowledged leaders and elders in attendance in his opening comments:

When we look at the beginnings of this process with Peter Russell, we saw it was a process of building consensus. People in the region are as a result knowledgeable and supportive of this process. We need to know the interests of governments in this process. We need to be open with each other. This process builds on Treaties 8 and 11. The purpose of this process is to build two parallel trails – one for us and one for the non-Aboriginal people. The vision of the elders is to maintain our way of life. We want to live according to our values and principles. Through this process we are trying to implement that vision. That was the view in 1921 [when Dehcho Dene entered into Treaty 11] and it continues to this day. So we need to resolve issues of sovereignty, ownership, and jurisdiction. The Crown asserts ownership over this land. And so on that we have to agree to disagree. One of the principles is that we agree to educate each other. We give information about our ways and they will provide information on models or ways things are done [in land and governance agreements] across Canada.

Every once in a while there is an impasse. We need to move away from fear to make progress.

This process is unique. No other region or First Nation has achieved what we have so far, especially in the progress on interim measures. And with respect to models, our uniqueness is pronounced at this point. We have watched other [NWT] groups who are at the [negotiating] table [with Canada]. We DFNs were the Dene Nation for a long time. We stayed. We didn't walk [he is referring to Gwich'in and Sahtu peoples negotiating regional claims on their own beginning in 1990 instead of remaining as part of the Dene Nation negotiations]. Recently in Yellowknife we have seen the agenda of the Dene Nation. It has become a very claimant-group [oriented] agenda. We are wondering if we should stay there. There are regional routes ... We are wondering if we should do that. We see the Inuvialuits [sic]. They have created wealth in their country. We see that. It's the same with the Gwich'in and Sahtu. For us here – what will the Dehcho gain from a pipeline? The honest truth is that we are not there yet. The Interim Resource Development Agreement is being negotiated here today to guarantee us benefits of any development ...

This government [we are negotiating] will be based on our values and principles. We need to work on the basis that the Dehcho government has always been the government in this region ... Right now in the media there is an emphasis on development – but despite the promises of money from development there are still social problems in this region. The basis for this is that we have a treaty and it is unfulfilled. (Dehcho negotiation sessions 2002)

Grand Chief Nadli's comments exemplify the resort to narrative as described by Young (2000) previously. Just as government discounted DFN concerns despite the negotiation setting, Grand Chief Nadli's greeting exercise includes a narrative establishing DFN authority and legitimacy to hold its opposing position. Moreover, his words reinforce DFN insistence in speaking outside of government terminology and frames of understanding. It stands as an example of the ways in which Indigenous governments and representatives are forced to use multiple languages and narratives – legal, political, cultural, and emotional – to convey the frame of reference and scope of variables within which negotiations are situated.

Grand Chief Nadli's eloquence educates the negotiators and observers about the DFN perspective and its rationale, while giving thanks and honouring elders and their place in Dehcho experience and worldview. Through it, Nadli situates the progress of the Dehcho within the ongoing struggle of the Dehcho peoples for rights recognition and recognition of their authority and belonging to their lands. The message stresses coexistence and that the difference between Dene and non-Indigenous existence stems from not only culture and values but also the Dehcho peoples' rightful place as stewards of Dehcho territories. Stewardship elements are not only jurisdictional but also cultural and spiritual. His words, typical of speeches given by elders and leaders in similar situations, are without ambiguity or euphemism. The narrative situates intergovernmental relationships within a specific sequence of events, indicating how difficulties and successes owe more to approaches to issue resolution than the specific issues themselves: the fear that blocks negotiations progress, the consistency of the DFN in their approach to negotiations, the pressures arising from differences in material conditions of regions. His narrative detail conveys explicit information to Canada, highlighting Dehcho conceptual understandings as starkly different from government manners of speech, going beyond law and policy to recognize emotional, spiritual, ideological, and moral forces at play.

At the same time, Grand Chief Nadli finesses difficult truths. Canada at the time was continually pressuring the DFN to support a Mackenzie Valley pipeline and devolution negotiations. And, consistent with its policy, it emphasized the importance of Canada's economic interests despite their impact on Dehcho rights recognition. Grand Chief Nadli responds firmly through his statements, establishing conditions requisite for DFN support of a pipeline and territorial devolution negotiations. He indicates that "we are not there yet," that getting there must be done by the Dehcho on its

own terms, and that the DFN have not been afraid to take the path of greater
resistance in similar situations, such as opposing rather than acquiescing
to rights extinguishment. Grand Chief Nadli in this way subtly links the
most pressing issue for the Dehcho region: daily conditions of many people's lives, "social problems," with the purpose and desired results of the
negotiating process. He also raises the underlying issue of the unfulfilled
treaty, the material dispossession and political marginalization which is
at the root of the poverty and suffering in the region. In contrast to Canada's history-less, future-focused approach, Grand Chief Nadli situates
Dehcho interests squarely within the Dehcho experience and lived reality – the things that Dehcho peoples know for sure.

In another way, Grand Chief Nadli responds in kind to Canada's consistent rebuffs of DFN proposals and rationales on resource revenue sharing.
Just as Canada indicated it was "prepared to wait" on the DFN acquiescing to Canada's formula on proposed resource revenues, Grand Chief Nadli
indicates that the DFN have proven they are capable of similar waiting,
as they have been in securing a Dehcho process rather than agreeing to
a comprehensive claim process. Moreover, this waiting is not simply posturing; rather, it is a simple fact: the Dehcho are "not there yet." Without resources to address its priorities, or meaningful recognition of the
DFN perspective in the process, or recognition of the DFN's right to participate in directing and benefiting from development, support for a
pipeline does not exist among Dehcho peoples. This is in contrast to other
Dene, Métis, and Inuvialuit who are in a position to take advantage of
megaproject developments, such as a Mackenzie Valley pipeline, rather than
be overwhelmed by them.

# Dehcho Negotiations

Mike Nadli (left) and INAC Minister Robert Nault speak at the Dehcho IMA signing. File photo courtesy of INAC.

Mike Nadli (foreground) and Peter Russell at a workshop at Trout Lake. File photo courtesy of INAC.

## Conclusion

This chapter has provided insight into how Aboriginal policy's conflation of injustice and the past and its consequent separation from suffering function with respect to discussing revenue sharing, an essential element of financing governance. The discussions provide insight into the rationale, strategy, and differences in perceptions of the negotiating parties. For Canada, comparability with other agreements and control over the end results – such as ensuring revenues are used strictly for governance – shape its mandate. For the DFN, agreement provisions on revenue sharing must provide a basis for Dehcho independence from other governments, a conviction rooted in experiences of injustice, suffering, and government control of programs and services. The DFN position is also rooted in an ethic resonant with the Indigenous resurgence paradigm, for the fundamental principles informing that ethic are ones that speak to the necessity for Dehcho First Nations being able to live as Indigenous peoples on their terms, rather than as Aboriginals as determined by the Canadian state.

The understandings of Canada and the DFN differ in terms of rationales for negotiation mandates, practical and psychological significance of potential outcomes, and implications for intergovernmental relationships. The negotiation process is a forum for reaching practical arrangements of power sharing, but as Young (2000) argues and Chief Nadli acknowledges it is also the site of mutual education and compromise toward building a mutually respected frame of reference within which agreement can be reached. A critical challenge lies in reconciling divergent perspectives in order to reach an agreement, through creating a "total social knowledge." The accounts of exchanges between negotiators above do not offer evidence of the sort of openness and potential necessary for that mutual respect to develop. Perhaps the greater challenge is that efforts to establish a common framework will only continue to founder in a forum where the DFN voice is marginalized: through the restrictions placed by policy and need for comparability with other agreements at the outset, the refusals of Canada's negotiator to recognize the relevance of injustice, and the coercion used in an effort to turn the DFN to accept Canada's negotiating positions.

One of the most important elements of any self-government agreement is financing. The previous discussion has provided a limited glimpse into basic interests shaping financing negotiations mandates. Once basic principles can be established among the parties, they must be translated into policies shaping funding of specific programs, capital infrastructure improvements, cost escalators, and incremental and one-time implementation costs. It is at the stage of broad principles where what is included or excluded can make all the difference in future financing discussions. For example, if resource rev-̇enue formulas are tied to governance costs, the definition of governance will have to be comprehensive and anticipatory if the DFN hope to ensure that their own interests are met through that definition.

This also raises the difficulties inherent to translating basic principles shaping the DFN mandate into dollars and cents. For example, the DFN interest that financing should promote decreased dependence on transfer payments from Canada may translate into negotiating financing agreements based on a complex formula allowing for several years of funding guaranteed in advance, block funded (as opposed to funding predetermined on a program basis by Canada), and including escalators (adjustments compensating for increases in inflation, population, etc., affecting program funding needs). It is through financial discussions that degrees of DFN independence will be determined. If their negotiators secure a deal that makes the new governments more accountable to Canada and the GNWT than their own constituents, generous jurisdictional and revenue provisions will make little difference if program funding and standards cannot accommodate the DFN visions of Slavey language school instruction or support for elders to participate on resource management boards.

This chapter has provided an example of how the injustice-as-history conflation combines with a refusal to hear the Indigenous suffering narrative or need-based arguments in negotiations. It sets the stage for looking at how the same phenomenon functions within negotiations taking place in Délînê, north of the Dehcho territory. As we will see in the next chapter, the analysis of Canada's future focus orientation taken with the Dehcho is further developed through examining Child and Family Services negotiations between the GNWT and Délînê Dene. The next chapter highlights the deep roots of the ironic denial of injustice as a source of social suffering, accompanied by government's use of evidence of social suffering to deny Indigenous control of Indigenous lives and communities.

### Soaking Moosehides in Brain Water

From Field Notes, Tanning Camp, July 2002
The small white canvas bag hung from the trees beside the tent for several days before it was taken down. Everyone gathered around a washtub of water heating on the fire as Jane shaved half a bar of Ivory soap into a small pot of warm water on her lap. Only Ivory soap should be used, she said, as she shaved thin slices from the small white bar with a

paring knife, using a whisk to periodically dissolve the shavings in the water. She poured the solution into the washtub, then reached up to remove and open the canvas bag. Reaching in with a small cloth, she scooped some of the contents into the cloth and twisted the ends together at its top to make a pouch and immersed it into the washtub, squeezing it with her hand to dissolve it slowly. Most of us stepped back, laughing, at the pungent smell of rotted moose brains. Jane spoke:

> These brains were boiled a few days ago, and then Marie had them hanging up in the willows for the sun to rot them. That way they are out of reach of animals and the smell is away from the camp. Once your hides are ready, you make this brain water. You shave a half bar of that soap into little flakes, then whisk them like this in a small pot or coffee can. Once the water is warmed a bit, you pour the soap into it. As the water heats, you put these brains in a cloth like this. Don't touch them with your hands. Then you take the cloth and work it in the water, so that the brains are dissolved through the cloth, into the water. This is your brain water. Be very careful with it. Don't spill any of it. You warm your water like this every time you go to soak the hide. Then without warming it, you leave your hide in the brain water overnight. From now on, you only soak the hide in this water, not in fresh water.

We treated the water with care. Moose brains, after all, are not easy to come by. Moose often weigh more than a thousand pounds, so hunters are selective about what they carry back out of the bush after a kill. Moose heads, if they are packed out of the bush, are usually kept for elders, and people who appreciate the various parts considered delicacies – eyes, nose, tongue – are reluctant to give them up. Caribou brains or even cow brains could also be used, but those are usually just as difficult to obtain.

The hides were left in the brain water to soak overnight. Each morning we wrung them out over the large plastic storage tubs. At that stage the hides are snowy white and slippery to the touch – raw wet hides beginning to decompose. The brain water solution assists in the breaking and drying of the skin's fibres, along with the smoking and twisting and stretching of the hides. Slits are cut around the edges of the hides at an early stage to allow them to be stretched and twisted. Half the slits are used to secure the hide to a wooden hook attached to a tree, with the other half folded carefully onto a wringing stick. The tanners then must wring out the hide by twisting and pulling it until it folds into a series of loops, bunched up to and secured against the hook. Each morning, after twisting the hide, we poured the brain water into a metal washtub to be warmed over the fire, then poured it back into the plastic tubs for the hide to soak in before it was wrung and then smoked repeatedly throughout the day. After each smoking, hides were stretched and pulled.

As the days progressed the hide's heavy, slippery whiteness gave way to a lighter, yellow, chamois cloth-like consistency, and with each wringing dry patches grew larger on its surface. As the hide grew lighter and more pliable, and easier to work, it was tempting to refuse the assistance of others in the process. A combination of satisfying progress and anticipation made us overconfident, independent, inadvertently slowing down our pace, sometimes breeding frustration. Although we resisted, working together continued to be necessary, and Jane reminded us not to rush, to focus on here and now. She reminded us that the hides would only be tanned correctly if we took the time to tan them correctly: working together, focusing on what the hide needed at this stage based on what we had done together so far to tan it, and not being distracted by what would come later.

# 4
# Délînê Child and Family Services

As the Royal Commission states in its final report, before the renewal of the relationship can begin, "a great cleansing of the wounds of the past must take place." It is for this reason that *Gathering Strength* begins with a Statement of Reconciliation in which the Government of Canada formally acknowledges and expresses regret for the historic injustices experienced by Aboriginal people.

> – Government of Canada, Department of Indian Affairs, *Gathering Strength: An Aboriginal Action Plan* (1998, 3)

You know how every August Délînê has a spiritual gathering. Dene people come from all over to Délînê, to the gathering. I remember one time these Dogribs [Tłîchô] came. They came to have a handgame[1] with Délînê at the community centre. I went over there to see, and all along one wall of the gym there were the Dogrib players, lined up and waiting to play. Then I looked at the opposite wall, where Délînê players were supposed to be. There, all along one wall, were the widows of the men who died of cancer after working in that mine. There were no men in front of the women, no men waiting to play. All those men died. There were no handgame players for Délînê. You know, I spent so much time negotiating with government about that mine, to fix things.

That's when it really hit me: there were no men standing there for Délînê.

I had to go outside for a minute, to leave the room. It really hit me. I just about had tears in my eyes it was so powerful.

> – Danny Gaudet, Délînê self-government negotiator and Délînê Uranium Team negotiator, October 2003

These two quotations juxtapose profoundly different understandings of injustices experienced by Indigenous peoples in Canada. Government acknowledgment of injustice is often set in general and broad terms. Indigenous peoples, however, in speaking of injustice, often articulate specific events or categories of experience. There are no ambiguous wounds of the past, obscured by time's forgetful memory. Instead, there are specific circumstances, requiring change and substantive measures for healing.

In this chapter, self-government negotiations over Délîne Child and Family Services are used as a window into how negotiations discourse silences narratives of suffering while simultaneously invoking suffering as a rationale for ongoing government control of programs. We learn about the centrality of Dene culture and ways in the community's approach to self-government and vision of self-determination and of relations between Canada and Délîne Got'îne that background that approach and vision. The relationship is informed not only by colonization but also by specific events causing suffering, including residential schooling, and the perceived health, social, and spiritual impacts of a nearby uranium mine. The consistency with which suffering's meaning is silenced during interactions with the state and its agents assists in scoping out what is identified as the state's dysfunction theodicy. As elaborated later in this chapter, the state's dysfunction theodicy identifies Indigenous peoples as authoring their own suffering through a combination of self-inflicted "dysfunction" and the inherently non-modern nature of indigeneity itself. The state, in reality the cause of much suffering, remakes itself through the theodicy as a source of redemptive healing and modernization through Aboriginal policy and various social, legal, and political programs targeting Indigenous peoples. This chapter looks at how the theodicy's combination of assumptions and state positioning vis-à-vis Indigenous suffering plays out within negotiations discourse.

### Prophecy, Self-Government, and the Atomic Bomb

Délîne Got'îne have lived on and around Great Bear Lake, their source of culture, well-being, and existence, for millennia. The community's landscape is dominated by this body of water, as is the rhythm of life there. Winter remakes the water's surface into ice several feet thick, crossed by trails onto the land and an ice road to the neighbouring community of Tulita; people travel by skidoo and dogteam onto the lake to set fishnets and beyond it to hunt and trap. In summer, sport and subsistence fishing takes place on the lake and at various camps and places along its shores. Sometimes the catch is brought back to be shared, eaten fresh, or smoked in the teepee-shaped smokehouses covered with wood or tarpaulins sitting in well-tended yards, beside neat stick-built and log houses that line the community's gravel roads. There are women who continue to spend many of their days tanning moose and caribou hides, and it is common for men to hunt and fish for much of their families' food. For many people this is necessary, since food and consumer goods prices are approximately double those in Yellowknife, owing to the community's fly-in-only access for ten months of the year. While Délînê has successfully capitalized on the pristine state of fresh-water Great Bear Lake and its world-record-size trout yields through sport fishing, economic development opportunities are limited, and increasingly mineral and resource exploration have become economically significant. As in many other communities in similar circumstances, poverty and high unemployment are common, with government services providing most of the local wage-earning opportunities. North Slavey is the language spoken by most Dene in this community of 650, both at home and at work (see Government of the Northwest Territories, Bureau of Statistics, 2006).

Délînê is the site where Sir John Franklin wintered between 1825 and 1827 on his expedition mapping the Arctic coast, supplied with meat and goods by Dene people. Located near an important fishery site for Dene, the community is one of five Sahtu (Hare, Bear Lake, and Mountain) Dene/ Métis communities and a signatory to the 1993 Sahtu Dene/Métis Comprehensive Land Claim Agreement. The Sahtu claim is administered by the Sahtu Secretariat Incorporated, which is supported through community-based land corporations. The Sahtu land claim agreement is unique compared with that of the Gwich'in and Tlîchô in two ways: it explicitly recognizes Métis people and institutions alongside those of the Dene, and it anticipates that self-government agreements will be community based rather than having one regional agreement.[2]

In 1996, the community of Délînê embarked on the first single-community self-government negotiations process in the NWT. Since then, other Sahtu communities have begun discussions with Canada on individual self-government agreements. Meanwhile, other Dene peoples have approached self-government talks on a regional basis. Délînê negotiations have taken place while the community struggles with significant suffering and loss due to cancer-related deaths. In the minds of many residents, the cancer and its aftermath are owed in large part to the lasting effects of the nearby Port Radium uranium mine that operated for several decades between 1932 and 1982 (DFN 2005, 9). Balancing this negative experience has been a parallel motivational force: a commitment to structuring self-government according to Dene values and ways, in the spirit of the teachings of the revered Dene prophet Ehtseo (Grandfather) Louie Ayah. Prophet Ehtseo Ayah lived between 1857 and 1940. Originally from Behchok'o (Fort Rae), he married Rosalie Origilie from Fort Good Hope; most of their life was spent in Délînê. Since his passing, each summer the people of Délînê hold a spiritual gathering to celebrate the prophet's life, attended by members of the community and people from Behchok'o as well as many other Dene people.

The community's rationale for negotiating self-government is unique. The community's elders have determined that many of the issues experienced by the community, such as uranium mining impacts, a perception in the community that health services are inadequate, and constant tensions between government agencies and residents over program approaches and content, stem from a combination of fragmentation of decision making and cultural non-understanding on the part of the state's decision-making agencies operating in the community. The uranium mine's perceived aftermath stands as an example of how lack of local control combined with a diffusion of decision-making power among external agencies (e.g., federal and territorial governments, mining companies) could result in serious harm to the community over the long term. A major focus for Délînê's self-government vision is to achieve one decision-making organization that will represent the community to external agencies. The intention is to have "one government" making decisions and thereby eliminating multi-agency miscommunication, fragmentation of authority, and consequent suffering.

The Délînê self-government negotiating mandate is set in broad terms by the vision of Ehtseo Ayah.[3] He was recognized by Dene peoples as a man of wisdom and vision, and during the yearly spiritual gathering people pray at a shrine dedicated to him in his former home in Délînê, known as the Prophet's House. Ayah's picture is found in virtually every building in the community and in the community's school, which is named after him. In Dene culture, "prophets were wise men who possessed special spiritual powers and were able to help others to find answers to troubling problems" (Dene Nation 1984, 20).

Anthropological theory often views prophecy as heralding the breakdown of social order (generally postcontact) which cannot cope with changes brought by outsiders. However, it has been observed that prophecy has general utility, for example providing insight into the relationship between and significance of interactions between people and things Indigenous and non-Indigenous. For example, among people of the Upper Yukon, prophecy provides "evidence not of failure but of successful [Indigenous] engagement with change and detailed foreknowledge of events" (Cruikshank 1994, 149). That interpretation finds validation in the case of Ayah's prophecy, which focuses not on Armageddon-like cautionary tales but on social transformations requiring the full potential of Dene knowledge and action for successful Dene continuity.

Ayah's teachings are kept vital through their interpretation by Délînê self-government elder advisors Leon Modeste, Alfred Taniton, and until his passing in 2005 Paul Baton, who are knowledgeable in Dene ways, particularly with respect to matters of governance and treaty making. Their presence at negotiations reminds participants that the Délîne negotiator speaks with the full authority and support of a community that values Dene ways. As a result, self-government negotiations and related community consultations and events are conducted in ways incorporating Délîne Got'îne knowledge and practices. At negotiating sessions, the elders clarify and expand on arguments in their language (with the audience aided by a translator), just as they would at meetings in Délîne, where North Slavey is the dominant everyday language in Dene institutions. The elders' advice includes identifying links between proposed self-government authorities and the wisdom of Dene oral tradition and in particular the teachings of Ayah's prophecy. The power of the prophecy lies in the veracity of predictions that have come to pass and its ability to illuminate and locate experiences and events in reference to Délîne Got'îne lifeways and culture.

At negotiating sessions elders discuss negotiating proposals in the context of the prophecy. While the content of the prophecy has literal understandings associated with it, general principles applicable to changing circumstances are also frequently drawn from the prophecy.[4] For example, interpretations of Ayah's visions of the shores of Great Bear Lake being crowded with boats and people from all over the world in search of clean water has focused community concern about Great Bear Lake's ecosystem management. The way the prophecy is used to distill Dene principles and values echoes the perspective of other Indigenous peoples that an explicit purpose of oral tradition is a tool for thinking about changing conditions and challenges, no matter how different the circumstances, era, or experiences of the listener (Cruikshank 1998, 25). Délîne elders similarly relate aspects of Ayah's prophecy in a way that is meant to turn the minds of negotiators to the moral imperatives embodied in Délîne Got'îne cultural knowledge and practice.

For example, during negotiations Ayah's teachings are analyzed for principles applicable to the matter at hand, such as having only one governing institution in the community or seeking jurisdiction over lands and resources. The elders say that one of Ayah's teachings is that the people are strong when they work together as one and speak with one voice. After the land claim was signed, the First Nation, Délîne Land Corporation, and community council each represented various different public and Aboriginal-specific interests of Délîne Got'îne. The elders see this as fragmenting responsibility and accountability, mirroring some of the less admirable traits of the state, and weakening the community's purpose and functioning.

Their interpretation of the prophet's teachings requires bringing together all institutions in the community which represent Délîné Got'îné, a concept resisted by Canada for several years at negotiations. This resistance was based in part on Canada's own legal and bureaucratic structures being incommensurate with the cohesion sought by the community. The one-government concept exemplifies how elders work with the negotiating team to ensure that proposed authorities and power sharing are evaluated within a matrix of knowledge and interests that include Délîné Got'îné Aboriginal rights and interests, treaty and legal entitlements and obligations, Dene values and beliefs, and the teachings of the prophecy.

The importance of maintaining strong values, ways, and culture as the foundation for a self-government agreement is a result not of blind adherence to the prophecy or a yearning to return to "precontact" circumstances. Délîné's self-government mandate has as its basis the same Dene values and worldview shaping the content of the prophecy: self-reliance, self-awareness, and awareness of the needs and interests of others with whom the community is connected. This includes recognizing change and innovation as long-standing elements of Dene culture and using empirical knowledge of the perils of the imposition of non-Dene values to navigate changing circumstances. The philosophical approach of Délîné Got'îné to negotiations is grounded in both Dene culture and experiences of colonization.

**The Uranium Mine**

Ayah's prophecy has been proven in part in the foretelling of the consequences of Délîné Got'îné involvement in uranium mining activities. The experience of the community in relation to the Port Radium uranium mine on Great Bear Lake's southeastern shore has been instructive for the community as it considers its ideal relationship with other governments as part of its overall vision of self-determination.[5] Uranium used in nuclear testing was mined there, foretold in Ayah's vision of the destruction that would be wrought through Délîné on "the people who look just like us." During the life of the mine, radioactive ore was carried out of the mine on the backs of a generation of young fathers and husbands from Délîné. At the same time, government documentation of the health hazards lay unheeded in Department of Mines offices in Ottawa, as evidenced by memorandums advocating ore-handling safety precautions due to the threat of its cancer-causing properties.[6] A symbol of frontier progress, the mine was celebrated in a 1938 painting by famous Canadian Group of Seven artist A.Y. Jackson. The painting depicts an idyllic scene of mine buildings, roads, and barrels neatly laid out, set against clouds suspended over a massive

*Port Radium Mine,* 1938, by A.Y. Jackson. National Gallery of Canada, courtesy of the Estate of the late Dr. Naomi Jackson Groves.

sky over snow-covered Great Bear Lake. The images evoke an imagined north, brilliant sunshine and pure white snow imparting a sense of pristine peace and solitude, a deceptive contrast with the mine's devastating effects for generations of Délî̂nê Got'î̂nê.

A newspaper story, "A Village Thrown into the Nuclear Age," from *News North* dated October 25, 1999, reflects the lived experience of those who had worked at the mine site and the continuing effects on people's lives and perceptions. The article recounts the central role of the Port Radium mine in supplying uranium, a metal at that time valued at $10,000 per ounce, to the Manhattan Project in the United States, which eventually produced the first atomic bomb. Included is a description of the experience of several men who lived and worked at Port Radium. According to Huey Ferdinand, workers such as his father were issued safety glasses and gloves when working with materials from the mine. Uranium tailings were dumped in the bay on Great Bear Lake next to the mine. The tailings were also used to fill a sandbox in which children of Dene workers played. According to Elder Paul Baton,

The workers never knew the seriousness of pollution back then, and it was cheaper to dump the waste material in the lake than take it out on a barge, he said.

"When they cleaned the barge, they'd just sweep it into the lake," he said. "They'd throw all kinds of garbage into the lake. There's lots of barrels in the water, too."

"Nobody goes there anymore, but I usually go every summer," Ferdinand said. "I'm not afraid to eat the fish and the caribou."

Paul Baton worked at the mine for five years. He said the cleanup/ containment should have happened a long time ago.

"It should have been done in the first place," Baton said. "They should have dug a hole in the bush and buried it real good."

Baton worked on the barge, toting the bags of ore on and off the barge.

"I worked on the boat going back and forth," he recalled.

"We'd load the barge with these little bags," he explained, his hands about a foot apart. "But they were heavy – about 120 pounds."

The men worked 12 hour days, Baton recalled.

"We'd get up and eat at six and work at seven," he remembered. "They'd say, 'Boys you gonna have a drink you only get 10 minutes, if you take 15, you're fired.'"

"They only paid us three dollars a day," he added.

"All day lifting those bags ... our arms were just red here, boy," he said, rubbing his forearms.

Although the government knew about the harmful effects of radiation, Baton said they were never warned of a possible danger.

"Nobody told us," Baton said.

"People drink the water and eat the fish," he said. "It made it really bad for the people."

During 1999, a year after Délîne community representatives attended a peace ceremony at Hiroshima, where they formally apologized for their role – however unwitting – in the creation of the atomic bomb, the Canada-Délîne Uranium Table was established at the request of the community. It resulted in a research and negotiation process aimed at determining social, environmental, and ecological impacts of the mine and obtaining a mine cleanup commitment from Canada. The call for action was strongly motivated by the ongoing suffering of the community wrought by cancer deaths, perceived to have been caused mainly by uranium mining activity.[7]

The vitality of Délîne Got'îne culture is woven as tightly through the self-government agreement as the traumatic effects of the uranium mine are woven through the life of the community itself. These two critical concerns are linked through Ayah's vision of the future, which portends yet more difficult times and choices for Délîne Got'îne. The experience of the uranium mine has not only brought death, grieving, and loss; it has also fostered a unity and strength of purpose to the goal of Délîne Got'îne reorienting governing toward Dene values. The experience has created a loss of trust in Canada to make decisions or reparations regarding Dene interests. For years, as cancer ravaged the community, no targeted measures were taken by the government to mitigate potential risks, such as comprehensive screening or monitoring programs or an increase in health resources related to cancer and cancer-related loss. Cancer assails the community still; the unnatural "sickness," as people refer to cancer, is omnipresent. Many believe that it is preventable, that it still rages due in part to the government's denial: of the risks of the mine; of governmental responsibility in assessing, mitigating, and communicating risks; and of the connection between past mining activities and current reality.[8]

### The Context for Negotiating Child and Family Services

Between the 1920s and the early 1980s, children were removed from Délîne Got'îne families to faraway residential schools. Negative effects often included language loss, cultural and familial dislocation, and in some cases childhood experiences of physical and sexual abuse.[9] Guilt and shame associated with what happened at the schools are felt not only by survivors but also by the parents and grandparents forced to submit to the authority of the police, priests, and Indian agents who removed the children. The residential school experience compounds with experiences such as that of the Port Radium mine effects, solidifying a profound lack of trust in the government. The residential school experience has resulted in a particular distrust in government services relating to children. Throughout Canada in recent years, there have been increased sensitivities around Indigenous children in care as Indigenous peoples assert authority in this area. This is in part a reaction to routine placements of Indigenous children in non-Indigenous homes and in part due to Indigenous children in care coming to harm as a result of incompetent case management by government authorities. Distrust of the government is significant, despite attempts by the GNWT to provide culturally sensitive and appropriate care arrangements for children where possible.

Child services were on the agenda at the Délîne negotiating session during April 2003 in Yellowknife. At issue was whether the community would have jurisdiction in the area, including designing and operating a Child and Family Services agency. The GNWT had previously refused to vacate the jurisdiction, and after a year-long hiatus the subject was the last on the table to be dealt with one month before the negotiators were scheduled to recommend the Agreement-in-Principle for signing by their respective political leaders. Canada's negotiators acted as observers: the jurisdiction was that of the GNWT; therefore, Canada had no formal participation in formulating proposals, though its chief negotiator strongly backed the GNWT position.

In response to a request for a description of the current system, the GNWT had provided copies of publicly available Child and Family Services legislation. After a subsequent request for information, the territorial governments' main estimates – detailing government expenditures in each department – were provided. What was glaringly absent was information which could be used as the basis for analyzing program effectiveness. For example, no information was made available on agency structure, services available or planned, types and quantity of staff requirements and job descriptions, service funding and guidelines, policies guiding service provision, or statistics on service use or needs within the community. No information assessing the quality of services provided was offered.[10] Fortunately, Délînê's chief negotiator was knowledgeable of the community's Child and Family Services system, and I had assisted in researching and negotiating the same subject matter previously for the Inuvialuit and Gwich'in self-government negotiations. With minimal preparation due to resources and time constraints, discussions went ahead.

### The GNWT Child and Family Services Proposal
During the previous year, the NWT premier, Stephen Kakfwi, as the territorial Legislative Assembly member for the Sahtu constituency including Délînê, had been strongly lobbied by the community to improve on the GNWT's original proposal of minimal administrative authority for the community. The premier took action, and the GNWT made a new offer. Its principal features were that Délînê would be able to have jurisdiction over its Child and Family Services after it had successfully operated a Child and Family Services agency under GNWT law for a period of ten years. At that point, Délînê would be able to make laws that had to meet or surpass GNWT standards, and final decision making on child protection would be made by the GNWT's director of Child and Family Services, located in Yellowknife. Ultimately, if things did not work effectively in the opinion of the GNWT director, responsibility for inoperable functions would revert back to the GNWT.

Délînê's response through the chief negotiator focused on three issues. The first issue was the ongoing consequences, including suffering and guilt, ensuing from the community's previous loss of care for its children. This issue informed the social and psychological context for regaining authority: jurisdictional authority would assist in healing and repair capacity through providing community control. The second issue was the significance of the contemporary relationship between Child and Family Services jurisdiction and the overall governance capacity of the community. Without having control in this area, the power and authority of the Délı̨nę Got'ı̨nę government as a tool of social and cultural self-determination would be undermined. The third issue was to question the arbitrariness of time as a measure as to when the jurisdiction could be exercised. Délı̨nę's negotiator emphasized that determining jurisdictional readiness based on a time period rather than a qualitative assessment of capacity simply made no sense.

The negotiating session where the subject was discussed was held soon after the Délı̨nę Land Corporation and First Nation had hired new staff to assist the chief negotiator, Danny Gaudet. Danny had been chief negotiator from the initiation of negotiations in 1996. He had been selected by the community leaders based on his experience in government and his track record negotiating and liaising with governments and private enterprises on behalf of the community. The session was the first in which he was accompanied by me as an advisor; we had known each other since attending the same high school in Inuvik, where I had grown up and where Danny had attended high school, staying at the local residential hostel along with other Indigenous students from the smaller communities. We had also kept in touch regularly when I worked for the Inuvialuit and Gwich'in self-government negotiations. Lawyer Brian Crane had also been recruited to assist; based in Ottawa, he had provided legal advice to the Sahtu during Dene/Métis land claim negotiations.

The session began at 9 a.m.; each party sat in groups of six or seven around the long oval table in the seventh-floor boardroom at the GNWT's Ministry of Aboriginal Affairs offices in Yellowknife. Several officials from the GNWT Department of Health and Social Services were in attendance. Casually dressed participants arrived shortly before the session began, exchanging pleasantries as they filled their coffee mugs near the back of the room, filling small plates with fresh fruit and pastries. Most representatives from the Délı̨nę Land Corporation and First Nation, including three elders, sat behind or at the table with their negotiators, making Délı̨nę's contingent the largest at about twelve people. The room was full, with members of the various teams seated in fabric-covered padded chairs, adding to the sound-proof quiet of the book-lined room. The GNWT negotiator provided a welcome and informed participants that smaller meeting rooms were available for caucusing and other amenities such as phones and fax and photocopying machines. The mood was comfortable and genial. Since there was no translator present, throughout the discussions Danny regularly requested time to caucus with his team to translate the English discussion for the elders and discuss the proposal and possible solutions with them, translating their advice from Slavey back to English for Brian and me. The government teams took such opportunities to take breaks at a café across the street or to caucus or catch up on phone messages and other work.

Danny, like the elder advisors and the community representatives, was noticeably calm throughout the discussions, which I found surprising, as I found myself frequently angered during the talks owing to several indefensible positions of the GNWT. When I asked Danny why, and how, he held his temper in check, he told me that the elders were adamant that all discussions had to be held with a calm mind. Central to the negotiations, they said, was to communicate effectively, which anger would prevent.

The session began with introductions; then each chief negotiator gave a brief update of issues or developments within their organizations with respect to negotiations or related matters. The session then turned to discussion of Child and Family Services. In response to the GNWT's proposal, Danny had this to say:

Délînê: You heard us for seven years tell you about how elders and kids don't talk to each other – it's all about having to go away to [residential] school, losing language, etc. That's what thirty to forty years of assimilation and integration has done to us. Traditionally and culturally we care for our elders and children more than anyone, that's the way we survive. Now the survival of Aboriginal people is dying. We have had more damage done to us in forty years just by allowing people to change us, than over 2000 years. Now we don't even understand the principles that we stood by for 2000 years, we need to try to get back to that ...

An important issue for us in terms of principles is that we are trying to prevent ever being in a situation where we are apprehending and protecting a child. Elders are saying: everyone at one time worked together solving problems; look at it now, it is fragmented, all these areas are supposed to work together ... If you can convince people to work together at the community level then it [co-ordination] filters up.

Generally there is a need for our people to include their way of thinking and being in the system, there needs to be more recognition of that. To interpret what is best for the child the GNWT has to put their minds around Aboriginal beliefs and wishes ... I'm just saying it's [the child protection system] not perfect when it deals with a different group of people, as this is built on a European system. That system moved through Canada, then it was applied to Aboriginal people. The system needs to reflect that Aboriginal people are different ... Given all the restrictions [of the GNWT proposal] what is left for us to do? We are supposed to be so self governing. Our people have been doing that for 2000 years. If the children die then we all die as a race. With a government system that does not include culture, we might be saving the children but we are killing off the identity of the children. (Délînê negotiation sessions 2003)

Danny's response cites residential school and assimilation as damaging forces continuing to threaten and impair Indigenous identity and well-being. It conveys an understanding of authority's nature as not only instrumental but also essential to the identity and well-being of the community. Toward this end, the response questions the hollow authority offered by the proposal, seeing it as a mockery of what the community understands to be self-government. Danny argues that real authority, the ability to make decisions and be fully accountable for them, is necessary to begin to heal and revive collective responsibility for raising children and having healthy families. Living these commonly held values would have positive implications on a larger scale, beyond this one subject area.

### Time Limits or Capacity?

The effectiveness or track record of the GNWT's management of Child and Family Services was not a matter for discussion at the table, ensured by the lack of empirical information on programs. Instead, government positions made the assumptions that its authority was legitimate and that program delivery was competent. Later in the day, discussion turned to the ten-year period when Délînê would exercise its authority according to GNWT policies and standards. The GNWT negotiator repeatedly argued that time was the only objective measure which both it and Délînê would likely be able to agree to as an indisputable index of competence. Instead of offering statistics similarly indisputable such as numbers of children apprehended, frequency of apprehensions, criteria for apprehensions, or evidence directly related to social conditions leading to a need for Child and Family Services (such as school attendance, youth crime, youth achievement), time was asserted to be the only satisfactory measure for the organization's competence. Curiously, if GNWT internal discussions had taken place establishing this as the only possible measure, this fact was not conveyed by the GNWT negotiator. Instead, arguments challenging time's objectivity were angrily dismissed without even a superficial exploration of alternatives.

Délîne: We don't agree with how you have a ten year period before we can exercise jurisdiction – is it a matter of time or capacity?

NWT: You are right – we used time as a measure – just because no one can debate when time lapses. Our interest was that Délîne have time to take this on – not just to demonstrate an ability to do things but you need the experience – experience is gained over time – staff turnover, experience with a variety of situations and circumstances is needed – over time you gain that experience – we think it's valuable to keep ten years in there but if we all think things can be advanced we are willing to look at greater flexibility there.

D: What if we hired people with experience?

NWT: That could work for two or three years – you would then be faced with the challenge of staffing up again – people in these jobs tend to burn out after two or three years then quit.

D: My point is that you gain experience by doing it yourself or by hiring it – you don't just keep starting with people who don't have experience.

NWT: In that case we can consider longer – we don't know how we could come up with objective criteria to measure that.

D: ... You can't link it to a time frame, it's based on experience – I would just like to see it linked to capacity building.

NWT: (Starts getting angry) How do you measure that? I don't know – if you think you can come up with a way to objectively measure it – we are taking a risk with ten years – if more seems too long or if more seems reasonable we are willing to look at that.

D: We always talk about how we are only learning – look at 2000 years of people looking after their own – for me it's silly when you have a culture and whole society and group of people who have done it for 2000 years and now you say well now we need you to learn some more. I understand the best interests of the child are important – but if people who have done this already want to do it again they are capable of it. And that's why I have problems with some of the stuff you are telling me – it bothers me when you make these kinds of statements. (Délîne negotiation sessions 2003)

Délînê's resumption of jurisdiction is framed as a condition required to return to normalcy and continuity. Although time is invoked by Délînê's negotiator – "for 2000 years" – as a temporal index of authority familiar to government negotiators, it is made meaningful through identifying it with the qualitative experience it bounds: the previous forty years have been a period of assimilation and attendant destruction of peoples' values, and ways of being, contrasted with 2,000 years of competence. Tension builds as the negotiators talk around the central issue: the people in the community, individually and collectively, have been seriously impaired by assimilative practices of the past forty years. For Délînê that destructive experience is a rationale to resume authority over a critical aspect of collective life, the caring for and well-being of children, essential to re-establishing a cultural foundation nurturing a sense of Dene identity and self-worth in the children as well as the community.·

However, for the GNWT the suffering arising from forty years of assimilation is a rationale to restrict the authority of the community in dealing with its most vulnerable population, children experiencing neglect or abuse. For the GNWT, once the community establishes the capacity to take on authority, it must then prove consistency over a longer term to meet GNWT standards. To an outsider, and to GNWT bureaucrats themselves, such concern may be viewed as reasonable and prudent. However, the foreign values, practices, and demands embedded in GNWT standards, experienced by Délînê Got'înê in their different forms in government programs generally, have been a consistent source of cultural weakening and social stress. Had the negotiations included discussion of how standards might be implemented in ways addressing flaws in the child welfare system, the two sides might have been able to recast the discussion as one about mutually acceptable outcomes or progress measurements – a prospect flatly rejected by the GNWT proposal.

Délînê Got'înê, expecting an opportunity to become self-governing according to Dene culture and values, are left to contemplate operating a system that "kills off" the identity of the children. Délînê's negotiator argues that the approach must ensure that the ultimate goal, no children apprehended or in need of protection, is achievable, primarily by reinstituting a framework of participatory responsibility in which "instead of having two or three social workers you have the whole community, 650 people" (Délînê negotiation sessions 2003) working toward family wellness. This reflects the principle that developing capacity within the community in a holistic sense underpins the Délînê Got'înê philosophy of self-determination, in all areas of jurisdiction. Fundamentally, the GNWT system is not a Dene system. Délînê's position is that the GNWT system has proven incompatible with Dene ways of being and is wholly unsuited for providing services that might simultaneously build community capacity, effectively care for children, and contribute to restoring governance authority to Délînê people. Ironically, it is continuing government intervention in governance that is part of the source of social suffering that contributes to the social ills affecting children.

## Silencing Experience

The GNWT and Canada did not acknowledge the relevance of arguments relying on the significance of Délînê Got'înê culture, sense of identity or self-worth, or experiences of colonization for the community's resumption of authority over child welfare. Instead, the conversation hinged on the lack of acknowledgment of Délînê's perspective by the GNWT negotiator, owing to the GNWT's view that conditions extant in the community could lead to a catastrophic failure of a Child and Family Services system. Just as the GNWT failed to provide basic information describing the child welfare system, and withheld statistics or analysis indicating its efficacy or weakness, so too a description of why Délînê was expected to fail was not forthcoming.

Government's failure to acknowledge suffering experiences of communities is common. I have also witnessed similar incidences at negotiating sessions of the Inuvialuit, Gwich'in, and Dehcho. In discussions with Indigenous peoples and government negotiators at tables across Canada, similar stories surface. Heart-wrenching testimony of personal experiences results in a flood of silent gestures of resistance from government negotiators: the set jaw and blank stare of refusal to acknowledge; sighs and eye rolling to indicate the boredom of repetition; the downcast eyes of the infrequent government attendee, not yet immune to the suffering narratives underpinning arguments from communities burdened with a long history of damaging government policies, forced to seek relief through negotiating processes controlled by governments and weighted against them.

None at the table would dispute the truth of suffering narratives related by Indigenous negotiators; they constitute an undercurrent of truth whose power must be avoided. Their power is emotional, potentially explosive, and challenges the authority and competence of Canada and the GNWT to govern. The narrative is similar across communities and lived experiences among generations of Dene, Métis, and Inuvialuit people who experienced similar Aboriginal policy initiatives during similar time periods. This type of suffering narrative, however, is understood to be as irrelevant as it is true: it has no specific bearing as a determinant on jurisdictional or program arrangements. For this reason suffering narratives are marginalized, remaining beyond the acceptable discourse. Their power is disqualified from the legally and bureaucratically bounded and contained discourse, defined primarily by specific policies and ground rules to which all parties have explicitly or tacitly agreed. These include formal policies of government and the state presumption that its role, while benevolent, is to ensure its own interests are paramount.

Government negotiators' direct responses to suffering narratives sometimes take the form of a strategy of non-response by distraction, or variations on this theme: if Indigenous peoples' negotiators agree to the government position, Indigenous governments will gain enough control to realize change. This line of persuasion holds that, once seemingly meagre resources or levels of control are transferred to Indigenous governments, there will be little that the GNWT or Canada can do to shape how services are delivered, as long as mutually agreed standards are being met. There is careful avoidance of discussing the painful experiences of community members, either individually or collectively, or acknowledging how experiences weave through the ongoing indignities of the present. The subject heightens emotions, causing discomfort to the usually male negotiators, whose only permissible extreme emotion is aggressive anger.

Suffering narratives are met with silence when used to educate government bureaucrats about Indigenous motivations and aspirations. Narratives are extremely effective in providing emotional testimonies and empirical evidence about the need for changes in existing circumstances. And it is important to note that sometimes government negotiators are not without sympathy in the face of such narratives. Lacking avenues for engagement, suffering narratives are stripped of any power to teach or to scaffold a new way of being beyond their own existence, reduced to a rhetorical device, a past and unreachable event, a regrettable yet ultimately irrelevant story.

### The Dysfunction Theodicy

In *Critical Events: An Anthropological Perspective on Contemporary India,* Das (1995) argues that discourses of state agencies produce an underlying theodicy similar to that provided by religion, legitimizing state mechanisms perpetuating suffering and social injustices. In its strictly religious sense, a theodicy vindicates God's goodness and justice in the face of the existence of evil, often by rationalizing some moral failing on the part of sufferers as a cause of suffering-inducing evil. In Das's usage, God is replaced by the state, and in that context the notion of theodicy describes how the state rationalizes politically induced social suffering as the fault of sufferers' actions. The state simultaneously minimizes its own role in causing suffering, while positioning itself as a beneficent institution with the capacity and duty to ameliorate suffering through programs aimed at addressing social pathologies. The notion of a dysfunction theodicy I put forward here, captures the dynamic where the state effectively shifts responsibility for suffering onto the sufferers, establishing itself through discourse and action as a necessary and legitimate interventionist agent in the lives of Indigenous people alleged to lack the capacity to recognize or alter what the state alleges to be their own suffering-inflicting actions.

In one case study Das examines medical, legal, and administrative discourses of state officials involved in court proceedings following the Bhopal disaster of 1984, where up to forty tonnes of methyl isocyanate (cyanide) were released overnight in the city. Approximately 2,500 people died, and thousands more were disabled as a result. Subsequently, the state took over the legal case for damages against the chemical manufacturer responsible, Union Carbide. By examining controversial judgments of India's Supreme Court during 1989 and 1991 that favoured Union Carbide regarding liability and reparations, Das shows how the "professional transformation of the suffering of the victims ... can become an occasion for the legitimation of power ... exercised through the mediums of science and state" (1995, 138). Through this example Das shows how interpretations of official discourses as theodicy offer a powerful tool for analyzing ways in which the mechanisms and symbols of the state's sovereign power and institutions such as the courts and state legislature draw upon disparate legal and social tools to appropriate and represent the suffering of victims. Deconsructing the way the state first blames then characterizes its own efforts to help victims creates what Das calls a "master dialogue" (see 137-74), which makes suffering and survivors separate abstractions, which once separated can be manipulated in ways that release the state from responsibility for suffering while maintaining its legitimacy with respect to its authority over its subjects, the sufferers, particularly in diagnosing and determining amelioration of their pain.

Applying this approach to examining self-government negotiations and Aboriginal policy discourse offers insight into how suffering is used as a rationale for continued state intervention as opposed to a rationale for decreasing state control. After Max Weber, Das explains how a theodicy is a religion's answer to "an existential and cognitive problem of loss of meaning to the individual" (1995, 137). Just as suffering generates doubts (if God exists, how can he allow such evil?), a theodicy provides a justification for suffering. (138). What Das investigates is "experiences which are actively created and distributed by the social order itself" (138). The applicability of the concept of theodicy to socially and politically produced

suffering for analyzing colonization in Canada rests on the complex of asser-
tions and assumptions of the state which taken together characterize
Indigenous suffering as exclusively historically and self-induced, rendering
suffering's causes as beyond the state's control. As discussed in the previous chapter, during self-government negotiations state discourses are
received as scientific and neutral, a phenomenon identified by Young
(2000) as an important element of marginalizing non-dominant views.
Positioning its arguments as objective and neutral allows the state to legitimate its discourses, gaining broad acceptance for the state's focus on
addressing the symptoms of suffering toward creating a better future, without having to examine its historical or ongoing role in suffering's production or take drastic actions toward changing institutions and systems
producing ongoing suffering.

Experiences such as colonization and, inherent to it, the denial of injustice by the state through both silence and communicative marginalization are another site of theodicy creation necessary to legitimate the production of suffering through both state institutions and the social order
itself. Statistics evidencing widespread and ongoing social pathologies in
Indigenous communities that far outstrip incidences of those found in the
rest of the Canadian population are an expected result of colonization.[11]
Multiple collective and individual injustices suffered, ongoing dispposes-
sion of lands and resources, continued control of Indigenous communities and lives, denial of self-determination through such mechanisms of
the state as the Indian Act and its associated policies and programs, and
consequent social tensions and marginalization – all of these work together
to create conditions profoundly disabling for Indigenous communities
and individuals. In such conditions, success stories are extraordinary, and
suffering and associated behaviours begin to make sense when viewed as
coping mechanisms in situations of ongoing injustice and oppression.[12]

Despite documented pathologies among Indigenous peoples, including
poverty, alcoholism, low education levels, et cetera, the government denies
a colonial present. Instead, it acknowledges only a colonial past. The logic
of the theodicy determines that Indigenous experiences of colonial suffering must be *misunderstood* by the sufferers if they are attributed to present causes. According to the government, the difficulties experienced by
Indigenous people do not arise from dispossession and injustice. They are
authorized solely as problems of either (1) *legacies* of past decisions and
colonial administrations (historical injustice), including *dysfunction*
specific to indigeneity rather than suffering specific to oppression, or (2)
the clash between *Indigenous* ways of life and *modern* ways of life (indigeneity as premodern).

In support of the first point, one only need read the introductory section in the Gathering Strength Policy, which includes the following:

Sadly, our history with respect to the treatment of Aboriginal people is not something in which we can take pride. Attitudes of racial and cultural superiority led to a suppression of Aboriginal culture and values. As a country, we are burdened by past actions that resulted in weakening the identity of Aboriginal peoples, suppressing their languages and cultures, and outlawing spiritual practices. We must recognize the impact of these actions on the once self-sustaining nations that were disaggregated, disrupted, limited or even destroyed by the dispossession of traditional territory, by the relocation of Aboriginal people, and by some provisions of the Indian Act. We must acknowledge that the result of these actions was the erosion of the political, economic and social systems of Aboriginal people and nations.[13]

The second point is borne out later in the same policy: "Factors also speak to the importance of building capacity for both individuals and communities. As self-government becomes a reality, Aboriginal communities will require increasingly sophisticated policy and program skills and administrative structures to support good governance" (Government of Canada, Department of Indian Affairs 1998)

Uncovering the dysfunction theodicy illuminates how "the social mechanisms by which the manufacture of pain on the one hand, and the theologies of suffering on the other, become the means of legitimating the social order rather than being threats to this order" (Das 1995, 138). Silencing suffering during negotiations is part of a larger state strategy encouraging Indigenous peoples to see themselves as the principal authors of their suffering: there is much talk about "social problems," "dysfunction," a need for "building capacity" – terms and phrases implying a lack of "normalcy," of flaws inherent to the subjects of oppression and their functioning rather than the circumstances in which they exist. Contrast this with the label "suffering." Suffering indicates that there are unjust circumstances that people react to and cope with, that they suffer. The concept of suffering does not adhere sources of pain to the actions or inherent characteristics of the sufferers. This distinction is important as the "suffering" label widens possibilities not only of the causes of suffering but also for understanding the nature of the pathologies themselves, which are not simply the results of lifestyle choices but also the expected outcomes of ongoing oppression.

This combination of non-understandings of Indigenous peoples and their circumstances gives rise to swelling federal bureaucracies providing a constellation of programs aimed at addressing "Aboriginal issues" (self-government is one such program). Much is made of the amount of money spent on Indigenous peoples each year, expenditures that by 2006 amounted to over $6 billion.[14] This amount promises to grow as resources are dedicated to servicing suffering perpetuated by injustice, a never-ending task as long as the focus is suffering alone rather than its underlying causes.

It is important to address the obvious state interventions appearing to undermine the claim that Canada justifies and perpetuates injustice toward Indigenous people. Despite the evidence of suffering, many point to the billions of dollars spent in Aboriginal programming as evidence that colonialism is dead. What such analyses miss is that, if the billions of dollars spent each year on programs to address suffering were effective, would we not see a decline in suffering? And, were resources and specific efforts aimed at Indigenous issues effective, why is it that the same issues arising decades ago continue to persist: conflicts over land rights, calls for greater self-determination, agitation for increased Indigenous control of Indigenous lives, the inadequacy and inherent colonialism of the Indian Act? At the same time, measures put in place to address injustices are often ill suited to or ineffective in their purpose: the bungling of the reparations for residential schools which saw over 90 percent of funding go toward the bureaucracy administering claims rather than settlements to survivors,[15] specific and comprehensive claim processes where Canada is responsible for deciding on the legitimacy of claims to be heard, then acting as defendant, judge, and negotiator/jury in their adjudication?[16] More recently, Canada refused to support the United Nations Declaration on the Rights of Indigenous Peoples and reneged on a commitment to the Kelowna Accord, a deal supported by all provincial premiers dedicating major resources to specific Aboriginal initiatives.[17]

Yet it must be noted that the Canadian state at least makes an effort to put such processes in place. Canada's Aboriginal policy is perceived as progressive in comparison to that of more repressive states. By comparison, Indigenous peoples in Canada are fortunate. However, compared with non-Indigenous citizens in Canada, the only valid comparative group, Indigenous peoples in Canada are far worse off. Ultimately, the statistics that attest to the suffering of Indigenous peoples speak for themselves. According to an article published by a team of medical researchers in the *Canadian Medical Association Journal*,

> Compared with the general Canadian population, specific native populations have an increased risk of death from alcoholism, homicide, suicide and pneumonia. Of the aboriginal population of Canada 15 years of age

and older, 31 percent have been informed that they have a chronic health problem. Diabetes mellitus affects 6 percent of aboriginal adults, compared with 2 percent of all Canadian adults. Social problems identified by aboriginal people as a concern in their community include substance abuse, suicide, unemployment and family violence. Subgroups of aboriginal people are at a greater-than-normal risk of infectious diseases, injuries, respiratory diseases, nutritional problems (including obesity) and substance abuse. (MacMillan et al. 1996, 1569)

The persistence of social suffering among Indigenous peoples cannot be ignored or explained away with victim-blaming simplifications. Although causes may have deep historical roots, sources of suffering are ongoing and in that sense are most certainly contemporary. Causes of persistent widespread collective suffering of Indigenous peoples require attention if alleviating suffering is an object of Aboriginal policy.

During self-government negotiations, the state's dysfunction theodicy provides a rationale for government mandates justifying negotiating Indigenous rights at the same time that they seek to restrict Indigenous authorities. In other words, the subtext of these mandates is that, although Indigenous peoples surely have legal rights, the reality is that fully implementing those rights is tempered by positioning Aboriginal "dysfunction" as a rationale for ongoing state intervention. As such, suffering is ironically used to legitimate rather than undermine social and political order, maintaining the primacy of state interests. According to this approach, fixing capacity deficits, in terms of social wellness, skilled human resources, capital, and infrastructure, must be done in a way that will promote integration into the dominant culture. Therefore, the state asserts that communities cannot take on too much responsibility until they are rebuilt through programs that address deficits on their merits, without addressing deficits' origins. Moreover, the rebuilding process includes "training" and institutional development mimicking the state's own bureaucracies, required if Indigenous communities are to conform to government standards to which they must adhere as a condition of their authority. The use of suffering as a rationale for ongoing state intervention underscores how the institutions and bureaucratic practices of the state are reaffirmed and re-entrenched within Indigenous communities in a way that consolidates state authority and dominant cultures over Indigenous ones. The Inherent Right and Gathering Strength Policies brand this as a process of "modernization" of Indigenous peoples and communities, implying that change by Indigenous peoples, particularly by "modernizing," will allow greater self-determination through sophisticated, modern (as opposed to

Indigenous) governance practices. Characterizing consolidation of state control as "modernization" also functions to ensure expressions of self-determination conform with state priorities and orientations rather than Indigenous ones. For example, the requirement that Délîne Child and Family Services programs must be determined wholly by GNWT legislation and policies for the first ten years of operations ensures that Délîne Got'îne are forced to institute cultural expressions of program delivery within frameworks prescribed unilaterally by the state.

The underlying message is that what must change for a better future is not state institutions or injustice. Indigenous people must change, be "cured": modernized, able to fit into and with the mainstream society, to obtain a better quality of life. This sort of understanding may be bolstered, however unintentionally, by those supportive of Indigenous self-determination yet unquestioningly deceived by the state's temporal positioning of Indigenous peoples. For example, political scientist Alan Cairns (2000, 103) interprets Indigenous change as "modernizing Aboriginality," a label indicating that Indigenous cultures no longer must be "rooted in the past." Although this change is not labelled assimilation, the intent is to produce people, institutions, and processes consistent with and legitimating those of the mainstream society and aligned with state interests seeking maintenance of its legal and constitutional order and authority. The theodicy's subtext is that the root of Indigenous suffering is indigeneity's inherent inability to fit into society: a difference which is not simply cultural but also explicitly non-modern. Political philosopher Jeremy Waldron's (1992) arguments that injustice is superseded by time's passage also reverberate within the theodicy's subtext, exhorting Indigenous peoples to move away from their historical claims from an *imaginary*, primitive time and instead engage with present suffering, as if that suffering had no origin other than indigeneity's presumed clash with the modern world.[18]

Government rhetoric promising that Aboriginal programs allow Indigenous people to strengthen their Aboriginal traditions while acquiring modern skills clearly demarcates things Indigenous from things modern. For example, we see below that traditional ways are differentiated from accountable ways: "Moving to new solutions means ensuring that the authority, accountability and responsibility of each of the parties are established. It means recognizing traditional customs, including their role in governance; celebrating Aboriginal languages, heritage, and culture; assisting to build the capacity of Aboriginal institutions to handle new responsibilities; and working to establish mechanisms to recognize sustainable and accountable Aboriginal governments and institutions" (Government of Canada, Department of Indian Affairs, 1998, 4). The theodicy's subtext constructs

Indigenous peoples as people of the past, the vanishing race, its message reinforcing the concept of Indigenous as history. It is this perceived "pastness" which is taken as the basis of difference, a difference that is sanctioned as an embodiment of cultural diversity, yet that must ultimately give way to "modernity" in arenas such as governance and rights. Government is cast as a benevolent support in overcoming the dysfunction it encounters; its benevolence will result in promoting Aboriginal culture in ways compatible with the legal and policy status quo.

The only thing that this requires from Indigenous peoples? To modernize, become more sophisticated, build capacity. To change. From being Indigenous into something else.

However, the lived reality of Délî̧nê Got'î̧nê contradicts all of the assumptions about Indigenous peoples on which Aboriginal policy and the dysfunction theodicy are based. The Port Radium mine experience demonstrated how loss of control of lands and resources could have ongoing negative impacts for the health of both people and the land. Residential schools demonstrated how policies premised on improving individual lives instead devastated both individuals and collective generations in various ways. Despite those events and their aftermath, the community continues to thrive, due in no small part to the strength of culture that persists. And at the centre of that cultural strength is the wisdom of elders and the prophecy of Ehtseo Ayah, vitalized by the energy of youth and resourcefulness, and specifically Dene knowledge applied to both issues and opportunities. In circumstances where government control and interventions yield results ranging from culture loss to disease and death, being Dene is logically the safest place to be. As Raymond Taniton, former Délî̧nê Land Corporation president, was quoted as saying in the first chapter, "what they [the government] haven't understood yet is that we are Dene, and nothing will change that." Remaining strong in their convictions as Dene in the face of potentially damaging government control is a matter of both rational behaviour and survival. It is more intuitive and common sense than self-conscious. In that sense the Indigenous resurgence paradigm echoes the ethics and actions of Délî̧nê Got'î̧nê. Self-government negotiations bring all of these contextual strands together, laying bare the inherent contradictions of the situation (why would Délî̧nê negotiate for an agreement that continues state intervention in their affairs?) and the situation's inevitability (the desire to decrease the level of state intervention that currently exists). Gaining self-government authority over Child and Family Services is an example of all of these cumulative experiences, knowledge, and convictions of the community finding validation and expression.

### Negotiators Living the Theodicy

In response to a question about what the hardest part of her job was, a government negotiator had this to say:

What are the hardest things to deal with?

Well, you represent a structure which has been so damaging to First Nations. So in a negotiation, you may be the first person from that structure who is willing to sit and talk to them. A lot of the content of negotiations is airing grievances. People come to the table with a lot of anger, and generally this is the first time they have had anyone to talk to. As a person it's really hard to hear all that anger and pain. And it's really difficult not to take it personally, but you can't take it personally. What you are doing there is in part giving them the respect that they are due. Finally – and maybe for the first time for them. One of the hardest things for me personally is often I wonder if I'm on the wrong side of the table. I remember when we had to give our position on heritage in the negotiations. I gave the message I had to give, and then – I just couldn't look up at the First Nation negotiators. I was just too ashamed. That's hard. Or there are situations where elders come and talk about the treaties and what the treaties mean to them. I find some provisions of treaties obviously so strange, how at the time these were negotiated that to have expected Aboriginal people to understand what was in them is beyond me. I'll give you an example – in one treaty one of the benefits are hatpins. What the fuck is that?

The abuse and damage issue is hard to take. I completely understand how it is so present all the time – they are not wrong to raise it. On the other hand, I can't do anything. I can as a person acknowledge and understand what you are saying. I can't do anything about what happened – I'm there to negotiate self-government, that's what I'm there to do. (Federal negotiator, interview, 2002a)

The negotiator quoted above demarcates clear distinctions between her role as an individual serving the broader policy of silence and the theodicy necessary to justify the separation between reality and solutions. There are no directions within her mandate about how to respond to suffering. She is forced to refocus on the specific task at hand, which is to negotiate the nature and extent of legal rights in the form of jurisdictions and authorities over specific subject matters.

This negotiator's reaction conveys a strong sense that what she is hearing is so visceral and heartfelt that she alone has been the first government representative to listen to Indigenous suffering narratives. This perhaps more accurately reflects the destabilizing impact of that reality on her own preconceptions than the frequency with which the same suffering narratives have or have not been related to other government representatives. The official refusal of suffering results in a separation between the negotiator's compassionate personal views and her role as a messenger. The non-response to suffering denies its existence and validity; yet for the negotiator the non-response is one of sheer helplessness rather than being part of some grand design of ongoing oppression.

What this helplessness signals is that, unwittingly, the negotiator is positioned as an obstruction to mutual understanding between the state and Indigenous peoples: how could a system possibly change if the front-line negotiators have no way to include suffering narratives within the total social knowledge required for renewing relationships through self-government agreements? When she meets people in communities, the negotiator recognizes the perception of her presence as an opportunity for people to create meaning of their suffering, to confront power with its inherent illegitimacy. Yet the silence then relegates suffering to meaninglessness within the official negotiations discourse. Both she and Indigenous negotiators are at a loss. And officially her mandate requires that she does not address specific suffering causes – that would be the responsibility of representatives from other government departments, such as a residential schools claim resolution negotiator or a child welfare agency official.

Although Canada's negotiators may not be empowered to address specific suffering events, for example residential schools, within their mandates sometimes large-scale suffering (without exception as a result of either court decisions or the threat of court action[19]) is validated, albeit very carefully as *legacies,* consistent with the overall temporal situatedness necessary to keeping injustice at a distance. Historicizing injustices is crucial to narrowing potential redress. For how can the state be responsible for oppressive actions taken hundreds of years ago? And as emphasized in the work of Waldron (1992), it apparently is impossible to reconstruct what it is that should be redressed, particularly since the original sufferers are long dead (Waldron 1992). This is a rationale for symbolic (rather than substantive) redress, coupled with a focus on present suffering rather than trying to right persisting injustice, which is the source of that suffering.

The Canadian state's dysfunction theodicy cannot be found neatly packaged within any specific policy. Rather, policies such as the Inherent Right Policy or the Gathering Strength Policy are pillars orienting government agencies, committees, decision makers, and bureaucrats, the powerful who create and legitimate the discourse that creates a government reality and truth. The discourse, like the dysfunction theodicy itself, is created through policy and discussions at negotiating tables, in academic works on self-government, and "the Indian problem" writ large. It is found through tracing threads which emerge and submerge through a disparate collection of conversations, debates, and pronouncements on Indigenous issues.

## Recognizing Suffering Discourse

Whatever boundaries silences may set, the narrative of suffering persists. Some phrases hold worlds of meaning. For example, the phrase "residential schools" has become a signifier of a low point in Canadian Aboriginal policy and synonymous with stories of the worst sexual, physical, psychological, cultural, and spiritual predation on helpless Indigenous children by holy men and women of the mainstream society. Grammatically jarring and deeply felt phrases are powerful markers of the inexpressibility of suffering – for example, the previous discussion at negotiations, where Danny Gaudet argues that "the survival of our Aboriginal people is dying." At negotiations, awkward phrases, all the more arresting for being spoken by men of sovereign demeanour, indicate what Das calls the "mutilation of language" (1995, 184), struggling out of accumulations of painful images, momentarily overwhelming, tangling inexpressible emotions and words.

In her book *Critical Events*, Das (1995) examines various sites of violence and suffering in India, including the Bhopal disaster, Indian partition, and the assassination of Indira Gandhi, where language is mutilated in this way. Similarly, Morrow and Hensel (1992), in "Hidden Dissension: Minority-Majority Relationships and the Use of Contested Terminology," examine how language is used in a way where, in the context of negotiations between the government and Alaska Natives about resource management, while government and Indigenous peoples may use the same terms, their meanings are distinct. In the same context, the authors argue that Western paradigms are presented as scientific and therefore value-free, whereas Alaska Native paradigms are seen as anecdotal. This issue is further addressed in the context of colonial power relations by Nadasdy (1999, 2003).

Rooted in the narratives of violence survivors in India, the mutilation concept conveys the inability of victims to describe or communicate experiences of pain through common uses and structures of language. Foreign to the audience's experiences of daily life, the pain is indescribable, its expression confused, beyond the grammatical syntax or voice of survivors themselves. Essentially, mutilated language is the point at which unimaginable yet experienced pain meets attempts at verbal expression of its recollection, further strangled by the simultaneous pain of remembering. Mutilated language is also language emerging from an inability to contemplate the indescribable experience in any terms other than those that deny its meaning. In self-government negotiations I have attended, these are constituted by grammatically incorrect English phrases used by people fluent in English and by the tones and gestures accompanying the speech act itself. I recall and continue to witness many examples in negotiations. One includes a negotiator's frustrated and increasingly loud and emotional repetition of a specific phrase which seemed oddly out of place, requiring far more explanation than the person offering it could muster: "But this is our section 35 right! That's in your constitution! Read your constitution section 35!" (Field notes, Inuvialuit and Gwich'in negotiations, April 1998). The intensity of the Indigenous negotiator's expression outstripped the meaning of the words, just as the coping mechanisms of government negotiators steered them from assigning importance to the intensity of expression to questioning the relevance of the constitutional reference to the point under discussion. This sort of reception from government officials serves to compound the frustration of the speaker, who is effectively left without words to bridge the void in the discourse created by the inexpressibility of suffering.

Suffering narratives surfacing in self-government negotiations may be used differently during discussions as circumstances require. As Young (2000) explains, the variety of purposes of such narratives include teaching, expressing specific idioms, and conveying a wider horizon of truth. As Danny Gaudet argues in his response to the GNWT negotiator, although decades of assimilation visited irreparable damage upon Délîné Got'îné, it did not decimate cultural knowledge or the ability of individuals to a point of no recovery. Rather, the persistence of Dene culture despite the systematic attempts at its destruction is a testament to the strength and vitality not only of the culture but also of people's ability to resume their rightful authority over their own lives. This testifies not only to the suffering endured but also to the resilience of Indigenous knowledge and culture despite suffering.

Suffering narratives are not only focused on painful experiences. They may also detail triumphs over suffering. The focus of triumphal suffering turns on conveying examples of the innovation and resourcefulness of people within often unjust and disabling circumstances. The sorts of narratives offered to contextualize self-government discussions are varied and may have strength and success as their themes as often as pain and oppression. For example, the previous remarks providing a rationale for Délîné reasserting its authority for children in care draws heavily on the assertion that, prior to usurpation of this responsibility, the care of children was a source of strength and a testament to the capability of Délîné people, an existing capability. It is this knowledge which, in part, makes colonization that much more senseless and its weight so keenly felt.

## Conclusion

At the May 2003 negotiating session, the Délînê team was told to take or leave the Child and Family Services proposal. The GNWT negotiator stated that an election would happen in the fall, and there was no guarantee that the Sahtu MLA would again be premier. According to the GNWT, if the deal was rejected, negotiations would resume on the basis of a previous offer Délînê had rejected. In caucus, we quickly debated the options. Despite concerns that the disrespect by government negotiators in action and speech had prevented full discussion, it was decided to proceed cautiously and accept the GNWT's proposal with a few modifications. There was an expectation that toward the end of negotiations, when politicians are anxious for outcomes, outstanding concerns with the proposal might be resolved in Délînê's favour at a political level.

This chapter is not meant to establish colonization or suffering narratives as specific to self-government or as a trope invoked to establish or undermine the legitimacy of any party engaging in self-government negotiations. The intent is not to reinscribe Indigenous peoples as victims in a story where they have long been made to be and appear powerless. Rather, suffering narratives draw out powerful yet unacknowledged subtextual tensions pervading self-government negotiations. Acknowledging this subtext allows for tracing ways in which government non-response to suffering tensions and narratives signals and enables specific approaches to negotiations. Moreover, the continuing presence of suffering despite extensive government interventions through programs attempting to address ongoing suffering testifies to government programs' inadequacy. The inadequacy lies not within an inability to address pathologies as intended (although programs often fail) but within their irrelevance to the underlying conditions giving rise to suffering. It is my contention here, based on the foregoing discussion, that self-government is yet another program destined to dull the symptoms of suffering rather than cure underlying causes.

At one point in her discussion of the Bhopal disaster, Das (1995) describes how doctors hired by Union Carbide gave courtroom testimony that victims increased their own suffering in various ways: for example, malnourishment made victims more vulnerable to the poison than they might have been. The victims are blamed for their own suffering. Such excuses and victim blaming often attest to the inability of the state to sanction admissions of its role in suffering's causes. These victim-blaming tactics prompt questions of the state's explanations. Is it really the case that Indigenous people are entirely the authors of their own suffering? Was it really the case that Bhopal victims bore responsibility for damaging their own lungs by being malnourished or running from the poisonous clouds that suddenly surrounded and choked them? Perhaps it could be considered that certain circumstances overwhelm people, preventing escape, circumstances that should never have been permitted.

# Délînê Negotiations

The signing of the Délînê Self-Government Agreement-in-Principle, 2003. Left to right: (back) Ethel Blondin-Andrew, MP; Stephen Kakfwi, NWT premier; INAC minister Robert Nault; Chief Raymond Tutcho; and John Tutcho; (front) elder advisors, Elder Alfred Taniton, Elder Leon Modeste, and Elder Paul Baton. Leon is signing the occasion's commemorative moosehide. Photo: Morris Neyelle.

The Délînê self-government negotiating team confer during a negotiating session in Yellowknife, June 2008. In this picture, clockwise from left, are Jane Modeste, Elder A.J. Kenny, Morris Neyelle, Elder Leon Modeste, Dolphus Tutcho, Fred Kenny, Elder Alfred Taniton, Brian Crane, and Danny Gaudet. Photo: Tawna Brown.

Danny Gaudet, self-government chief negotiator for Délînê, at a June 2008 event in Délînê celebrating the agreement of chief negotiators on a final draft of the Délînê Self-Government Agreement. Photo: Tawna Brown.

Elder Leon Modeste, self-government advisor, drumming during a hand game in Délı̨nę, June 2008. Photo: Tawna Brown.

Men and boys participate in a hand game at the Ehtseo Ayah School gymnasium in Délı̨nę, June 2008, part of the celebrations to mark achieving a final draft of the Délı̨nę Self-Government Agreement. Photo: Tawna Brown.

Sunset behind teepees in the yard of the Prophet's House in Délı̨nę. Photo: Morris Neyelle.

A prayer song is drummed and sung by men in Délînê at a fire feeding ceremony, June 2008. Pictured from left to right are Peter Menacho, Sidney Tutcho, Andrew John Kenny, Leon Modeste, Charlie Neyelle, Morris Mendo, Gordon Taniton. Photo: author.

## Postscript: Western Science as Universal Truth

During August 2005 I arrived at the Yellowknife airport to take a flight to Délînê, where the self-government team was conducting a Dene laws workshop. Several people on the flight were staff of the Délînê Uranium Team (DUT). The DUT had been established by the community to research physical, social, and environmental impacts of the uranium mine on the community, in co-operation with Canada. The team also represented the community interests in discussions with Canada about mitigating mine impacts. A researcher who worked for the team provided an update on the DUT research findings. She told me that the science indicated that there was no connection between the mine and cancer in the community. It was clear from her manner that she approved of the findings, which contradicted perceptions in the community, whose members attributed cancer deaths in the community to the involvement of Délînê Got'înê in mining activities (Field notes, Yellowknife, August 2005). This news was stunning. It seemed the final report was still in preparation, and a number of different studies, referred to as "the science," contradicted the community's experiences and perceptions of the mine's effects. The next day, August 12, 2005, CBC Radio broadcast a news story:

Uranium Exposure Insufficient to Cause Cancer in Délînê Workers: Report
A report says scientific data does not show a link between cancer rates in Délînê and the Port Radium mine.

Men from the N.W.T. community were hired to carry sacks of uranium ore from the mine, which opened in 1929 and operated for decades. Cancer cases started showing up and the community became known as the "Village of Widows" receiving widespread attention.

But, the report, which looks at how much uranium a worker may have been exposed to over time, says those employees' exposure levels weren't high enough to cause cancer, contradicting widely held opinions by many local people. Dr. Douglas Chambers, a radioactivity expert hired to double check the team's scientific data, says he believes the science is solid.

"The Délînê [workers] to my knowledge never worked underground at Port Radium. The potential risk of cancer associated with transporting the ore concentrate is extremely small and in fact so small it would not be detectable in the variability of natural cancers and factors of effect cancers such as smoking," says Chambers.

The contamination controversy prompted the creation of the Délînê Uranium Team five years ago. The team, made up of federal officials, members of the Délînê community and scientists, spent $6.5 million doing studies, including this soon-to-be-released report.

Not all the studies involved in the project are based on hard science. Traditional [knowledge] studies, including oral histories, environmental surveys and mental health reports are also part of the final report. Residents say those studies also need to be taken seriously ("Uranium Exposure Insufficient to Cause Cancer in Délînê Workers" 2005)

The same day, Danny Gaudet, who was also the DUT chief negotiator, spent most of the day preparing a response to the CBC story. Visibly upset, he explained some of his concerns. Of primary concern was the well-being of the widows in the community. Throughout the DUT process, reporting of results had followed a protocol where the team would meet with the widows first, then the elders, then the community; then the information would be available to the public. This approach was due to the painful and very personal nature of the situation. The news story ignored that protocol; community meetings to discuss results had not yet been held. Moreover, Gaudet did not agree with the interpretation of the findings.

Review of the research for the DUT shows that significant pieces of information and scientific studies had not been conducted. For example, Canada Eldor Incorporated, the Crown corporation that owned the mine, refused an original DUT request, and then an access-to-information request about whether any Dene people had worked in the mine or as contractors, an information gap interpreted as no Dene having worked in or at the mine, despite oral histories contradicting that account. A forensic study had not been conducted in the community, due in part to concerns of elders about exhuming bodies for testing. Dosage reconstruction studies did not conclusively determine effects of non-work-related exposures, for example children playing in tailings or people eating fish or animals in and around the mine site as recounted in oral histories. A report condemning lack of government action on preventative cancer screening and mental health support in the community was not "approved" as acceptable research by the governments who were part of the DUT process.

According to Danny Gaudet, at one point the community had been experiencing "a death every six months" due to cancer. People were so overwhelmed by the losses they were unable to properly grieve or recover. In the report of an initial workshop held at the beginning of the Uranium Table process, two health consultants conducted a psychological assessment yielding the following results:

A preliminary community-based health needs assessment recently conducted for the CDUT by two Public Healthcare consultants, Dr. Rafik Gardee and Mr. John Jackson, revealed a number of areas where healing and mental health issues should be addressed. Through a series of interviews with healthcare practitioners, community leaders and people directly affected by Port Radium, the consultants found that the psychological needs of individuals in the community are not being addressed in a systematic manner. Cancer, simply referred to as the "sickness," is of such a high profile in Délîne that it leads to obvious anxiety and distress within certain sections of the population. The individual and collective grief of the community appears to be manifesting itself in symptoms of depression, and the absence of cross cultural bereavement counseling and support for people carrying long-term losses represents a major deficit in the health services provided in Délîne.

A program of bereavement and grief counseling, as well as professional psychological counseling, should be instituted in Délîne to address the obvious psychological and emotional distress and suffering being endured by widows and other people affected by cancer deaths. Such a program should be run in conjunction with a series of workshops and retreats conducted by Délîne's Traditional Healer, Charlie Neyelle (with the possible assistance of outside organizations). It is important to adopt a holistic approach to healing and to promote psychological well-being throughout the community.[20]

The findings of the links between the mine and cancer incidences in the community bring closure to this chapter in unanticipated ways. At the initial time of writing, the community's perspective of the mine and its effects were grounded in the experience of the mine itself: from the toxic effects being originally kept secret from the community, to the eerie accuracy of the prophecy borne out by the use of Délîne uranium in the making of atomic bombs, to the many cancer deaths of loved ones, friends, and valued community members.

While "the science," as it was referred to, did not confirm the uranium mine had a significant causative effect on cancer rates within the community, it did not confirm other causes, such as smoking, as speculated by the scientist quoted in the news report. In that report, the science was presented as conclusive that mining-related activities did not cause cancer but that the community engaged in high-risk activities that probably did. It is curious that scientists such as the one quoted in the article are very careful to ensure people accept that carrying around radioactive ore does not increase cancer risks significantly but freely speculate that cancer is more likely due to smoking, without knowing whether any of the cancer victims actually smoked or what their exposures to tobacco smoke over their lifetimes might have been.

At the beginning of the Délîne uranium process, a workshop was held in the community. Some of the proceedings of the workshop were reflected in a report of the workshop results released by INAC, including the following:

> The community of Délînê is severely affected by the issues addressed during the workshop. Not only is the presence of the Port Radium mine in their traditional territory a threat to them, but their past experiences as mine workers, ore carriers or families living near or at the mine site had important repercussions on the entire community. The concerns are particularly related to human health but also to the health of their environment. The Dene rely strongly on their environment for their survival and their connection with the land is strongly reflected in their language and spiritual culture: *"If the land, the water, the fish, the caribou are healthy, us Dene people will be healthy."* The Great Bear Lake area is the larder of the Dene peoples to whom traditional food is essential.
>
> Chief Leroy Andre expressed during the Experts and Community Workshop that several years had been spent by the community trying to find answers to their problems but that the government was not receptive to the urgency of the situation and did not want to take responsibility for what had happened. During the course of the workshop, several community members shared their fears and concerns. One of the most critical issues appears to be the re-establishment of trust between the Délînê Dene and the government of Canada. Even though an official promise to "heal the land" was made, the community remains skeptical. More than twenty years after the mine closure, little activity was deployed to address their concerns, and several questions are still unanswered. The need for an acknowledgment of the problem and an official apology from the government was raised by several members of the Dene community and appears to be a potential significant contributor to their healing process. (Canada-Déline Uranium Table 2002)

The CBC news story, taking its tone from the findings of the final report, reporting that the uranium mine is not linked to the cancer deaths, the "sickness" that plagues the community, was a cause of significant upset within the community. The insinuation of both the report and the scientist interviewed that Délînê residents should look exclusively to their lifestyle choices (such as smoking) instead of trying to determine links between their community's unusually high cancer rates and the radioactive uranium ore effects on humans and the environment is typical of strategies promoting self-blame in the face of injustice. Once again, Indigenous peoples are reaffirmed as makers of their own misery. That radioactive ore

carried by unprotected men, scattered about the mine site and transportation route into the ecosystem, and within tailings dumped by the
tonne into Great Bear Lake itself should not be a cause of cancer or significant concern is a proposition defying serious consideration. In this
case "the science," questionable in terms of both scope and quality, and a
quick sound-bite from a scientist silence suffering, make meaningless the
collective knowledge and experience of the community with respect to
the mine, and insinuate that the suffering experienced has more likely
been brought on by individuals' behaviours than from cumulative exposure to radioactive uranium ore at work, at play, in the fish and caribou
consumed, in the air, in living life in a poisoned place.

Once again we are put in mind of the doctors testifying about the health
of the victims of the Bhopal disaster: if the victims had not been malnourished in the first place, or run from poison surrounding them in the
dark, they may not have died. Constructing Indigenous peoples as primary authors of their own suffering overshadows the fundamental issue:
exposure should never have happened. And it could have been prevented.

That it should not have happened is the only thing we know for sure.

### Tanning Tensions

**From Field Notes, Tanning Camp, Inuvik, July 2002**
"Have you done this before?" I asked. Joe had taken the scraper yet
again, taking over the task at the hide.

It had now been smoked three times a day for five days, and after
wringing it was always completely dry. The main focus now was to
scrape the hide soft with the long-handled steel scrapers, to make the
whole a clean, uniform softness in preparation for final smoking.
The work was repetitive, requiring a constant steady effort. It was
complicated in no small part by the lack of knowledge we had – there
was no example of what it should look or feel like at this stage, just the
cursory instructions of the elders as they worked, demonstrating
scraping techniques.

"No," he replied. "You make too many mistakes."

The scraper went through the hide as he spoke. He swore quietly and
moved to a different part of the hide.

"Those ladies don't like you, you know. You don't pay enough
attention to what you're doing. You wrecked one of their knives."

The thing about the knife was true. I had ruined the edge on Marie's best knife the week before, attempting to sharpen the knife on my own. I had done it at Joe's request, even though I had known I should have asked beforehand. It had been difficult and embarrassing to keep asking for help every half hour, and I wanted to do something on my own. It had backfired; Marie had been upset. Other than that, my attention span and development of skills seemed to be fine in comparison to the other tanners.

I walked away from the hide, taking a break before returning. It was puzzling: the other participants kept showing me how to do things – even things I was competent with – and when asked they without exception would say it was also their first time working with hides.

Later that day, Janice wanted to talk.

"Joe is being asked to stay in town for the rest of the week," she said.

I was surprised, but the news was also unexpectedly welcome. "But why?" I asked. "He's working as much as anyone else."

Janice continued, "Yes, but he's gossiping and being mean to people. We're all tired of it, so it was decided he shouldn't come tomorrow. He had a big fight with Marie and was swearing at her and Jane."

"But he's been like that with me since day one. That's just the way he is." There would be extra work if Joe were to stay in town.

"Yeah, for a while it was okay when it was just you. Now he's bothering the rest of us."

Initially, I felt annoyed at that comment. On reflection, I considered that the elders had been observing everyone's behaviour and interactions. That would have included any conflict between Joe and me. And I was not the one being asked to leave.

Later, Jane sat down beside me. "You've been working hard," she said. Despite working from early morning until late at night on hides and then her own sewing, Jane never seemed tired. She was very focused on the hides, and although she would occasionally joke with us she had an air of quiet authority and leadership in all things. Everyone admired and respected her, a sentiment that deepened with interaction.

It was several hides later that conversations with Jane moved beyond tanning, and she revealed that as a young teen she had left residential school to return to her small community and care for her ailing grandmother on her own. Without any money or help, she had relied on her own hard work to get by and provide for them both. At the camp, she would get up at 6 a.m., go out to get spruce branches, then work on her own hide, then once people began their day's tasks help those who needed it. Throughout the day she rarely took breaks, often missing lunch or stopping only for a short time to eat. In the evenings after dinner she would take out her beadwork and sew until retiring for the night, talking with others who would gather at the main cabin, translating the English into her Dene language for her mother throughout. Clearly, the work ethic she had developed as a young girl had not been abandoned in her late middle age.

Jane smiled. "Mom was watching you earlier and said next time those ladies in town come to have her tan their moosehide she's going to tell them there's a white lady from Yellowknife who can even tan hides good. Anyone could do it. Boy, they'll just feel ashamed."

We laughed. It was funny. Suddenly, I understood all the extra instruction in a whole new light.

# 5
# Inuvialuit and Gwich'in Culture and Language

A previous chapter showed how the state's conflation of injustice and history coupled with the marginalization of the Dehcho voice in negotiations rationalizes Canada's position on resource revenue sharing. Exploring the conflation of injustice with history preceded an examination of how the state's dysfunction theodicy denies the existence of state-induced suffering, while simultaneously using that suffering as a rationale for maintaining state control in discussions with Délînê about Child and Family Services. Residential schools, briefly mentioned in that chapter, are further examined below.

Contextualizing the implications of the theodicy through the lens of a specific event, the residential school experience is used as an example of state-induced suffering not being comprehended as relevant by government negotiating mandates, in this case during discussions on culture and language at the Inuvialuit and Gwich'in negotiations. At the time the Inuvialuit negotiator was Vince Teddy, who continues engaging with the life-long effects of childhood and subsequent ongoing disconnection from his Inuvialuit culture after attending an English residential school at Inuvik during the 1960s. His story provides a sense of the way people's lives in the present, including their attempts to make meaning of their suffering, are diminished by government silence in response to suffering. This chapter brings together the ways in which past decisions create ongoing suffering and how that suffering is silenced by both communicative practices of the dominant in negotiations and elements of the dysfunction theodicy used as a silencing rationale. Residential school is a primary example of the profound failure of Aboriginal policy predicated on changing Indigenous peoples, as evidenced in the collective suffering it has caused.

During 2006, the Inuvialuit and Gwich'in decided to negotiate separate self-government agreements. This chapter focuses on the personal experience of the Inuvialuit negotiator during joint Inuvialuit-Gwich'in negotiations, a process that took place between 1999 and 2006. Given the resonance of the issues for both Inuvialuit and Gwich'in, and the lack of distinction made between the two by governments when applying policy in the negotiating context, the chapter retains a focus on both peoples.

## The Inuvialuit and Gwich'in

The Inuvialuit are Inuit; the Gwich'in are Dene; these two peoples live in close contact in communities of the Beaufort Delta region, in the northwest corner of the Northwest Territories.

The Inuvialuit (the Real People), descendants of both Alaskan Iñupiat and Inuit designated in older anthropological literature as the Mackenzie Delta Eskimos, occupy traditional territories, including the Mackenzie Delta, Beaufort Sea coast, and Arctic Islands. The population has fluctuated since the early 1800s, resulting mainly from disease epidemics (such as influenza and tuberculosis) and in-migrations of Alaskan Iñupiaq. Between 1889 and 1906, a period of intense whaling activity in waters off the Beaufort Sea coast, the population was reduced to the point of extinction, at which point Iñupiaq from Alaska moved into traditional territories to take up hunting and trapping (see Smith 1984).

In the Beaufort Delta region, Inuvialuit communities include Sachs Harbour, Ulukhaktok (Holman), Paulatuk, and Tuktoyaktuk; farther south, Aklavik and Inuvik are home both to Inuvialuit and Gwich'in. In Inuvik, almost half of the population of approximately 3,484 (current to 2006) consists of non-Indigenous people. Like many Indigenous peoples in the NWT, Inuvialuit people engage in a combination of wage labour and subsistence lifestyles, speak English or their language, Inuvialuktun (or both or others), and practise their culture. Determining factors for cultural vitality may include issues relating to accessibility to land-based pursuits and availability of opportunity, depending on the location and the economic and personal circumstances of individuals. Inuvialuit originally inhabited areas along the Beaufort coast with seasonal migrations both farther north and inland to gather berries, trap, and hunt caribou and other mammals. Beluga whale hunts from Shingle Point and Kendall Island remain essential subsistence activities. Families gather for the summer months at their camps to hunt whalesand prepare the meat for the winter. In addition, spring hunting for geese, fishing, and fall and winter caribou hunting take place throughout Inuvialuit territories.

Inuvialuit culture and language have benefited from the establishment of the Inuvialuit Cultural Resource Centre, responsible for culture and language preservation and development as well as associated research. Among the Inuvialuit,[1] the Inuvialuktun language is considered to be in decline. Of the Inuvialuit communities, Holman has the highest percentage of language retention, with 76 percent of Inuvialuit speaking their language; in communities such as Tuktoyaktuk, Sachs Harbour, and Paulatuk, this number drops significantly, to between 19 percent and 28 percent (see Government of the Northwest Territories, Bureau of Statistics, 2006). The Inuvialuit Cultural Resource Centre has developed a variety of programs and materials to address language retention. The centre's efforts are aided by the Inuvialuit Regional Corporation, recognized as the Inuvialuit representative organization upon the signing of the Inuvialuit Final Agreement with Canada in 1984. In 2008, of about 5,600 Inuvialuit, the corporation had approximately 3,800 beneficiaries (Inuvialuit over the age of eighteen) enrolled in the agreement. The corporation has been a major supporter of cultural activities such as Inuvialuit language education in schools, funding for drummers and dancers in each community, and sponsorship of arts and cultural events. The Inuvialuit are active members of national and international Inuit organizations such as the Inuit Tapiriit Kanatami and the Inuit Circumpolar Council.

The Gwich'in (People of the Caribou) are Dene and live to the south of Inuvialuit, with traditional territories extending into the Yukon. The Gwich'in people are closely related to other Gwich'in peoples living throughout the Yukon and Alaska; their connections and unity are maintained in part through organizations such as the Gwich'in Council International. Numbering approximately 3,200, Tetlit, Gwich'ya, Nihtat, and Ehditaat Gwich'in who are resident in the Northwest Territories live in the communities of Fort McPherson (Tetlit Zheh), Tsiigehtchic, Inuvik, and Aklavik respectively.[2] In the older anthropological literature, they are known as Loucheux, a French translation of the Sahtu Dene name *degede*, or by the designation Kutchin.

Introduction of European disease during the 1800s resulted in what is thought to be a population low of 1,000 Gwich'in throughout what is now Alaska, the Yukon, and the NWT during the year 1860 (see Slobodin 1981). Similar to the Inuvialuit experience, Gwich'in continue to practise a combination of wage-earning and subsistence lifestyles, opportunities in both ways of life having expanded since the signing of the Gwich'in Land Claim Agreement in 1992. Subsistence activities include trapping, caribou and moose hunting, gathering berries, and netting and drying fish. While most speak English, there are still some Gwich'in speakers, but language use is in decline: estimates range from 16 percent to 26 percent of Gwich'in people speaking their language (Government of the Northwest Territories, Bureau of Statistics, 2006).[3]

Fortunately, the Gwich'in, through the Fort McPherson Language Centre, the Social and Cultural Institute, and the Gwich'in Tribal Council, have embarked on a variety of projects aimed at increasing language and culture retention and development, with a particular emphasis on youth and elders. These projects include the development of language and culture curriculum materials for schools, language classes and camps, and research projects, such as the ethnography of the Gwichy'a Gwich'in of Tsiigehtchic titled *Gwichy'a Gwich'in Googwandak,* a collaboration between Gwich'in and non-Gwich'in researchers and the community's elders.

Self-government negotiations began subsequent to the Inuvialuit and Gwich'in Land Claim Agreements. The Inuvialuit negotiated a regional claim with Canada between 1974 and 1983 (see Map 1). The agreement exchanges undefined and exclusive use of Inuvialuit territory for defined rights, cash compensation, land, and participation in resource management. At that time, Canada did not recognize political self-determination as an Aboriginal right. However, the Inuvialuit secured clause 4.3, guaranteeing Inuvialuit participation in reshaping of public government in the region.

The Inuvialuit agreement establishes five bodies co-operating as an integrated wildlife and land co-management system. Six community corporations manage local land claim responsibilities and benefits, co-ordinated by the Inuvialuit Regional Corporation based in Inuvik. Although the original $45 million cash compensation was reduced after the repayment of $9 million in negotiating loans, over the past twenty-five years the Inuvialuit have increased the value of the holdings of the Inuvialuit Regional Corporation to over $300 million, employing over 1,200 people, many of whom are beneficiaries. The Inuvialuit Regional Corporation website describes specific land claim provisions under the Inuvialuit Final Agreement:

> The Inuvialuit would have legal control over their land (see map) with ownership of 91,000 square kilometres (35,000 square miles) of land including 13,000 square kilometres (5,000 square miles) with subsurface rights to oil, gas and minerals. Furthermore, the Inuvialuit established the right to hunt and harvest anywhere in the claim area, particularly as primary harvesters on certain lands known to be rich in wildlife. They also secured the responsibility for ensuring good wildlife management, becoming part of a wildlife management team with the government. The IFA was based on sustainable development.[4]

The Gwich'in agreement, signed in 1992, provides for the exchange of undefined Aboriginal rights within Gwich'in traditional territories together with specific Treaty 11 rights and interests, in exchange for defined rights. These include cash compensation, land, and participation in resource co-management (co-ordinated with other land claim regions in the Mackenzie Valley through the Mackenzie Valley Resource Management Act). Specifically, the Gwich'in became the recognized owners of 16,264 kilometres of lands within their traditional territory, which extends into the Yukon, with a combination of surface and subsurface rights. The Gwich'in received $75 million in cash compensation. Land claim interests are administered in each of the six communities by Designated Gwich'in Organizations (DGOs) and regionally by the Gwich'in Tribal Council, based in Inuvik. Although the Gwich'in band councils negotiated the claim on behalf of their members, Canada's resistance to recognizing political self-determination at the time meant that the Indian Act band councils remained in place. They discharge responsibilities under the Indian Act, alongside the DGOs and Tribal Council, which operate under the Gwich'in land claim. In this way, representation of a variety of Gwich'in rights and interests is institutionally fragmented. However, the land claim does contain a framework for subsequent self-government negotiations in Chapter 5 and Appendix B. Under self-government, the Gwich'in band councils would be dissolved, and the Indian Act bands would be replaced by Gwich'in governments operating in accordance with the self-government agreement.

During the early 1990s, the Inuvialuit and Gwich'in began to discuss in earnest the possibility of forming a regional government, known then as the Western Arctic Regional Municipality. Both the Inuvialuit and the Gwich'in had settled land claim agreements, and their leaders were anxious to move toward greater political independence for the region. Eventually, the proposal evolved into a joint self-government negotiating process. Negotiating parties included the four Gwich'in band councils recognized under the Indian Act, the Gwich'in Tribal Council established through the Gwich'in Land Claim Agreement (1992), and the Inuvialuit Regional Corporation, representing the six Inuvialuit community corporations. The Inuvialuit and Gwich'in joint self-government negotiations were guided by a mandate developed in 1998 through consultations with the leaders and people of all Inuvialuit and Gwich'in communities. In a series of community surveys and workshops, people were asked to identify key principles and priorities to be negotiated. The results, simultaneously promoting consensus building and Inuvialuit and Gwich'in participation in negotiation planning, were synthesized into a mandate, regularly reviewed and updated by leaders.

During 2006, the Gwich'in decided to pursue their own self-government agreements. The split from the Inuvialuit was preceded by increasing concerns of band councils over Indian status and treaty rights and how they would be affected by the contemplated combined public-Aboriginal governments that were to be created under the self-government agreement. The Agreement-in-Principle, reached during 2003, was based on having a strong regional public government with guaranteed Inuvialuit and Gwich'in representation, drawn from community-based Aboriginal-public governments. In communities such as Aklavik and Inuvik, with large minorities of both Inuvialuit and Gwich'in, guaranteed representation was reduced from 50 percent of councillors, as in cases of communities dominated by either Inuvialuit or Gwich'in, to guaranteed representation of 25 percent of councillors for each of the Inuvialuit and Gwich'in populations. Although many other factors came into play in the decision to pursue a Gwich'in rather than a joint Gwich'in-Inuvialuit agreement, issues around representation and uncertainty about the protection of rights through combined Aboriginal-public governments had consistently arisen as prominent concerns during community consultations. Although the now separate Gwich'in and Inuvialuit negotiations are based in part on aspects of the agreement negotiated jointly, structures of government in particular are being rethought, since necessary issues arising from a joint approach such as shared obligations, responsibilities, entitlements, and decision making no longer exist.

## The Negotiator's Question

Inuvialuit and Gwich'in self-government negotiations, like most others, were usually held in participating communities. During December 1999, the boardroom we were meeting in was on the top floor of a skyscraper in downtown Calgary, its floor-to-ceiling windows framing both the foothills and the Rocky Mountains beyond, sprinkled with the first snows of winter.

The first item on the agenda was culture and language, one of the many subjects contained in the Process and Schedule Agreement, which described subjects to be discussed, the process of negotiations, and mutually agreed time lines for major milestones. It was signed at the outset of negotiations by all parties. Prior to the session, basic interests had been exchanged, allowing each of the parties to consider the ideas and aims of the others, and the morning's discussion was to be the start of substantive negotiations. After three years of negotiations, the GNWT had recently appointed a new negotiator, who had not quite found his feet in this subject matter.

At the time, as senior analyst, I sat between our legal counsels Bernie

Funston and Charles Hunter; Charles has the distinction of being the first Inuvialuit lawyer. Beside Charles sat Vince Teddy, Inuvialuit negotiator, and Bob Simpson, the chief negotiator representing both Gwich'in and Inuvialuit. The GNWT negotiator sat a few chairs away from Bob, on the same side of the table. The director of the heritage and culture section of the GNWT Department of Education was present, as were several other officials. The federal chief negotiator and his team faced us on the opposite side. The boardroom, at the law offices of Charles's firm, was spacious and suitably well appointed. The teams were more smartly dressed than for a community meeting, with most people wearing business attire, and the atmosphere was polite and formal.

The session began in a congenial manner, making introductions, exchanging pleasantries, and discussing administrative items. After about fifteen minutes a consensus emerged to move into substantive discussions. The GNWT negotiator began the discussion. He wanted to start, he said, by posing a question: "Why, exactly, do Inuvialuit and Gwich'in need control of culture and language? These are policy based programs, I don't see the point in why we are discussing them. There is no jurisdiction here. So I just want to understand why discussing this seems to be so important when there is really nothing here" (Inuvialuit and Gwich'in negotiation session 1999). For a few moments no one spoke. The entire Inuvialuit, Gwich'in, and federal teams stared in shock at the new negotiator. Vince stood up and walked to the back of the room to refill his coffee, stony resignation filling his face. He remained there. Bob also vacated his seat to take up a position beside Vince – something he had never done before nor has done since during active discussion at a negotiation session. The federal team, in unison, pushed themselves back from the table where they sat, as if trying to put physical distance between themselves and the territorial negotiator. The question hung in the air.

After some long moments of silence, Charles began to speak. In a remarkably steady voice, under the circumstances, he outlined in detail the multifaceted assault on language and culture occasioned by residential schools, the provisions of the Indian Act, and the societal marginalization of Indigenous people in Canada generally over the previous 200 years. It was clear to us all that the GNWT requirements of their negotiators included neither tact nor appreciation of the history and reality of Indigenous-state relations in Canada. Nor even necessarily honouring the basic agreements structuring negotiations, namely the Process and Schedule Agreement, and the Gwich'in Comprehensive Land Claim Agreement, where it had twice been agreed the subject was an item for negotiation.

The territorial negotiator's question could be read as a perfectly innocent one. It may have been based, at best, on a lack of knowledge of Indigenous-state relations and a failure to contextualize the negotiations within that reality. The question indicated a sense that culture and language are naturally determined rather than socially or politically determined. It also indicated a belief that a central, non-Indigenous government retaining control of cultural programs for Indigenous people was not a significant incursion into Indigenous self-determination. The question was also based on a policy position shaping self-government negotiations: negotiating practical self-government arrangements relating to specific subject matters. No connection was made by the negotiator between the importance of self-government to Inuvialuit and Gwich'in experiencing ongoing suffering with respect to residential schooling and similar policies. Nor was it connected with dissatisfaction over current government action. There was no recognition of Indigenous peoples' lack of trust in government or of the ravages of experiences of colonial assaults on Indigenous languages and cultures informing Inuvialuit and Gwich'in perspectives on negotiations.

Instead, the question was based on policy – consistent with a negotiating mandate predicated on maintaining as much jurisdictional authority for the GNWT as possible.[5]

# Inuvialuit and Gwich'in Negotiations

Negotiators at a main table session of the Inuvialuit and Gwich'in joint self-government negotiations, at the Gwich'in Tribal Council boardroom in Inuvik, November 1998. Photo: author.

The Gwich'in and Inuvialuit self-government negotiating team, Inuvik, summer 1999: from left to right, Bob Simpson, author, Charles Hunter of Inuvik, Vince Teddy of Tuktoyaktuk, and Charlie Furlong of Aklavik.

The federal negotiating team assigned to the Inuvialuit and Gwich'in self-government negotiations; from left to right, Carla McGrath, Kim Thompson, and John U. Bayly, Queen's Council,
summer 1999. Photo: author.

## Experiencing Residential School

Inuvialuit negotiator Vince Teddy's preparation for his negotiating respon-sibilities began at the age of six, when Vince was chosen from among his siblings to be sent away from his community to the residential school in Inuvik to learn English and get a "white" education. Having known only the acceptance and safety in his family's camp on the Arctic coast where he was born, then later in the home of his family in the community of Tuk-toyaktuk, the regimented solitude and bare clinical spaces of the English-only school came as a shock. He was forbidden to speak in his own words, and English soon completely replaced Inuvialuktun, the language of his early childhood spent with parents and grandparents and his extended family. As Vince tells it,

> At that time I didn't know why I was being sent away. I didn't want to go. Back then you didn't question if your parents or an elder told you to do something. I sometimes thought about why it was that I was the one to be sent away.
>
> I don't remember the first two years. I just remember that I didn't know what they were saying to me. They just lined us all up, and being little I just got in line, and they started shaving our heads, then after that I don't remember for two years. I just remember different images, but nothing makes sense. We would go home during the summertime; we were kept at the Grollier Hall in Inuvik from fall until summer. Mom made us good clothes, brand-new clothes, but they took them away and dressed us all the same in uniforms. During summer when I went home I couldn't under-stand Mom and Dad when they were talking. They had to start speaking English with me. I know that when we were at home when I was a little boy we all understood each other, but after that first bit of school it was different, and it's only in looking back that I realize at the time I didn't even notice that. I thought we were all speaking the same; I guess that happened to every family. During the summer it was good to be back home, but there was always suspicion on the parents' side about whether or not we would still know them. It was kind of a shock on both sides ...
>
> There is a story I heard. Some kids had a very violent and negative expe-rience. In one community they had a band meeting where there were two ladies, adults in their thirties. They had always had a troubled life in their community, and people saw them as good for nothing. When they were young they were okay. People did not know what happened, but some of them in a way knew what happened. At this meeting the people were talk-ing about an issue around religion or the Roman Catholic Church. One lady stood up and told her story of sexual abuse. It was really emotional,

she was talking about sexual abuse she went through as a young girl and was crying. Then the other girl was going to tell her story. The amazing thing was that there was a group of elders there too, and they got up and told them to shut up and told them not to talk that way about the priests and nuns. It shut the meeting down. You know, in many places the elders had similar experiences, and for some it must have been traumatic. Those girls, the girls were their children, so they felt responsible. In my community it's sort of similar sometimes; people talk about abuse in a round-about way, not as personal history, instead they always end up talking like a third person, as if it didn't happen here. With the boys and [Grollier Hall] court cases, it has finally come out ...[6]

We come to the conclusion we just have to accept [that] it happened and move forward in a positive way, and that is where we need the elders, but when we say things sometimes the elders are not there [to back us up], so we kind of don't do anything, because that's our elders, and if they don't say anything then we can't move forward as a community ... That is the way to do it, we have always been told whatever the elders' way is you do that, so we are sort of caught between two worlds and want to do what's right.

Today when government talks about self-government, wanting to move forward and not recognize the past, and they say they can't do anything about it, it's ironic, because sometimes our elders are like that too. It's comical in a way but sad; if you don't have humour, you have nothing. It's difficult for communities to heal, because one generation denies it, then my generation steps up to tell the truth about it all. Even though we step up, it's not our place to move forward without the whole community. Some elders do say it's good that we are moving forward, but others say there are so many negative things around, and how do we move forward with the negative things there? It's like they are kind of saying, "how can [your generation] be trusted to move ahead if you are not trusted by us because of the negative things you say?"

A lot of it also goes with the traditional knowledge part. We were away from home for more than three-quarters of a year, and then we come back home to communities and families without being taught the traditional knowledge that was always there. So there is that missing critical piece of information of culture and language. As soon as I got back home [from university], my older sister took me and said, "you have to learn to live here and off the land," and I said, "okay, good, I'm ready." That was the most important part of my learning process, being with the hunters and people who went out on the land.

... Through my older sister, and my wife's family, I learned all the survival on the land, learned the land, the seasons, enabled to survive, and that's something I know I could pass on to my children. I know I don't know my language, but I respect my language and my culture ... Twenty years ago our people used to call us down for [having lost our language at school], but now they are saying they are sorry for having done that. That was the positive part of the last ten years. That recognition had to do with the sexually abused survivors coming forward; until then everyone was wondering why residential school kids could not speak our language, so it's all coming out now. I tip my hat to those guys who came forward even in a negative way, but the truth came out about the sexual and cultural abuse and all the other abuses.

There were a few kids who were kept at home [from residential school], and those are the ones we go to now for traditional knowledge and for help when we need it in doing things traditionally and culturally ... While we were going to school, we made fun of them for not going to school, and now it is full circle: my education helps them, and their traditional knowledge helps us. It becomes a whole community when we are together ... We function now as equals. At community meetings, for example, on self-government when we talk about putting culture and language back into programs and services, people like my sister [who was kept at home] are a critical part of it, and yet we [who were sent away] are too. That is where there is hope in a healing process as the next stage. (Vince Teddy, interview, 2002)

For the community, individuals who could speak the white man's language and knew his ways were considered essential to collective survival in the future. It was thought that young educated people could act as bridges between the community and representatives of government and industry, educating newcomers in Inuvialuit ways and fostering positive relations between whites and the community. It was only years later, after returning to his community, that Vince learned how his fate had been so intertwined with his elders' aspirations for the community. The years spent at the English-only residential school came at a price: Vince lost his language, connections with his culture, family, and community; and groups of children kept at home and the ones sent away to school each had to develop defence mechanisms justifying their relative positions, creating divisions in the community. All these were keenly felt consequences of attending residential school. At the negotiating table, the consequences are motivation for ensuring that in future such experiences will not be repeated: Inuvialuit should be in a position to maintain and develop Inuvialuit language and culture.

Vince's residential school experience represents aspects of a spectrum of experiences among residential school survivors, which are well documented elsewhere. In the case of the Gwich'in experience, Gwich'in novelist Robert Alexie Jr. chronicles residential school years and their aftermath for individuals in a fictitious Gwich'in community in his critically acclaimed novel *Porcupines and China Dolls* (2002). Generally, and particularly in the wake of Canada's Statement of Reconciliation in *Gathering Strength* (1998) and high-profile class action lawsuits against churches which administered residential schools, it has been accepted that the residential school system was probably the most powerful state-sponsored instrument used to systematically destroy the language, culture, and practices of Indigenous communities, the foundations of existence as individuals and peoples. A residential schools settlement reached during 2007 between Indigenous peoples' representatives and Canada replaced a botched attempt by Canada to administer its own state-determined settlement process. Part of the recent settlement includes a Truth and Reconciliation Commission, where the testimonies and experiences of survivors are made public.[7]

## Implications of Residential Schools for NWT Political Development

The 1998 Gathering Strength Policy acknowledges a widely held negative view of residential schools. The pedagogy at the schools was often racist, using violent and destructive tools and methods of assimilation. Although prevalent, and revelatory of a view of the schools as a key source of intergenerational social suffering in the communities where I have worked, this view is by no means the whole story about the residential school experience among Indigenous people in the NWT. This section provides a series of reflections of individuals on their experiences, providing insight about how residential schooling shaped aspects of NWT political development. The following reflections do not represent the complete spectrum of experiences or a complete picture of the experiences of each individual. These reflections were chosen for their relevance to how residential schooling shaped individuals who would go on to become actively involved in self-government negotiations and related political initiatives.

Initially, mission schools, run by Catholic and Anglican churches, provided homes to children orphaned by disease epidemics, who found themselves suddenly without extended families or even distant relatives who could care for them as a result of the massive death tolls of the epidemics (see McCarthy 1995). According to one Inuvialuit elder who attended the Aklavik school during the 1930s,

I was born at my parents' whaling camp near the coast [of the Beaufort Sea]. My mother died while I was small. My father was a whaler; he didn't know how to take care of us kids. So we went to mission school at Aklavik, where they took care of us. I don't know what would have happened to us if we hadn't gone there. It was a good place. We were fed, and they cared for us, we learned the Bible and to cook, to sew, us girls. I was grateful for having a place. We met kids from all over. Lots of Indians from even past Yellowknife. It was a hard life in a way but a good one; back then life was hard for everyone. At the school with the priest and the sisters it was strict, sure they might use that strap if they needed to, but they had to be that way. It was a hard life for them, white people living like that, and with all those kids to look after too. (Inuvialuit elder, interview, 2002)

As the government increased its presence in the North, the schools were organized more systematically and the curriculum standardized to emphasize academic rather than the primarily vocational skills imparted to Indigenous students up until the 1950s (see, e.g., Dickerson 1992; and McCarthy 1995). By 1960, residential high schools were centralized in Inuvik, Yellowknife, Hay River, and Fort Smith. Students were drawn from small communities to the regional centres, often returning home for the summers, as absences from home spanning several years common in the early 1900s were alleviated after the 1950s through the increased number of schools and improved transportation infrastructure in remote locations. The mixing of students from disparate geographic locations had unintended consequences for NWT political development:

What the government didn't realize was that these schools were where we all met each other, Indians and even the Eskimos, from all over. We got to know one another, and found out sometimes that we were relatives, and realized we had a lot in common, and as we got older talked about some of our common experiences as Indian people. This was the basis for our future working together, like on the land claims and the Berger Inquiry. So in the late 1960s, when us young Indians started to organize, our networks and a lot of the groundwork [were] already in place, because we all knew each other from the hostel in Inuvik or wherever [residential schools]. (Gwich'in beneficiary, interview, 2002)

However, many students also experienced the worst sorts of abuse of power practised by those charged with their care and well-being. Sexual abuses sometimes occurred, their extent described by the media articles below. The disclosures of the 1990s about such incidents sparked the establishment of a Grollier Hall Healing Circle, promoting healing and recovery of adult survivors of the Inuvik-based residential school.

Grollier Hall Abuse Scandal Grows[8]
Inuvik, N.W.T. – Police are charging three former supervisors at the Grollier Hall residential school in Inuvik with nearly 30 new sex-related offences. Paul Leroux, 63, Jean Louis Comeau, 69, and 66-year old Martin Houston have all been charged.

Paul Leroux faces 11 new charges. Jean Louis Comeau faces five, and Martin Houston faces thirteen. They are charged with gross indecency and indecent assault. That's what these offences were called at the time they are alleged to have happened. The crown prosecutor's office is saying very little about the case. There is a publication ban on the identity of the complainants.

Leroux's charges cover a time period between 1967 and 1979. Paul Leroux was convicted of 14 sex charges in 1998. They relate to his time as a boys supervisor at the residential school. He was sentenced to ten years in prison. Comeau was convicted of two counts of indecent assault in 1998. The Crown's office doesn't know when the three men will appear in court to answer the charges.

Since the late 1990s, such disclosures have resulted in growing awareness of the extent of problems in the church- and government-run residential schools. The Aboriginal Healing Foundation, an independent national agency with responsibility for providing funding to communities to recover from such abuses and consequent ongoing effects within communities, was established in 1999 with a five-year mandate as part of Canada's response to the Royal Commission on Aboriginal Peoples *Final Report* (1996). The foundation has been active in the NWT, contributing millions of dollars to community-based projects. Many projects focus on healing through cultural renewal targeting survivors, their families, elders, and helping professionals. These projects range from healing circles to support to attend conferences and therapeutic events such as workshops and healing gatherings.

Among the residential schools in the NWT was an elite program for Indigenous youth who had demonstrated superior scholastic potential, established by Catholic bishop Piche in Fort Smith. The Grandin College school was named after a former Catholic bishop, Vital Grandin, who established the mission at Fort Providence in 1861; six years later the Grey Nuns established the residential school there. During the 1960s the most promising Indigenous high school students undertook a rigorous academic program in an atmosphere fostering competition and self-discipline. One former student, Rosa Van Camp (1989), noted in a biography of Bishop Piche that Indigenous languages were openly spoken at the school, and its students were constantly challenged to achieve their best, using the tools of both Indigenous and non-Indigenous societies. According to another former student,

> If you look at where we [former students of Grandin College] are today, most of us are in leadership positions: the former premier [Stephen Kakfwi], the former member of Parliament [Ethel Blondin-Andrew], some MLAs, chiefs, negotiators. All of us went to Grandin College. It was a training ground for what they hoped would be good-model assimilated Indians and Eskimos. Instead, it produced leaders who wanted to change the system, and the weapon to do that was the white man's own education. We got some good strict training from the priest and brothers. It's too bad they don't have a program like that now; it would be really good especially as all regions have to work together even more now that land claims are being settled. It would have been good if today's youth had that kind of opportunity like we had. (Gwich'in beneficiary, interview, 2002)

The impact of the schools was multi-faceted, yet the emotionally gripping stories of abuse and consequent compensation by churches and governments responsible are outcomes justifiably garnering most public attention. Little attention has been paid to how the situation into which children were thrust was later used to their own advantage, specifically by turning to networks built as youth to undertake shared political goals after returning to their communities. The schools facilitated political networks critical to the success of Indigenous political mobilization of the 1960s and 1970s. The connections between individuals created personal networks based on shared experiences, leading to effective Indigenous coalitions spanning diverse regions, despite the absence of kinship or geographical ties. The positive aspects of residential schools were as politically significant – albeit differently significant – as the negative outcomes and treatment experienced by many individual students.

### The Past Is the Present: How Events Shape Reality
Residential schooling in many respects set the tone and trajectory of the relationship between the state and Indigenous peoples. This was true not only for those surviving the schools themselves but also for the cultural and psychological effects felt throughout families and communities as a

result. Shaping children from an early age, the approach to education prepared survivors and their families and communities for a continuum of approaches to Aboriginal policy and its implementation predicated on assimilation of Indigenous peoples into the mainstream society in all respects. The underlying message of assimilation, that things will be better for Indigenous peoples if they change to adopt dominant ways, is the same assumption underlying the state's dysfunction theodicy.

Each self-government negotiation can be understood as part of a larger relationship between the state and Indigenous peoples. Indigenous and Canadian realities meet in a discussion forum that is intended to create positive change in the state-Indigenous relationship. As with any relationship, recollections, meanings, and understandings of the whole are created through progressive interactions, animated and contoured through critical events. These critical events are moments great with tension, revelation, insight, the points at which a relationship and its foundational structures are laid bare. Those moments are signposts, boundaries, and turning points intertwined, the existence of which alters the landscape of both mutual understanding and self-understanding. The negotiating event focusing this chapter's discussion was a moment of clarity. It revealed an apparent gulf in understanding between government and Indigenous perspectives about how suffering should be understood. Specifically, a government view seemed to hold to a notion of injustices suffered as a distant memory versus an Indigenous sense of injustice as a formative experience shaping ongoing existence at individual and collective levels.

Two critical events are brought together within the life of one individual: one event of national resonance for Indigenous peoples (residential schooling), the other specific to the course of the Inuvialuit-Gwich'in joint self-government negotiations process (the negotiator's question). Their confluence as personal experiences in the life of the Inuvialuit negotiator provides insight into how seemingly unrelated experiences intertwine to shape the way in which new foundations are being laid and mislaid within the context of the new relationship being conceived at self-government negotiations. Similar to the way that impatient neglect of specific steps required in the tanning of moosehide can reduce the effectiveness of the overall tanning process, decontextualized policy approaches to negotiations can undo much effort at relationship repair both before and after the event. The negotiator's question takes a discussion of language and culture that stands to make meaning of residential school-based suffering in a completely different direction, leading with the assumption that whatever happened in the past at the hands of churches or governments has no bearing on discussions over who should control Inuvialuit and

Gwich'in culture and language. The negotiator's question effectively silenced suffering, which is a most compelling rationale for Inuvialuit and Gwich'in control over who they culturally are and could be.

The testimonies of residential school survivors create a multi-faceted sense of the implications of different experiences for individuals. Each individual quotation focuses on different aspects of the experience. Despite the complexity and diversity of experiences among the narrators, no justifications are made for the institution itself. That residential school was a primary tool of assimilation has been acknowledged by the Canadian state (Government of Canada, Department of Indian Affairs, 1998). The news article above illustrates the extent of damage continuing to shatter and shape the lives of survivors and their families and steps being taken to exorcise consequent suffering. These experiences often stand at the centre of concentric circles of suffering and healing efforts reverberating through communities. As a result, experiences have generally made both survivors and observers wary of government initiatives, officials, and representatives, of the outcomes and long-term effects of government involvement in the areas of Indigenous cultures, languages, and education.

Negotiators' mandates are informed by the general sense that their purpose is to minimize state intervention into community affairs. In general negotiators are pragmatic, often approaching negotiations with a certain amount of healthy cynicism. However, the negotiators' question shattered the Inuvialuit and Gwich'in team's assumption that Indigenous peoples' experiences of language and culture loss due to government control would be made meaningful for its relevance as a rationale for Inuvialuit and Gwich'in control of their own culture and language. Self-government's purpose is in part to promote language and culture as an essential and crucial aspect of governance. The negotiator's question, and the underlying threat that the government would not entertain Indigenous authority over language and culture, made very real the possibility that the cultural identity of future generations could be controlled by non-Indigenous governments. The searing insight that government views the ongoing experience of culture loss as something at best in the past or at worst irrelevant for a split second robbed the residential school experience of meaning. It silenced everyone in the room and rendered senseless and futile the participation of Indigenous peoples' negotiators in attempting to make sense of suffering and lay the groundwork for avoiding such suffering in future. As within the paradigm described by Young (2000), the norms of discourse and action needed a legal, bureaucratically conversant reason for discussing the subject matter, not personal experience or testimony.

By answering the question the way he did, with an overview of both officially and unofficially sanctioned repression of Indigenous cultures throughout Canada over the course of several hundred years, Charles's explanation relieved the pressure in the room. By contextualizing individual experience within the scope of state-Indigenous relations, the moment was depersonalized and refocused toward flaws and effects of government policy. By outlining how the shared and individual experiences of Indigenous peoples throughout Canada have resulted in a compelling body of evidence as rationale to restrict and withdraw governmental authority over Indigenous culture and languages, his appeal focused on issues of broad principles, legal obligations, and practicalities. Charles found a way to speak suffering, or at least an intelligible approximation of it, in the language of law and policy. From discussing the negotiation of a transfer of power, the discussion became one of educating the government negotiator as to why the subject was on the agenda in the first place, in a language intelligible to that negotiator. His response was an excellent and conciliatory negotiating tactic. Yet it required him to speak in the discourse of the dominant, to play by its rules, instead of being able to widen the total social knowledge of participants. The incident marked a low point in the relationship of the negotiating parties. The Inuvialuit and Gwich'in team knew that Charles had made the only choice possible by using the moment to continue to communicate an Indigenous experience in the discourse of the dominant, a tactic echoing the residential school survivors who, instead of becoming "good assimilated model Indians," used the knowledge gained through their residential school education to press for their own people's interests.

What silenced the rest of the team was knowing the question could not be answered in the only way that conveyed a living experience on its own terms: the Inuvialuit and Gwich'in needed jurisdiction over culture and language because Vince had lost his language at residential school; because a generation of young men who had attended Grollier Hall had their lives destroyed; because all the things the government says are in the past are so vibrant in the present. While Charles's explanation to the government negotiator turned a moment of despair into one of communication, the power of the truth was in a sense lost in that translation, limited by a discourse not designed to convey or accommodate experiences of suffering. That translation could never convey the suffering experience to those with the power to accept its meaning.

The fallout from the negotiator's question recalls the earlier observations of a government negotiator when speaking about the implications of ongoing suffering for how negotiators must conduct themselves: "They [Indigenous peoples] are dysfunctional, their communities are suffering, and it is very personal. So you have to set boundaries on a personal level as a way to facilitate getting through that. Then when you get non-Native negotiators who go in there and don't have the cultural awareness or know the history behind that – it's just a recipe for an explosion."

## Conclusion

This chapter describes how the ongoing nature of injustices suffered by Indigenous peoples is a filter through which Indigenous-state interactions, including self-government negotiations, are experienced and interpreted by Indigenous people. The clash between the residential school experience of Inuvialuit negotiator Vince Teddy and his GNWT counterpart's lack of awareness of the relevance of such experiences for negotiations becomes more than a simple misunderstanding. In that specific context, it exemplifies the power of the dominant discourse and underlying dysfunction theodicy to silence suffering, particularly in this case, where a government negotiator was simply acting according to government policy and mandate. The gulf between the Indigenous and government negotiators' realities creates a basis for discussing culture and language that can only accommodate the dominant discourse, which excludes the relevance of suffering.

As discussion unfolded that day, it was revealed that the territorial negotiator's puzzlement over why jurisdiction was desirable was a perceived difficulty of how a government might pass laws regarding "culture." His confusion arose from the fact that GNWT cultural and related language programs are policy-based, not jurisdictional. Logistical issues were also raised – would the Inuvialuit and Gwich'in finance their own museum facility to repatriate their cultural objects held at the territorial museum? Practical issues merited serious consideration, but the government negotiator's choice of approach to the subject excluded the relevance of governmental assaults on Indigenous culture and language that had been experienced by Inuvialuit and Gwich'in. Since these assaults arose mainly through residential schooling, they were understood as bureaucratically unrelated to the departmental responsibilities under discussion. As discussion progressed, residential schools were given as an example of the government's failures in relation to Indigenous language and culture. In response, the GNWT argued that residential schooling experiences would more appropriately be discussed in the context of education or perhaps not at all since education would focus on local rather than regional residential-based schooling.

Several difficulties in the negotiations process arise from future-oriented government policies. Indigenous peoples' negotiating positions are informed by their collective and individual experiences over the long term. Government policies may be unintentionally (though perhaps intentionally) based on not recognizing the relevance of experience. Because a government has apologized for an act such as creating residential schools, or was not responsible for residential schools at the time of an injustice, does not alter the ongoing experience of survivors. Generally, the individual perpetrators of that experience or their legal culpability is not relevant to how the experience affects Indigenous approaches to negotiations. What is relevant are the conditions which gave rise to the experiences, specifically non-Indigenous control over Indigenous lives, including language, culture, education, well-being, and custody of children. Non-Indigenous control over Indigenous lives has been proven destructive to the point of being fatal. It is this basic condition – non-Indigenous control over people and things Indigenous – that self-government negotiators seek to eliminate. Whether it was churches, governments, or independent administrators, all of these were non-Indigenous, were unaccountable to Indigenous communities, and wielded significant power over Indigenous peoples. A renewed relationship, for Indigenous peoples' negotiators, is based on conditions either where non-Indigenous governments are held accountable to and directed by Indigenous representatives chosen only by Indigenous people to represent Indigenous interests or where Indigenous people have direct control over the programs, services, and laws bearing directly on their lives.

Clearly, the GNWT negotiator had a view enviably free of an Indigenous experience, one where government could be trusted to do the right thing. Such a view is a luxury unavailable to Indigenous negotiators. Simply trusting government, which they are so often encouraged to do by government negotiators, would be an unethical act. The organizations and individuals that Indigenous peoples' negotiators represent do not give them a mandate to trust. Rather, negotiators act to secure protection from government intervention, to minimize risk of further suffering and its sources, and to ensure Indigenous peoples' control of their own lives to the fullest extent possible. That is a mandate reflecting the basic principles informing Indigenous visions of self-determination generally.

That Indigenous negotiators have as their fundamental directive a responsibility to limit Indigenous peoples' exposure to non-Indigenous governments' authority, brings into sharp relief the irreparable damage and lack of trust upon which an Indigenous-state relationship is based. Acknowledgment of that reality, and acceptance of responsibility in having created conditions where Indigenous peoples have suffered and continue to suffer injustice, are critical to renewing any Indigenous-state relationship. That acknowledgment can take many forms. In the context of negotiations, one method might be for government representatives to explicitly acknowledge the Indigenous reality that negotiating self-government is not only to achieve certainty and implement a right. It is also an aspect of separating from an unjust relationship toward creating conditions where Indigenous people achieve a more equitable position vis-à-vis the state. Such equity would have expression legally, politically, and financially. Indigenous peoples could thereby gain some control over the extent to which the state can be part of their lives and futures. This might be achieved by changes in government representatives' approaches to subject matters and development of mandates and by changes in fundamental philosophies underlying policies shaping negotiations.

The insistence of the GNWT that culture and language could be negotiated without reference to Indigenous experiences silenced the residential school experience. It also underscored a fundamental element of the dysfunction theodicy: that past events could not be undone, remedied, or significant to a different way forward. By focusing on practicalities – that there is no jurisdiction to be had, that museums are expensive to maintain – government arguments were presented as rational and objective. Residential school experiences were defined out of the discourse by insisting their relevance could be acknowledged in negotiations over education. The GNWT response indicated that the invocation of residential school experiences was either irrelevant or misplaced within a discussion about control over Inuvialuit and Gwich'in language and culture.

This chapter, following on two others that examine how specific government policy orientations mediate and shape negotiations, raises a variety of questions for consideration in drawing conclusions about the viability of self-government negotiations for a renewed relationship between the state and Indigenous people. The three chapters examine negotiations respectively affecting Dehcho financing, how a specific program authority is denied to Délînê, and the government's a-contextual approach to negotiating jurisdictional control of Inuvialuit and Gwich'in language and culture. We have seen how applications of policy within discussions can have effects at regional, community, and personal levels for the organizations and individuals involved. We have looked at ways philosophical orientations of government are expressed through overarching Aboriginal policy, policies shaping negotiations specifically, and the concrete expression of these through discussions at negotiating tables. Finally, the examples have drawn together similarities within narratives at three different negotiating tables attesting to experiences of social suffering as a primary rationale for negotiating new governance arrangements.

Through each case study there are consistencies. These include the marginalization of suffering narratives through silence and discourse norms. Discourse norms are created in part through policies placing injustice firmly in the past, separating its relevance from self-government negotiations. Historicizing injustice renders government negotiators faced with suffering narratives unable to respond in any meaningful way. They can do nothing. They are there to negotiate self-government. So much so that hard-line tactics in negotiations may be taken without regard for experiences, resulting in a surreal negotiations atmosphere: accusing the Dehcho of seeking to "get rich" from a revenue sharing agreement, an assertion mocked by the cold and modest room in which it is uttered; arguing that Inuvialuit wanting control of language and culture is senseless despite the reality of state-sponsored cultural genocide through residential schools. Yet government policy brands self-government as a route to "restoring dignity" to Aboriginal peoples (see Government of Canada, Department of Indian Affairs, 1995, 3), a dignity stolen by colonial policies of the state, which it now seeks to bestow as an act of its redemptive power over Indigenous suffering – the same suffering that it uses as a rationale to continue controlling Child and Family Services in Délînê and levels of resource revenues in the Dehcho.

The twists and turns of the dysfunction theodicy take negotiations into unexpected places. State control within the lives of Indigenous peoples remains vibrant. The next chapter considers whether some of the outcomes of Aboriginal policy such as land claims and self-government agreements fail to address both Indigenous suffering and its underlying causes.

## Thinning the Hide

### From Field Notes, Tanning Camp, July 2002

After the raw white hide has been shorn of hair and flesh, and the dark skin removed, it must be thinned. The main parts requiring thinning are the neck, the area which covers the kidneys, and the upper legs. Depending on the season in which the hide was taken, it may need more or less attention. I watched Marie methodically assess the gleaming wet flesh, feeling its thickness between her hands, periodically checking the flat board upon which it was being scraped, making sure there were no bits of grass or leaves beneath that could catch the knife and force it through the thin, delicate skin to create holes. Every few minutes she would stop, sharpen her knife, then return to her work. It looked so easy.

It wasn't. Gauging the thickness correctly, either by feel or by sight without having ever thinned a hide, was virtually impossible. The Dene way of teaching seemed to rely heavily on demonstration, with an expectation of close observation from a learner rather than questions or discussion. This cultural difference proved particularly frustrating as the knife I was using repeatedly went through the delicate hide. The technique required laying the hide flat against a curved board planed from a large spruce, which leaned into a solid surface such as a wall at a fifteen-degree angle away from the tanner, who knelt before it with the top of the curved board at about eye height. A ten-inch butcher's knife was then held against the hide at about a forty-five-degree angle, grasped with one hand by the handle and with the other at the curved tip, with thumbs on the blade facing the tanner, and slid in one slow cut down the length of the shorn hair side of the hide. Ideally, the soft grey shaving was a uniform thickness, revealing the perfectly smooth snow-white skin underneath.

That was what it should have looked like. With my first hide, after a couple of hours the knife was dull, the hide was slippery and not ungenerously marked with what would eventually become 128 holes, counted by all with some amusement at the last stage of tanning, when all the holes were sewn prior to the final smoking. The work was tiring and repetitive, and again and again the knife went straight through the hide to a wooden board underneath. At other times, opaque slivers of flesh were revealed where the cut made the hide too thin.

Jane appeared, to inspect the hide and offer advice. "There's holes, Steph," she said. She expertly flipped the hide around, revealing more holes and the over-thinned bits strategically shielded with folds of the hide from just such scrutiny. "See here," she pointed at the see-through thinness shining in the sunlight, "that part is too thin. When it stretches, it will make a hole for sure during scraping." She dropped the hide back in place and bent down to pick up the knife, feeling its dull edge.

"Here, I'll sharpen this knife," she offered, looking around for a sharpening stone.

"Do you want some tea?" I asked.

"Sure," she answered, focusing on making the right edge on the knife.

The mistakes being made required refocusing. Doing badly at this stage would ruin the hide, and it was already significantly damaged. It was frustrating and disheartening. Every stage was just as important as the next. All mistakes would come back to shape each step of the process now until it was finished. It would require extra care when stretching and twisting the hide and far more work sewing holes during the smoking stages. During smoking extra smoke would be required for the thicker parts, otherwise those parts would stay raw, since the thin parts and parts around the holes would tan faster. Extra scraping on the thicker parts would also be required to get the water out and to break the stronger fibres there. Scraping the thin parts would be difficult, because too much scraping might create holes. New holes developed during twisting and smoking would have to be sewn. Parts of the hide would be useless, because without a uniform thickness all over no sewer could use the whole thing. It would just look bad.

I walked back to Jane and handed her the cup of tea. She motioned to the sharpened knife lying on the spruce boughs with its blade toward the hide, beside the plastic-covered pillow used for kneeling on while scraping, and waited a moment. Neither of us spoke as I picked up the knife and began to scrape again. I had so many questions, wrapped up in even more frustration and embarrassment. She stood for a moment, then without a word nodded a thanks for the tea and went on to the next hide.

# Conclusion

We can't go back to the old ways. The new system is not
working. We are in limbo.
　　Our youth are killing themselves.

>　　　　　　– Inuit filmmaker Zacharias Kunuk, in conversation
> 　　　　　　with Shelagh Rogers of CBC Radio, October 20,
> 　　　　　　2006

The prospect of negotiating a new relationship through self-government
is seductive. Communities are provided with money to negotiate. They
are promised recognition and respect. They are promised power. Most
importantly, they are promised release from colonization. However, the
real effect of participating in these negotiations is that Indigenous peoples are forced to collude in their own disempowerment by agreeing to
institutional frameworks and implementation approaches predicated on
Indigenous assimilation. As shown in the previous chapters, Indigenous
peoples' participation in self-government negotiations is marginalized
through a dominant non-Indigenous style of discourse, power imbalances
favouring governments, and state policies that do not address ongoing
injustices that structure the foundation of the relationship between Indigenous peoples and the state.

　　This last point is the elephant in the room that no one wants to acknowledge. The approach of government negotiators assumes the state cannot
undo injustice, often simply because it exists on such a large scale that
to undo injustice would reorder Canadian society, presumably riddling it
with poverty, chaos, and starvation. Their approach, and the policies on
which their approach is based, express a profoundly unconscious colonial
attitude, one in which a dominant-subordinate relationship is the natural
order of things. Canada has power to "give" rights, authorities, recognition to *its* Aboriginal peoples. In the nineteenth century the colonial mas-
ters fought to bring Indigenous peoples to submission and assimilation.
In the twenty-first century Canada no longer relishes the challenge but
wearily bears the burden and seeks to maintain control without having
to attend to the details. This assumed dominant-subordinate relationship
manifests in the limits to which governments will tolerate indigeneity. If

self-government agreements are any indication, every area of authority and jurisdiction recognized is subject to a variety of limitations and conditions at the discretion of other governments.

In this situation, the colonial relationship is not undone but undergoes what Canada calls "modernizing." Modern colonialism retains assimilation as its subtext, the changing of Indigenous people as its object, and the maintenance of subordinate-dominant relations as its product. Self-government must fit within existing constitutional arrangements. Third-party interests (land owners, municipalities, non-Indigenous people) are protected. The original and ongoing dispossession of lands, resources, political autonomy, and cultural integrity is maintained through a restructuring of the relationship that ensures sources of money and authority required to operate self-governments are firmly within Canada's control.

This modernizing is purportedly obtained through a process of inclusion and negotiation, documented in the previous chapters, ostensibly satisfying legal requirements for reconciling Indigenous peoples' rights with state sovereignty. The purpose of negotiation is to legitimize state sovereignty – by securing surrenders and releases of Indigenous peoples' rights. But negotiations do not release Indigenous peoples from suffering or the ongoing injustices inducing suffering. The tragedy is that, although the state can be seen to be meeting its legal obligations, the end result is that the social suffering of Indigenous peoples will continue and probably worsen.

### Lifting People's Spirits

During June 2006, Janet and I were driving back to the moosehide tanning camp after having spent a night in town, and we were talking about her work on wellness programs for the tribal council. Our talk drifted to self-government and to the various economic development initiatives in the region, such as the Mackenzie Gas Project, which is resurrecting the gas pipeline proposal that had been shelved during the 1970s.

Janet emphasized that what was needed was beyond program money or rights or agreements with the government. What she sees in her work every day, what needs attention before all else, is what she called the "spirit of the people." To her, Indigenous people have become individually and collectively despirited, which shows itself as various forms of suffering. The first step toward self-determination, or making the most of economic development or any other opportunity, is creating conditions where people can feel good about being themselves as Indigenous people, as individuals, as families – a sentiment consistent with the basic premises of the Indigenous resurgence paradigm.

This is a question that has haunted advocates of economic development, and self-government for that matter, in Indigenous communities. Proponents of economic development, such as Chief Clarence Louie, say that you can lose your culture faster in poverty than in economic development. Another slogan is "you can't eat [moral] principles," a criticism of those who champion Indigenous peoples' refusing to negotiate on the colonizer's terms. Those sentiments make intuitive sense. What is often not examined in such conversations is looking at the terms on which economic "development" (often environmentally and socially degrading in its various forms) and self-government are offered.

A classic case is the situation of the Dehcho First Nations. The proposed Mackenzie Gas Pipeline will be an economic lifeline for the Inuvialuit in the Far North, and 40 percent of the pipeline route will cross Dehcho territory. The Dehcho will see little benefit from the pipeline itself, while allowing access rights and thereby possibly compromising their interests in control of lands and resources. Control over activity affecting their traditional territories and resources is the only real hope the Dehcho have of securing their own economic, social, political, cultural, and spiritual well-being now and in the future. Dehcho objections to the pipeline are aimed not at the concept of economic development itself but in large part at possible marginalization of Dehcho participation in decision making and control over traditional lands and resources. The current circumstances the Dehcho are in, without a land and resources agreement with Canada, and without assurances about their participation in decision making, mean that the Dehcho are being asked to accept development on dictated terms. Accepting that could adversely affect the Dehcho process negotiations. For the Dehcho, economic development on master-slave terms is not acceptable.

Sadly, much economic development is available only on terms that mimic colonial relationships, a model transferred, for example, to the relationships Indigenous peoples have with resource extraction companies. This is facilitated by resource royalty regimes and economic incentives devised by Canada without consultation or consent of Indigenous peoples. For example, the NWT royalty regime is the most favourable in Canada for extraction companies. The resource royalties that are paid on extracted resources go straight to Ottawa rather than to northern governments. That model of economic development contributes to the perpetuation of suffering and despiriting the people. Maintaining control of the money also ensures that Ottawa cannot disentangle itself from Indigenous affairs.

Even on terms that are recognized as modernized colonization, are there benefits to land claim and self-government agreements? During October

2006, while at negotiating session in Ottawa, I pursued this question during a conversation with two friends. Both are Indigenous and had been chosen by their communities to be chief negotiators on self-government negotiations. Our conversation turned to the realpolitik of negotiations and the impacts of agreements in communities. I asked why, when we all knew that self-government was just another colonial tool, they chose to negotiate. Joe, who is from the Yukon, had this to say:

> All you have to do is go to one of the communities in the Yukon that hasn't negotiated self-government, and you can see right there: *another lost generation*. You go to communities like my community now – fifteen years ago we were robbed blind by consultants, the store manager, you name it. Now we own all the buildings in our community that we rent to the government, we build those buildings, we own buildings in Whitehorse that make us money, we own an airline that's profitable. People in our community have jobs if they want them. They also live off the land if they want. People still hunt and trap. In the last year we paid out $30,000 in social assistance. A community further south on the road system, not a fly-in-only community like ours, with the same number of people but without self-government, paid out $300,000 in social assistance last year.
>
> It's not just about having a self-government agreement. It's the psychological effect of having control. If we want to do something we are in a better position to make changes happen – either in terms of credibility with other governments or having the capital in terms of money and people to do it. The self-government agreement itself is far from perfect in terms of what it contains and how it has been implemented. But people don't look at it as all of the answer, it's just one tool of many. (Indigenous self-government negotiators, interview, 2006)

Al agreed with what Joe said. He added that, for his community in the NWT, one of the main understandings about self-government was that it was only one tool of many that was being obtained so that the community would have choices now while building toward self-determination. According to him, everyone in his community is aware that government policies are mainly geared toward changing Dene people and that self-government is no different. Knowing that is an advantage, and besides, he said, Dene people cannot change into anything else than who they are already, so it is just a matter of waiting it out until the government understands. In the meantime, he said, we need to move forward, even if it is only a small step because that is all the government is prepared to do right now (Indigenous self-government negotiators, interview, 2006).

Many of us working for Indigenous peoples on land claim and self-government agreements regard these agreements as simply tools for modernizing and perpetuating colonialism. For a long time I could not figure out why the people I worked with – all Indigenous, generally without formal education beyond high school, but all of them scary smart and having that superstar quality common to all people who make things happen – would collude in their own colonization. What these negotiators and leaders all have in common is that they are people of vision, people who are and feel responsible not just for themselves but also for their communities in very personal ways. They are people who know what it is to be impoverished and hungry and who observe many people in their own communities struggling with poverty and hunger every day. Negotiators and leaders are people who act and take risks.

During the 1800s, one of the problems that plagued fur-trading companies was that Indigenous people quickly realized they could take their furs to different traders, inciting competition and postponing debt repayment (debt used strategically by fur traders to indenture Indigenous patronage) for longer periods than the traders anticipated. Sometimes the traders worked together to put a stop to the practice, but sometimes competing traders were helpless due to their own unwillingness to work together. This is the sort of resourcefulness that echoes in the actions of those choosing to negotiate self-government. There is a suite of tools on offer that can be taken, such as land claims and self-government. The challenge is finding how those can be used to achieve the goals of Indigenous peoples, in a situation where they are at an extreme disadvantage. In other words these agreements are desirable more for their instrumental value, how they might be used in unexpected ways and in conjunction with other resources, than for the value they hold as agreements. It is in a sense the political, social, and psychological capital such agreements have the potential to create that is part of their real value.

This is where I part ways with those who completely reject self-government and land claims as anything but colonial traps willingly entered by Indigenous collaborators. The situation is more complex than that. Although there may be some people who truly believe that self-government and land claims are the end of colonization, or establish a new relationship, they are in the minority, a minority that is shrinking. The formation in the past few years of the Land Claim Agreement Coalition indicates that Indigenous leaders know that the "modern" treaties are not working as well as they should. Agreements are not working well in part because Canada embarked on them without a clear policy guiding implementation, including no attention at all to preparing land claim members for taking on the technical and professional roles implementation required. As noted by Canada's own auditor general, these agreements are being implemented by Canada in a way that does not honour their spirit and intent. Indeed, if ongoing disputes are evidence (for example, court cases launched by the Gwich'in, James Bay Cree, and Nunavut), then land claims are being implemented by Canada in a way that does not honour legal obligations either.

Leaders who once thought that land claims or self-government would be the end of colonization have realized in the course of implementation that this is not the case. Former land claim negotiator, Dene Nation president, and NWT premier Stephen Kakfwi indicated a sentiment true for all of the communities and regions in which I have worked when he said at the Inuvialuit and Gwich'in Self-Government Agreement-in-Principle signing during 2003 that, the more Indigenous people do and achieve, the more needs to be done. It is curious that the only comprehensive evaluation of the impact of land claims or self-government conducted in this country has been by the auditor general, whose reports look at policy structures, institutional performance, and financial controls. That scrutiny only began more than twenty years after the first land claim agreement was signed. But perhaps it is not so curious. If these agreements were evaluated with a view to broader social impacts and the broader structures of bureaucratic implementation, support, and evaluation, we would see that generally the agreements have spawned whole new sections of the federal bureaucracy to monitor Indigenous exercise of powers formerly exercised by federal bureaucrats. It would show that most agreements have had a variety of false starts and serious difficulties in taking flight; it would also show that large numbers of non-Indigenous people benefit economically from land claim agreements, mainly through employment opportunities in the organizations themselves or the many spin-off business investments.

Evaluating these agreements at the community level is a completely different task altogether. Anyone working in the Indigenous rights industry in the North is familiar with the stories about how support in favour of land claims was gained. Some people believed that once the claim was signed there would be a new truck in every driveway or that, indeed, everyone would have houses where they could put driveways. That did not happen. The implementation of some agreements, signed with regions or communities where little understanding or capacity to administer the claims existed after the exodus of lawyers and consultants hired to negotiate them, floundered for years. People lived much as they had before the claim. When I was working in Inuvik in the late 1990s, *Globe and Mail* reporter Stephanie Nolen visited for a weekend, returning to Toronto to write a series of articles about the town. In it, she mused about the irony of land claim organizations heralding a new age of authority and independence of the Inuvialuit and Gwich'in – organizations whose employees were made up almost entirely of white twenty-somethings from the South, fresh from graduate school, earning higher wages than they would in government, making critical decisions about implementing the agreements. There was constant tension between the white land claim technocrats and the beneficiaries they served, beneficiaries who could not get hired by their own land claim organizations.

Experiences and events change perspective, and since the 1990s land claim organizations in the NWT have changed considerably. In this sense we can see how Joe's comments about the situation of Yukon First Nations are true. In some respects land claims, and self-government agreements, have been forces of positive change. Some people have been given hope and opportunity where none existed before. Land claim organizations have matured and now employ mostly beneficiaries in technical and professional positions. The beneficiary workforce seems to be a combination of Indigenous youth motivated to obtain education because they know there are jobs in the land claim organizations that are accessible and an influx of beneficiaries leaving the employment of government or moving back home from larger centres to work for the land claim organizations later in their careers. In towns like Inuvik, the next generation need not expect to be lost but can instead aspire to work in a variety of business, professional, and technical roles, primarily with and in the service of their own people. The next generations have hope not only of meeting their basic needs but also of living well and, most importantly, of having choices about how they wish to live without having to leave their communities and their traditional territories.

Critics may see this as the creation of a Native elite: a professional class that lives well while the majority of the people continue to live in poverty and suffering. It is a microcosm of globalization, where a few live well, most live in poverty, and the gap between the rich and the poor grows greater. At the same time, the new elite is the group of people making decisions that will affect the ability of the vast majority of people to live Indigenous lifestyles – choices between pipelines and traplines. A widely held perception is that those decision makers do not live on or even necessarily value living on the land. Critics may say that economic opportunity often occurs at the expense of being able to live on the land and according to Indigenous ways of life. In the North, particularly in smaller communities where people continue to live primarily off the land, some may not stand to benefit from embracing the educational opportunities and values offered by mainstream society and capitalism. Indeed, some individual's subsistence pursuits have been limited by encroaching requirements of the economic development facilitated by land claims.

The decisions being made, and the ways of life and points of view of the people making the decisions, are not easily characterized. Many of the new elite may have had as little opportunity to live on the land as subsistence harvesters have opportunity to live in cities. Some of the elite do have significant knowledge and appreciation of subsistence lifestyles. One example of claim organizations working to ensure people do have a choice to continue living on the land, or to take up that lifestyle, has been developed by the Tłı̨chǫ government. The Tłı̨chǫ have attempted to support traditional subsistence-based population with a novel approach to impact and benefit agreements. Recognizing that there are some Tłı̨chǫ who want to live on the land as Tłı̨chǫ, the Tłı̨chǫ negotiated an impact and benefit agreement with the diamond-mining company De Beersduring March 2006 that devotes significant resources to supporting Tłı̨chǫ continuing to live off the land. This is a departure from usual impact and benefit agreements emphasizing training and employment integrating Indigenous people into the wage economy. In this way the Tłı̨chǫ have taken the initiative to prevent the marginalization of "traditional people," those who live primarily on the land. The agreement marked a major move toward supporting in financial terms one of the main reasons the Tłı̨chǫ entered into their land claim agreement: to enable them to make decisions over their own lives, in ways that promote Tłı̨chǫ culture and language.

It is evident that promoting and supporting Indigenous culture is a priority for regional land claim organizations in the NWT, indicated by the resources from claims being dedicated to cultural promotion and activities. Wealth generated by land claims, and the authority of claim organizations within and vis-à-vis resource management structures, have ensured that Indigenous culture and values are taken into account, to some extent at least, in everything from land use planning to negotiating impact and benefit agreements. Cultural institutes have been established, as have funding sources for cultural education and activities.

Land claims and self-government have not resulted in situations where the interests of people living off the land take primacy over economic development. Part of the intent of land claims and self-government is to promote economic development to alleviate poverty and its attendant suffering. Often the economic opportunities afforded by the recovery of single-digit percentages of original land bases and resources by Indigenous peoples through land claims lock leaders into situations where every and any opportunity for development is an opportunity that literally cannot afford to be missed. This fact circles this discussion back to the example of the Dehcho First Nations, whose determination to ensure participation in megaprojects such as the Mackenzie Gas Pipeline directly impacts the immediate economic opportunities of the Inuvialuit. Or, to look at it in a different way, the economic aspirations of Inuvialuit stand to threaten the Indigenous way of life and the chances for greater Dehcho control over its own traditional territories.

This is the irreconcilable difference between economic development dependent almost entirely on non-renewable resources, structured by the demands and imperatives of a dominant capitalist society, severely restricted by the symbolic rather than substantive recovery of ownership of lands and resources, and political authority, through land claims and self-government agreements. Economic development choices for Indigenous peoples are often not choices at all. Given the rampant social suffering in most communities, economic development opportunities are more akin to lifelines that cannot be refused.

Having recovered through land claims and self-government small parcels of developable lands and resources, minimal access to resource revenues, and limited authorities to make decisions, leaders are faced with having to live up to often unrealistic expectations of what land claims and self-government powers can actually accomplish. These leaders see high levels of unemployment, witness the anomie wrought by colonization, and know that high school graduates may have to leave the community to make better lives for themselves economically. In the face of that, it is understandable how it would be difficult for a leader to say, "no, we do not want that economic development opportunity that could create jobs because it will mean cutlines through Joe's trapline and will mean a few people will be in a job environment where they will have to conform to white ways of doing things." Sometimes the manner of resource exploitation is so repugnant, or the economic benefits such a pittance, that it is possible to say no. Often, saying no is not easy.

What the Tłîchô example indicates is that Indigenous governments are finding ways to move beyond the narrow range of opportunity provided by the limited sources of wealth that land claims provide. Ultimately, such strategies do not alter a basic relationship between Canada and Indigenous peoples where Canada remains in control of and retains ownership of most of Indigenous lands and resources and the wealth those lands and resources generate. Meanwhile, Indigenous peoples are forced to exploit their resources and lands according to the interests of multi-national resource developers, in an attempt to provide their people with basic needs, opportunities for a comfortable life, and support for those who still wish to live a land-based lifestyle within ever-encroaching economic and social interests of the dominant capitalist society.

That is the fundamental problem with land claim and self-government agreements. They embed colonialism as the structure regulating Indigenous-state relations. They do not undo ongoing injustices. They do not alter the circumstances of Indigenous peoples in terms of sources and resources of power and self-determination at a level that allows for real change – if the persistent social suffering in Indigenous communities with and without land claims and self-government is any indication. So the question then is what is the way out? What choices do governments and Indigenous peoples have to provide for a better future for Indigenous peoples? What of critics who say that Indigenous peoples are like all peoples – they aspire to greater wealth and well-being and seek to become equal and contributing members of the Canadian economy and society. If not land claims and self-government, then what? If Indigenous peoples cannot go back to the old ways because the world has changed too much, and the new system is not working, if people are continuing to experience the anomie and social suffering associated with living in limbo, where do we go from here?

Most scholars writing on the deficiencies of land claim and self-government policy are often criticized for not offering alternative "workable" solutions, an issue Paul Nadasdy (2003) addresses in *Hunters and Bureaucrats: Power, Knowledge, and Aboriginal-State Relations in the Southwest Yukon*, assessing land claim co-management structures in the Yukon. Many people forget that land claims and self-government were unheard of forty years ago. Land claims and self-government have brought some benefits to some people. They continue to structure and further embed the colonial relationship and the ongoing social suffering we can reasonably expect to result. Surely, policy choices cannot be limited to these ideas. A novel approach needs to be taken to finding alternatives. Perhaps it is time that white policy makers and settlers stop trying to come up with the answers based solely on state interests. What will lead us to viable policy alternatives is if the state recognizes ongoing injustice exists and is perpetuated by existing institutional and societal structures; if it stops asserting social suffering as unrelated to ongoing injustice; and if it recognizes the wisdom and knowledge of Indigenous peoples as wisdom and knowledge, and the aspirations of Indigenous peoples to live as Indigenous peoples, a viable alternative to living as colonized subjects. The Indigenous resurgence paradigm advanced by Indigenous scholars points to the necessity of changing existing circumstances while simultaneously strengthening Indigenous being. It would require that colonial mindsets, policies, actions, and attitudes structuring Indigenous-state relations be undone. It would require Indigenous peoples acting and leading by articulating alternatives to colonial-based policies, alternatives rooted in non-colonized Indigenous cultures and realities. At that point, policy makers should then consider the direction held in the words of former Dehcho grand chief Michael Nadli and move beyond the fear that holds us to places of brokenness and suffering, simply because they are familiar. At that point Indigenous and non-Indigenous peoples will be able to develop viable policy alternatives to colonization.

### Finding Dahshaa

I set out for the drive to Dettah from Yellowknife on a cold October morning. Through friends I had located an elder in Dettah to help with the final smoking of my third hide. Today was the first bright, sunshiney day, the best type of day to smoke a hide, so I had phoned Mary, who said to come to her house by mid-morning.

The moosehide had waited in my freezer for two years. I had agreed to tan it for a friend. The winter he sent it, I was pregnant and postponed tanning it until that summer. Then the demands of new motherhood meant postponing tanning for another year. The following summer I travelled to Inuvik with the hide, hoping to tan it over the course of a couple of weeks. It was a thick hide, and it was with some trepidation that I laid it on the grass before the elder I was working with, who walked around it, stopping at different places to feel its thickness. Kneeling beside the hide as she examined it, she looked up at me, concerned, and said "Don't walk away from this one, run."

Ann, the elder who had come from Fort Good Hope to Inuvik to help us with our hides that summer, obviously had finished assessing my two-year-old hide. She went on to say it was the biggest, thickest hide she had ever seen. She said it would take a long time to tan and be really hard work. She advised me not to tan it. She asked me why I would take a hide that thick and say I would tan it. The answer to both of us was obvious: I wasn't experienced enough to know the difference. I had my pride on the line – I had kept it for two years, there was no way I was giving up now.

"You're sure going to learn a lot," she said.

She was right. That hide took over my life, and I learned all sorts of things about tanning and commitments and pride. After spending ten days in Inuvik tanning it in the company of Janet and a group of other women, I spent another two weeks that summer scraping it, smoking it, wringing it out, and stretching it in my backyard in Yellowknife. That was after the fire department came to inspect the fire pit five times before issuing a burning permit, never having received a request for a permit to smoke a moosehide.

When I arrived at Dettah, Mary was in her smokehouse scraping a caribou hide. I introduced myself and gave her tobacco. She put away her hide and began setting up the moosehide for smoking. She looked through the *dahshaa* I had brought. Two large tubs of it, gathered over several days.

"It's too wet, this isn't the right kind," she said as she picked through what I thought was perfectly good *dahshaa*, rejecting most of it. My heart sank. I needed to finish this hide. "I don't think I have any around here," Mary sighed, looking through some boxes.

Undaunted, she mixed my wood with hot coals from the woodstove in a tin bucket, adjusted the hanging hide over it, and began telling me stories about final smokings of hides. I didn't feel so bad about my present misadventure as she told me about people whose hides had caught on fire, one that had been sewn so tightly ("just like yours!" she said) that it had *exploded!* After the exploding hide story, I nervously insisted we cut the stitches near the top to avoid the same fate. Mary alternated between tending the hide and picking over my wood, the reject pile mounting evidence that I had not found any *dahshaa*.

We continued talking. Several people came by to see her and say hello as we sat in the smokehouse with the hide. We shared some tea I had made. We talked about the characteristics of *dahshaa*, about tanning, and about how her mother had tanned hides all the time. After an hour or so she lifted the hide, checking the colour. It was still light yellow. The wood was hardly smoking.

"It's not working ... Help me take this down while I try to fix this fire," she instructed.

We draped the hide over a chair, and she began mixing more coals with the wood. She looked through the tubs once again and this time found nothing to put in the fire.

"Maybe I have some," she said.

Mary moved to a dark corner of the smokehouse, lifted some boxes off a chair, and reached underneath it. She brought out two small logs of brittle-dry rotten wood. They were beautiful. They didn't look anything like the wood in the two tubs I had brought. After working on three hides (my other final smokings had been done by elders) and spending countless days gathering wood, I still hadn't managed to find *dahshaa*. She held out the wood for me to look at.

"This is the wood you need," she said, "you go look for it in June." She added several handfuls to the fire and repositioned the hide over it.

Twenty minutes later the hide was finished, the *dahshaa* turning it a beautiful, rich brown.

We talked afterward, looking at her caribou hides and the worn bone scrapers her mother had passed on to her, yellowed with age and smooth with use. She showed me different kinds of wood and where to find it. I promised her I would look for *dahshaa* next summer and bring her some of what I found. I gave her a tub of the wood I had brought. She accepted it, saying it would be useful for regular smoking of hides.

On the drive back to Yellowknife with the hide, I reflected on the day, marvelling at how Mary had been so welcoming, at the knowledge she had shared. And how she had used her own *dahshaa*, which I knew was difficult for her, as an older lady, to go out and find. I had suspected she was holding out on me at first – none of the expert tanners was ever without everything she needed, including *dahshaa*, and they always planned ahead.

Instead of sending me home with instructions to find the correct wood, Mary took a few minutes and examined the hide, demonstrated how to hang it up on a pole, showed how to get the fire going, advised on the correct techniques, and patiently took the time to show exactly what would happen to a hide that was being smoked with regular rotten wood rather than *dahshaa*. Then she demonstrated how quickly and effectively the smoking was accomplished with the *dahshaa*. Her manner was marked by a graceful kindness and respect suffused with Dene values.

It was a way of being that tanning seems to bring out in people.

I learned a great deal from Mary that day. Her approach laid bare the way that tanning interaction and progress are based on values and imperatives starkly opposed to those structuring self-government negotiations. Tanning is a space of action and co-operation, its hallmark transparency. Nothing can transform a moosehide from a heavy, bloody mass of hair and flesh to a light, fluffy expanse of cloth prized for its utility and beauty, except concentrating and following correctly the tanning method's sequence. There is no double talk, no obfuscation or excuse, no looking to those who would sew the hide after the fact to make useful a thing disfigured with holes of incompetence, refusal, or compromise. Expert tanners can read missteps and competence on the hide in the same way that negotiators can analyze self-government agreements for the bottom lines and the trade-offs they contain.

What is striking about moosehide tanning is its embodiment of values and dynamics that provide a glimpse into what self-determination might be about culturally, psychologically, spiritually. This experience has convinced me of the vital importance of the resurgence paradigm as a way of understanding the importance of Indigenous peoples being able to live as Indigenous peoples – connected to each other and their lands and resources through Indigenous ways of being, values, and worldviews.

The success of moosehide tanning is rooted in the commitment of a community to support individuals to engage in a material production process that embodies what it is to live according to Dene values and worldview. The beauty of hand-tanning moosehide is that, although there are variations in method between regions, the keepers of the knowledge and the practitioners are Dene women elders, and the rules and norms of tanning are variations of the same basic principles. Tanning practices have been handed down to nieces, daughters, and granddaughters by aunts, mothers, and grandmothers. Some of the implements may have changed, and hides can now be tanned indoors, with greater convenience and comfort due to technology and innovation such as indoor plumbing and radios. However, when women need a hide, men must go hunting. Families must accommodate the attention hides demand, and men and women work in partnership, with men building structures and making tanning tools and women doing the work of tanning itself. When tanning together in groups, they make the work lighter by constant conversation and the camp alive with purposeful activity, and visitors come to admire and encourage their work.

Tanning, quite simply, lifts people's spirits. Its basis in a specifically Dene knowledge, drawing on knowledge of the land, the moose, its habitat, and the various natural elements necessary in the production process (such as the spruce boughs or *ah'*, the moose brains, the rotten wood), means that tanning represents a profound connection between Dene lands, people, and knowledge. People who have bush skills become leaders, the same people who may be unable to hold a job in town for more than a few days at a time. People who know their language and stories about their mothers and grandmothers tanning embody knowledge valuable to the process, with lessons and information benefiting the collective knowledge. Those who come to watch and admire convey a level of pride and support that is pure and unreserved. They recognize the difficulty of the work, the commitment it takes, and the profound Deneness of the enterprise. The group of tanners, the hunters, the people in the community, all rely on each other, need each other, and value each other's contributions.

The elders who first taught me to tan said that it usually takes at least five hides before a person becomes truly competent at tanning. Every hide is different, and the method for each hide must be adapted to its specific needs and peculiarities. The process of learning is unending, it seems, since every hide is different, and the places on the land that provide materials differ between regions and demand different types of knowledge. This variety of knowledge retention requires integration with one's way of being on the land and in the world.

If those two tubs of no-good wood I took to Dettah that morning are any indication, the most elusive aspect of this body of knowledge is that required to be able to find *dahshaa*. It requires knowledge of the land, a sharp eye, and the ability to filter away distractions while spending hours walking through the bush in the heat of summer while staying attuned to the signs that indicate *dahshaa* might be found. The process of finding *dahshaa* is time consuming and demands patience, vigilance, and an absolute focus on the task at hand. It is *dahshaa* that imparts the distinctive, rich orange-brown colour to the moosehide, that makes it water resistant, that sets apart the finished hide as uniquely Dene. Finding *dahshaa* marks the moment at which patience, knowledge of the land, and dogged determination reach a confluence confirming a tanner finally has all of the material, physical, and mental tools required to complete the tanning process. And to give encouragement, assistance, and hope to those of us who are not yet able to recognize what it is that we are seeking, who have not yet found *dahshaa*.

# Notes

## Introduction

1 With respect to terminology, throughout I use the word "Indigenous" to refer to the First Peoples; although I am aware of the contested nature of the term (see, for example, Barnard 2006; Kenrick and Lewis 2004; and Kuper 2003a, 2003b), it is inclusive of the Dene, Métis, and Inuvialuit peoples and is an internationally recognized designation widely accepted by Indigenous peoples themselves. The term "Aboriginal" is used by the state in Canada and has been discredited by Alfred (2005) as comparable to having an orientalizing effect (Said 1976), as it is a designation from the perspective of the settler state. Wherever possible, I refer to specific peoples by their self-designations (e.g., Délînê Got'înê, Inuvialuit, Gwich'in, Dene).

2 The Indian Act, RSC 1985, c. 1-5; hereafter the Indian Act.

3 Governor General Adrienne Clarkson, Speech from the Throne, February 2004, Thirty-Seventh Parliament, www.pco-bcp.gc.ca/.

4 The Inherent Right Policy (Government of Canada, Department of Indian Affairs, 1995) describes authorities available for negotiation.

5 Detailed information on the coalition and copies of reports and presentations associated with its conferences can be accessed at http://www.consilium.ca/alcc2006/main.html.

## Chapter 1: Context and Concepts

1 *Re: Paulette and Registrar of Land Titles* (No. 2) (1973), 42 D.L.R. (3d) 8 at 33, 9 C.N.L.C. 307 (N.W.T. S.C.); hereafter the *Paulette* case.

2 *Calder v. British Columbia (Attorney General)*, [1973] S.C.R. 313, [1973] 4 W.W.R. 1; hereafter the *Calder* case.

3 As found at http://www.parl.gc.ca/.

4 This is detailed later in Chapter 4, for example in examining negotiations for jurisdiction over Child and Family Services in the Délînê self-government negotiations.

5 Works by writers such as Frantz Fanon (1967) and Albert Memmi (1990) establish the scope and nature of colonial suffering. More recent scholarship – including that of Duran and Duran (1995), Wayne Warry (1998), Linda Tuhiwai-Smith (1999), Taiaiake Alfred (2005), Glen Coulthard (2007), and the various contributors in Kirmayer and Valaskakis (2008) – documents the ongoing nature of Indigenous peoples' experiences of contemporary colonization. See also MacMillan et al. (1996) for specific statistical information.

6 Part 2, "First Nations," paragraph 2, www.ainc-inac.gc.ca/pr/pub/sg/plcy_e.html.

7 There are excellent discussions elsewhere of debates around characteristics, uses, and abuses of traditional knowledge; see, for example, Morrow and Hensel (1992), Nadasdy (2003), and various contributors in Scott (2001). In my own work with Dene communities having high levels of cultural retention (as measured by indicators such as frequency of cultural practices, language retention, etc.), specifically Dene knowledge is called simply "our knowledge" or "Dene knowledge" during internal community discussions,

with labels such as "traditional knowledge" used mainly when an external or non-Dene audience is present.

## Chapter 2: Tanning Moosehide

1  Throughout the moosehide tanning descriptions, pseudonyms have been used.
2  The tanning process is lengthy and complex, requiring a variety of techniques, equipment, and knowledges that vary between individuals, peoples, and hides. This book does not provide a comprehensive ethnographic description of tanning, nor is it intended to impart specific Indigenous knowledge about tanning.

## Chapter 3: Dehcho Resource Revenue Sharing

1  For full details, see the settlement backgrounder, July 12, 2007, www.ainc-inac.gc.ca/nr/prs/m-a2005/02689bk_e.html.
2  For a detailed discussion of the relationship between devolution, self-government, and resource royalties, see Irlbacher-Fox and Mills (2007).
3  For example, court cases in BC such as *Delgamuukw v. British Columbia*, [1997] 3 S.C.R. 1010; hereafter *Delgamuukw*; and *Haida Nation v. British Columbia (Minister of Forests)*, 2004 S.C.C. 73, [2004] 3 S.C.R. 511.
4  See, for example, the judgment in *Delgamuukw*.
5  September 1998, c. 14, www.oag-bvg.gc.ca/domino/reports.nsf/html/.
6  See, for example, Morrow and Hensel (1992), Nadasdy (2003), and Scott (2001).
7  See Bourdieu (1977, 1991) and Foucault (1994), who develop concepts around the situatedness of discourse; see also, generally, MacDonnell (1986) and Van Dijk (1985).
8  Young credits Tully (1995, 26) with formulating aspects of this argument.
9  See www.dehchofirstnations.com.
10  During their June 2008 assembly, the DFN delegates voted to explore "land selection" as a negotiating option, which is a central component of the comprehensive land claim process and is at odds with the land stewardship model in the Dehcho proposal.
11  For a comparative overview of northern, Canadian, and international royalty regimes, see Taylor and Raynolds (2006).
12  For example, see the annual report of the Implementation Committee, Gwich'in Tribal Council, www.ainc-inac.gc.ca/pr/agr/gwich/anrh_e.pdf. The Gwich'in have received varying amounts each year, ranging from just over $10,000 in 1992 to just over $500,000 in 2001.
13  According to the Department of Indian Affairs, the registered Indian population among the Dehcho First Nations band councils totals 4,231, as found May 24, 2008, at http://www.pse2-esd2.ainc-inac.gc.ca/FNProfiles/; this number does not take into account the Dehcho Métis who are members of the Métis Locals, estimated at approximately 300.
14  See "Dehcho – Population" in Government of the Northwest Territories, Bureau of Statistics (2007).
15  Based on field notes of conversation with DFN official, November 2001.
16  This is an approximate number – there are discrepancies between "Aboriginal" populations and registered members of NWT bands and land claim beneficiaries, who may or may not be resident in the NWT and who may or may not be eligible for assistance and services from their governments.
17  See Government of the Northwest Territories, Bureau of Statistics (2007).
18  See ibid.
19  Statistics Canada, "Latest Release from the Labour Force Survey," August 8, 2008, www.statcan.ca/english/Subjects/Labour/LFS/lfs-en.htm.
20  See Government of the Northwest Territories, Bureau of Statistics (2006).

## Chapter 4: Délîne Child and Family Services

1  The handgame is a Dene competition between men (though sometimes women participate). Hand signalling is used to challenge opponents to guess the location of objects hidden under covers in front of opposing players. Drummers accompany the action, intensifying excitement and speed. Detailed by Helm and Lurie (1961), it is frequently played in the Sahtu, Tłîchô, Akaitcho, and Dehcho areas.

2  A Métis land claim organization has not been established in Délînê.

3  Ayah is written about by respected Sahtu Dene oral tradition holder and elder George Blondin in *When the World Was New: Stories of the Sahtu Dene* (1990, 239–41); see also www.deline.ca.

4  The prophecy is extensive and touches on many matters important to Délînê Got'înê. I am not knowledgeable of its entirety, only of those elements discussed during community self-government meetings and negotiations. Although I have not made intense study of Dene medicine power or dreaming, my understanding is that prophetic, medicine, and dream knowledge is understood not as subconscious fantasy, as it is in Western culture, but as the result of rigorous mental and spiritual training and questing of gifted individuals, who are regarded as healers, knowledge keepers, and seekers. See, for example, Blondin (1990, 1999), Brody (1981), and Moss (2005).

5  The experience of the community and individual members is well documented in the book *If Only We Had Known: The History of Port Radium as Told by the Sahtuot'ine* (DFN 2005).

6  See DFN (2005, 154-55) for copies of memoranda stating that "precautions are necessary even in the handling of substances of low radioactivity."

7  *If Only We Had Known* (DFN 2005) details the mining and transport operations and experiences of Dene who worked for the mine and its contractors.

8  See the final report of the Canada-Délînê Uranium Table (2002).

9  For a clinical analysis of residential school syndrome and its etiology, see Brasfield (2001).

10  Although information may have been provided previously to the Délînê team, due to a change in staff for the Délînê negotiators, most information provided by the government at a previous date was no longer available.

11  The Canadian Community Health Survey by Statistics Canada on off-reserve Aboriginal Peoples Health found alarming disparities between health conditions of the surveyed population and non-Aboriginal Canadians, including higher incidences of depression, diabetes, as well as "smoking, obesity, and heavy drinking." See www.statcan.ca/Daily/English/020827/d020827a.htm.

12  Also see, for example, Duran and Duran (1995) for a discussion of how often mental disorders diagnosed in Indigenous peoples, when understood in the context of collective and individual traumas suffered by virtue of being Indigenous, may be viewed as logical coping mechanisms.

13  From www.ainc-inac.gc.ca/gs/chg_e.html#reconciliation.

14  As stated by Indian Affairs Minister Jim Prentice November 2, 2006, Address to House of Commons Standing Committee on Aboriginal Affairs and Northern Development on the Main Estimates of the Department of Indian Affairs and Northern Development, www.ainc-inac.gc.ca/nr/spch/2006/medp_e.html.

15  See the findings of the All-Party Canadian Parliamentary Standing Committee on Indian and Northern Affairs.

16  During 2007 legislation establishing an arm's-length specific claims agency was promised. The comprehensive claims policy and process, found by the Auditor General of Canada (1998) to be weighted against Indigenous participants, remains unchanged.

17  According to Patterson (2006, 1), "in November 2005 the Government of Canada pledged $5.085 billion over five years to improve the socio-economic conditions of Aboriginal people. The overall plan was to bring the standard of living for Aboriginal peoples up to that of other Canadians by 2016."

18  See Waldron (1992, 19); for an analysis of his heavy reliance on temporal characterizations of Indigenous peoples, see Irlbacher-Fox (2004).

19  For example, residential school reparations resulted from recognition by the Supreme Court that Indigenous peoples were entitled to reparations from the state and churches, similarly, most government policies recognize that specific Aboriginal rights have resulted from Supreme Court decisions; most recently, out-of-court settlements on issues of Crown consultation on infringements of Aboriginal rights have resulted directly from a growing body of case law finding in favour of Indigenous peoples.

20  See www.ainc-inac.gc.ca/ps/nap/consit/cdut/cdut-ch4_e.html#oplin.

**Chapter 5: Inuvialuit and Gwich'in Culture and Language**

1  Population statistics provided by Bob Simpson, director of Intergovernmental Relations at the Inuvialuit Regional Corporation, August 21, 2008.

2  The population numbers here are current to 2007, as found at www.gwichin.nt.ca/EnrollmentBoard.

3  The data contained in this report on languages are current to 2004.

4  See www.irc.inuvialuit.com.

5  See the GNWT Land Claim Negotiations Policy, March 1998, www.gov.nt.ca/publications/policies/executive/Aboriginal_Land_Claims_(11.51).pdf.

6  A series of court cases occurred during the late 1990s, when former residential school students began to disclose sexual abuse by male supervisors at the Grollier Hall residential school in Inuvik, resulting in several criminal convictions of former supervisors.

7  For details of the settlement agreement, see www.irsr-rqpi.gc.ca/english/irssa.html, the Government of Canada website detailing the settlement and implementation of negotiated measures.

8  From www.north.cbc.ca.

# References

**Interviews and Negotiation Sessions**
*During the course of research, the author conducted seventy-eight interviews and attended thirty negotiating sessions, community meetings, and NWT Aboriginal Summit meetings. Of these, the following have extracts quoted in the text.*

Dehcho negotiation session. 2001. November 12-16, Liidli Kue (Fort Simpson), NT.
Dehcho negotiation session. 2002. January 21-22, Liidli Kue (Fort Simpson), NT.
Délînê negotiation session. 2003. April 22-23, Yellowknife, NT.
Federal negotiator. 2002a. Interview by author. March 31, Yellowknife, NT.
Federal negotiator. 2002b. Interview by author. April 18, Yellowknife, NT.
Federal negotiator. 2002c. Interview by author. September 19, Yellowknife, NT.
Federal negotiator. 2002d. Interview by author. October 12, Ottawa ON.
Gwich'in beneficiary. 2002. Interview by author. October 11, Inuvik, NT.
Indigenous self-government negotiators (two). 2006. Interview by author. October 24, Ottawa, ON.
Inuvialuit and Gwich'in negotiation session. 1999. December 14-16, Calgary, AB.
Inuvialuit elder. 2002. Interview by author. July 12, Inuvik, NT.
Raymond Taniton (President of Délînê Land Corporation). 2005. Interview by author. March 19, Deline, NT.
Territorial negotiator. 2002a. Interview by author. March 3, Yellowknife, NT.
Territorial negotiator. 2002b. Interview by author. April 17, Yellowknife, NT.
Vince Teddy (Inuvialuit negotiator). 2002. Interview by author. April 22 and September 12, Yellowknife, NT.

**Other Sources**
Aarviunaa. 2004. "Vision + Leadership = Success: Salute to the Inuvialuit on the 20th Anniversary of the Inuvialuit Final Agreement." *Native Journal*, October: 10.
Abel, Kerry. 1993. *Drum Songs: Glimpses of Dene History*. Montreal: McGill-Queen's University Press.
Adams, Howard. 1999. *Tortured People: The Politics of Colonization*. Rev. ed. Penticton: Theytus Books.
Adelson, Naomi. 2001. "Reimagining Aboriginality: An Indigenous Peoples' Response to Social Suffering." In *Remaking a World: Violence, Social Suffering, and Recovery*, ed. Veena Das et al., 76-101. Berkeley: University of California Press.
Alexie Jr., Robert. 2002. *Porcupines and China Dolls*. Toronto: Stoddart.
Alfred, Taiaiake. 1999. *Peace, Power, Righteousness: An Indigenous Manifesto*. Toronto: Oxford University Press.
–. 2005. *Wasáse: Indigenous Pathways of Action and Freedom*. Toronto: Broadview Press.
Asch, Michael. 1985. *Home and Native Land: Aboriginal Rights and the Canadian Constitution*. Toronto: Methuen.

–, ed. 1997. *Aboriginal and Treaty Rights in Canada: Essays on Law, Equality, and Respect for Difference.* Vancouver: UBC Press.

Barnard, Alan. 2006. "Kalahari Revisionism, Vienna, and the 'Indigenous Peoples' Debate." *Social Anthropology* 14, 1: 1-16.

Belanger, Yale. 2008. *Aboriginal Self-Government in Canada: Current Trends and Issues.* Saskatoon: Purich.

Berger, Thomas. 1977. *Northern Frontier, Northern Homeland: Report of the Mackenzie Valley Pipeline Inquiry.* 2 vols. Ottawa: Supply and Services Canada.

Berkes, F. 1999. *Sacred Ecology: Traditional Ecological Knowledge and Resource Management.* Philadelphia: Taylor and Francis.

Berkes, F., and T. Henley. 1997. "Co-Management and Traditional Knowledge: Threat or Opportunity?" *Policy Options* 18, 2: 29-31.

Blondin, George. 1990. *When the World Was New: Stories of the Sahtu Dene.* Yellowknife: Outcrop.

–. 1999. *Yamoria: The Lawmaker.* Calgary: NeWest Press.

Borrows, John. 2002. *Recovering Canada: The Resurgence of Indigenous Law.* Toronto: University of Toronto Press.

Bourdieu, Pierre. 1977. *Outline of a Theory of Practice.* Cambridge: Cambridge University Press.

–. 1991. *Language and Symbolic Power.* Ed. John B. Thompson. Cambridge: Polity.

Bourdieu, Pierre, Alain Accardo, Gabrielle Balazs, Stephane Beaud, Francois Bonvin, Emmanuel Bourdieu, Philippe Bourgois, Sylvain Broccolichi, Patrick Champagne, Rosine Christin, Jean-Pierre Faguer, Sandrine Garcia, Remi Lenoir, Francoise Oeuvrard, Michel Pialoux, Louis Pinto, Denis Podalydes, Abdelmalek Sayad, Charles Soulie, and Loic J.D. Wacquant. 1999. *The Weight of the World: Social Suffering in Contemporary Society.* Translated by Priscilla Parkhurst Ferguson, Susan Emanuel, Joe Johnson, and Shoggy T. Waryn. Cambridge: Polity.

Brasfield, Charles. 2001. "Residential School Syndrome." *BC Medical Journal* 43, 2: 78-81.

Brody, Hugh. 1981. *Maps and Dreams: Indians and the British Columbia Frontier.* Vancouver: Waveland.

Cairns, Alan. 2000. *Citizens Plus.* Vancouver: UBC Press.

Cameron, Kirk, and Graham White. 1995. *Northern Governments in Transition: Political and Constitutional Development in the Yukon, Nunavut, and Northwest Territories.* Montreal: Institute for Research on Public Policy.

Canada-Délînê Uranium Table. 2002. *Action Plan: To Address Concerns Raised by the Community of Déline about Risks to Human and Environmental Health from Exposure to Radiation and Heavy Metals from the Former Port Radium Mine, Great Bear Lake (NWT).* 2nd ed. http://www.ainc-inac.gc.ca/nth/ct/ncsp/pubs/cudt/cudt-eng.asp.

Cardinal, Harold. 1969. *The Unjust Society.* Vancouver: Douglas and McIntyre.

Chambers, Brian. 1996. "History of the NWT Dene/Métis Comprehensive Land Claim Negotiations." PhD diss., Scott Polar Research Institute, Cambridge University.

Coates, Kenneth, and W. Morrison. N.d. *Treaty Research Report: Treaty 11 (1921).* Ottawa: Treaties and Historical Research Centre, INAC.

Colchester, M. 2002. "Indigenous Rights and the Collective Unconscious." *Anthropology Today* 18, 1: 1-3.

Conference Board of Canada. 2002. *Setting the Pace for Development: An Economic Outlook Report for the Northwest Territories.* Ottawa: Conference Board of Canada.

Cook, Curtis, and Juan Lindau, eds. 2000. *Aboriginal Rights and Self-Government.* Montreal: McGill-Queen's University Press.

Coulthard, Glen. 2007. "Subjects of Empire: Indigenous Peoples and the Politics of Recognition in Canada." *Contemporary Political Theory* 6, 4: 437-60.

Cruikshank, Julie. 1994. "Claiming Legitimacy: Prophecy Narratives from Northern Aboriginal Women." *American Indian Quarterly* 18, 2: 47-67.

–. 1998. *The Social Life of Stories: Narrative and Knowledge in the Yukon Territory.* Lincoln: University of Nebraska Press.

Dacks, Gurston, ed. 1990. *Devolution and Constitutional Development in the Canadian North.* Ottawa: Carleton University Press.

Daniel, E.V. 1996. *Charred Lullabies: Chapters in an Anthropography of Violence.* Princeton: Princeton University Press.

Das, Veena. 1995. *Critical Events: An Anthropological Perspective on Contemporary India.* New Delhi: Oxford University Press.

Das, Veena, Arthur Kleinman, Mamphela Ramphele, and Pamela Reynolds, eds. 2000. *Violence and Subjectivity.* Berkeley: University of California Press.

Das, Veena, Arthur Kleinman, Margaret Lock, Mamphela Ramphele, and Pamela Reynolds. 2001. *Remaking a World: Violence, Social Suffering, and Recovery.* Berkeley: University of California Press.

Dehcho First Nations. 1998. *The Dehcho Proposal.* Fort Simpson: DFN.

–. 2000. *21 Common Ground Principles between Canada and the Dehcho First Nations.* Fort Simpson: DFN.

–. 2002a. "Dehcho Interim Measures Agreement Main Table Rolling Draft." January.

–. 2002b. *Options for Governance in the Dehcho.* Fort Simpson: DFN.

Délînê First Nation. 2005. *If Only We Had Known: The History of Port Radium as Told by the Sahtuot'ine.* Délînê: Délînê First Nation.

Deloria, Vine, Jr. 2004. "Philosophy and the Tribal Peoples." In *American Indian Thought: Philosophical Essays,* ed. Anne Waters, 3-12. Oxford: Blackwell Publishing.

Dene Nation. 1984. *Denendeh: A Dene Celebration.* Yellowknife: Dene Nation.

Dene Nation and Métis Association of the NWT. 1981. *Public Government for the People of the North.* Yellowknife: Dene Nation.

–. 1988. *Devolution of Powers to the Government of the Northwest Territories: Provincehood and Aboriginal Self-Government.* Yellowknife: Dene Nation.

Dickerson, Mark O. 1992. *Whose North? Political Change, Political Development, and Self-Government in the Northwest Territories.* Vancouver: UBC Press.

Duran, Eduardo, and Bonnie Duran. 1995. *Native American Postcolonial Psychology.* New York: SUNY.

Duran, Eduardo, Bonnie Duran, and Maria Yellow Horse Brave Heart. 1998. "Native Americans and the Trauma of History." In *Studying Native America: Problems and Prospects,* ed. Russell Thornton, 60-76. Madison: University of Wisconsin Press.

Fabian, Johannes. 1983. *Time and the Other: How Anthropology Makes Its Object.* New York: Columbia University Press.

Fanon, Frantz. 1967. *The Wretched of the Earth.* London: Penguin Books.

Farmer, Paul. 1997. "On Suffering and Structural Violence: A View from Below." In *Social Suffering,* ed. A. Kleinman, V. Das, and M. Lock, 261-84. Berkeley: University of California Press.

–. 2005. *Pathologies of Power: Health, Human Rights, and the New War on the Poor.* Berkeley: University of California Press.

Feit, Harvey A. 1998. "Reflections on Local Knowledge and Institutionalized Resource Management: Differences, Dominance, Decentralization." In *Aboriginal Environmental Knowledge in the North,* ed. Louis-Jacques Dorais, Murielle Nagy, and Ludger Muller-Wille, 123-48. Quebec: Laval University-Gétic.

Fixico, Donald. 2003. *The American Indian Mind in a Linear World.* New York: Routledge.

Flanagan, Tom. 2000. *First Nations: Second Thoughts.* Montreal: McGill-Queen's University Press.

Foucault, Michel. 1994. *Power: The Essential Works.* Vol. 3. Ed. James Faubion. London: Penguin.

Frank, Arthur W. 2001. "Can We Research Suffering?" *Qualitative Health Research* 11, 3: 353-62.

Fumoleau, Rene. 1976. *As Long as This Land Shall Last.* Toronto: McClelland and Stewart.

Government of Canada. 1984. *The Western Arctic Claim: The Inuvialuit Final Agreement.* Ottawa: Supply and Services.

–. 1992. *The Gwich'in Comprehensive Land Claim Agreement.* Ottawa: Supply and Services.

–. 1995. *The Sahtu Dene/Métis Comprehensive Land Claim Agreement.* Ottawa: Supply and Services.

–. 2001. *The Inuvialuit and Gwich'in Joint Self-Government Agreement-in-Principle*. Ottawa: Supply and Services.

–. 2003a. *The Délînê Self-Government Agreement-in-Principle*. Ottawa: Supply and Services.

–. 2003b. *The Tli Cho Comprehensive Land Claim and Self-Government Agreement*. Ottawa: Supply and Services.

–. 2005. *First Nations-Crown Political Accord on the Recognition and Implementation of First Nations Governments*. www.afn.ca/article.asp?id=1218.

Government of Canada. Auditor General of Canada. 1996. Chapter 33: Indian and Northern Affairs Canada – Funding Arrangements for First Nations. Ottawa: Supply and Services.

–. 1998. Chapter 14: Indian and Northern Affairs Canada – Comprehensive Land Claims. Ottawa: Supply and Services.

–. 1999. Chapter 10: Indian and Northern Affairs Canada – Follow Up. Ottawa: Supply and Services.

–. 2001. Chapter 12: Follow Up of Recommendations in Previous Reports. Ottawa: Supply and Services.

–. 2002. Chapter 1: Streamlining First Nations Reporting to Federal Organizations. Ottawa: Supply and Services.

–. 2003. Chapter 6: Federal Government Support to First Nations – Housing on Reserves. Ottawa: Supply and Services.

–. 2004. Chapter 8: Managing Government – Financial Information. Ottawa: Supply and Services.

Government of Canada. Department of Indian Affairs. 1969. *Statement of the Government of Canada on Indian Policy [The White Paper]*. Ottawa: Supply and Services.

–. 1995. *The Aboriginal Inherent Right to Self-Government: Federal Policy Guide*. Ottawa: Supply and Services.

–. 1998. *Gathering Strength: An Aboriginal Action Plan*. Ottawa: Minister of Supply and Services.

–. 2001. *Canada-Délînê Uranium Table Action Plan*. Ottawa: Supply and Services.

– (with Walter Nelson et al.). 1970 [1959]. "Report of the Commission Appointed to Investigate the Unfulfilled Provisions of Treaties 8 and 11 as They Apply to the Indians of the Mackenzie District." Reprinted by the Indian-Eskimo Association of Canada.

Government of Canada. Statistics Canada. 2003. *Aboriginal Peoples Survey 2001: Initial Findings: Well-Being of the Non-Reserve Aboriginal Population*. Ottawa: Minister of Industry.

Government of Canada. Treasury Board of Canada. 2003. *Main Estimates 2003-2004*. Indian and Northern Affairs Canada and Canadian Polar Commission. www.tbs-sct.gc.ca/rma/dpr/03-04/INAC-AINC/INAC-AINCd3401_e.asp#fint.

Government of the Northwest Territories. Bureau of Statistics. 2006. "Percentage of Aboriginal Population 15 Years and Older, by Ability to Speak an Aboriginal Language." http://www.stats.gov.nt.ca/Statinfo/Language/Language.html.

–. 2007. *Summary of NWT Community Statistics, 2007*. Yellowknife: GNWT.

Green, Joyce. 1993. "Constitutionalising the Patriarchy: Aboriginal Women and Aboriginal Government." *Constitutional Forum* 4, 4: 110-20.

–, ed. 2008. *Making Space for Indigenous Feminism*. London: Zed Books.

Halifax, Terry. 1999. "A village thrown into a nuclear age." *News North*, October 25.

Helm, June. 2000. *The People of Denendeh*. Montreal: McGill-Queen's University Press.

Helm, June, and Nancy Lurie. 1961. "The Dogrib Hand Game." Bulletin 205, Anthropological Series 71. National Museum, Ottawa.

Hylton, John, ed. 1999. *Aboriginal Self-Government in Canada: Current Trends and Issues*. 2nd ed. Saskatoon: Purich.

Inuvialuit Regional Corporation and Gwich'in Tribal Council. 1992. *Proposal for a Western Arctic Municipality*. Inuvik: Inuvialuit Regional Corporation and Gwich'in Tribal Council.

Irlbacher-Fox, Stephanie. 2004. "Indigenous Self-Government Negotiations in the NWT, Canada: Time, Reality, and Social Suffering." PhD diss., Scott Polar Research Institute, Department of Geography, Faculty of Earth Sciences, University of Cambridge.

–. 2008. "Justice Authorities in Self-Government Agreements: The Importance of Conditions and Mechanisms of Implementation." In *Moving towards Justice: Legal Traditions and Aboriginal Justice,* ed. John Whyte, 130-41. Saskatoon: Purich.

Irlbacher-Fox, Stephanie, and Stephen Mills. 2007. *Devolution and Resource Revenue Sharing in the Canadian North.* Toronto: Walter and Duncan Gordon Foundation.

Ivison, Duncan, Paul Patton, and Will Sanders, eds. 2000. *Political Theory and the Rights of Indigenous Peoples.* Cambridge: Cambridge University Press.

Jojola, Ted. 2004. "Notes on Identity, Time, Space and Place." In *American Indian Thought: Philosophical Essays,* ed. Anne Waters, 87-96. Oxford: Blackwell Publishing.

Kenrick, Justin, and Jerome Lewis. 2004. "Indigenous Peoples Rights and the Politics of the Term 'Indigenous.'" *Anthropology Today* 20, 2: 4-9.

King, Thomas. 2003. *The Truth about Stories: A Native Narrative.* Minneapolis: University of Minnesota Press.

Kirmayer, Laurence, and Gail Valaskakis. 2008. *Healing Traditions: The Mental Health of Aboriginal Peoples in Canada.* Vancouver: UBC Press.

Kleinman, Arthur. 1988. *The Illness Narratives: Suffering, Healing, and the Human Condition.* New York: Basic Books.

Kleinman, Arthur, and J. Kleinman. 1991. "Suffering and Its Professional Transformation: Toward an Ethnography of Interpersonal Experience." *Culture, Medicine, and Psychiatry* 15: 275-301.

Kulchyski, Peter. 2005. *Like the Sound of a Drum: Aboriginal Cultural Politics in Denendeh and Nunavut.* Winnipeg: University of Manitoba Press.

Kuper, Adam. 2003a. "The Return of the Native." *Current Anthropology* 44, 3: 389-402.

–. 2003b. "Return of the Native." *New Humanist* 118, 3: 5-8.

Ladner, Keira. 2001. "Negotiated Inferiority: Visions of a Renewed Relationship between Unequal Partners in Confederation." *American Review of Canadian Studies* 31, 1 and 2: 241-64.

MacDonnell, Diane. 1986. *Theories of Discourse: An Introduction.* Oxford Mills: Blackwell.

Macklem, Patrick. 2001. *Indigenous Difference and the Constitution of Canada.* Toronto: University of Toronto Press.

MacMillan, H.L., A.B. MacMillan, D.R. Offord, and J.L. Dingle. 1996. "Aboriginal Health." *Canadian Medical Association Journal* 155, 11: 1569-78.

Maybury-Lewis, David. 1997. *Indigenous Peoples, Ethnic Groups, and the State.* Boston: Allyn and Bacon.

McCarthy, Martha. 1995. *From the Great River to the Ends of the Earth: Oblate Missions to the Dene 1847-1921.* Edmonton: University of Alberta Press.

Memmi, Albert. 1990. *The Colonizer and the Colonized.* London: Earthscan.

–. 2000. *Racism.* Trans. Steve Martinot. Minneapolis: University of Minnesota Press.

Mihesuah, Devon A. 2003. "Decolonizing Our Diets by Recovering Our Ancestors' Gardens." *American Indian Quarterly* 27, 3-4: 807-39.

Miller, Bruce. 2003. *Invisible Indigenes: The Politics of Non-Recognition.* Lincoln: University of Nebraska Press.

Morgan, David, and Ian Wilkinson. 2001. "The Problem of Suffering and the Sociological Task of Theodicy." *European Journal of Social Theory* 4, 2: 199-214.

Morris, David. 1991. *The Culture of Pain.* Berkeley: University of California Press.

Morrison, W.R. 1983. *A Survey of the History and Claims of the Native Peoples of Northern Canada.* Ottawa: Department of Indian Affairs and Northern Development.

Morrow, Phyllis, and Chase Hensel. 1992. "Hidden Dissension: Minority-Majority Relationships and the Use of Contested Terminology." *Arctic Anthropology* 29, 1: 38-52.

Moss, Robert. 2005. *Dreamways of the Iroquois: Honoring the Secret Wishes of the Soul.* Rochester: Destiny Books.

Nadasdy, Paul. 1999. "The Politics of TEK: Power and the 'Integration' of Knowledge." *Arctic Anthropology* 36, 1-2: 1-18.

–. 2003. *Hunters and Bureaucrats: Power, Knowledge, and Aboriginal-State Relations in the Southwest Yukon.* Vancouver: UBC Press.

Newhouse, David, and Yale Belanger. 2001. "Aboriginal Self-Government in Canada: A

Review of the Literature Since 1960." Unpublished paper. Trent University, Peterborough, ON.

Ouellette, Grace. 2002. *The Fourth World: An Indigenous Perspective on Feminism and Aboriginal Women's Activism.* Halifax: Fernwood.

Pagden, Anthony. 1982. *The Fall of Natural Man: The American Indian and the Origins of Comparative Ethnology.* Cambridge: Cambridge University Press.

Patterson, Lisa. 2006. *Aboriginal Round Table to Kelowna Accord: Aboriginal Policy Negotiations, 2004-2005.* Ottawa: Library of Parliament Political and Social Affairs Division.

Penikett, Tony. 2006. *Reconciliation: First Nations Treaty Making in British Columbia.* Vancouver: Douglas and McIntyre.

Royal Commission on Aboriginal Peoples. 1996. *Final Report: Volumes 1-6.* Ottawa: Libraxus.

Russell, Peter. 2002. "Lands and Governance Workshop, Trout Lake 8 May 23-24, 2002." Report of facilitator, Trout Lake, NWT.

Ryan, Joan. 1995. *Doing Things the Right Way: Dene Traditional Justice in Lac LaMartre, NWT.* Calgary: University of Calgary Press.

Said, Edward. 1976. *Orientalism.* New York: Penguin.

Samson, Colin. 2003. *A Way of Life That Does Not Exist: Canada and the Extinguishment of the Innu.* London: Verso.

–. 2008. "A Colonial Double Bind: Social and Historical Contexts of Innu Mental Health." In *Healing Traditions: The Mental Health of Aboriginal Peoples in Canada,* ed. Laurence Kirmayer and Gail Valaskakis, 109-39. Vancouver: UBC Press.

Scheper-Hughes, Nancy. 1992. *Death without Weeping: The Violence of Everyday Life in Brazil.* Berkeley: University of California Press.

–. 1998. "Undoing: Social Suffering and the Politics of Remorse in the New South Africa." *Social Justice* 25: 114-42.

Scott, C.H., ed. 2001. *Aboriginal Autonomy and Development in Northern Quebec and Labrador.* Vancouver: UBC Press.

Scott, James C. 1987. *Weapons of the Weak.* New Haven: Yale University Press.

–. 1990. *Domination and the Arts of Resistance: Hidden Transcripts.* New Haven: Yale University Press.

Simpson, Leanne. 2006. "Birthing an Indigenous Resurgence: Decolonizing Our Pregnancy and Birthing Ceremonies." In *Until Our Hearts Are on the Ground: Aboriginal Mothering, Oppression, Resistance, and Rebirth,* ed. Memee Lavell-Harvard and Jeanette Corniere-Lavell, 25-33. Toronto: Demeter Press.

Slobodin, Richard. 1981. "Kutchin." In *Handbook of North American Indians, Volume 5: Subarctic,* ed. D. Damas, 514-32. Washington, DC: Smithsonian Institution Press.

Smith, Derek G. 1984. "Mackenzie Delta Eskimo." In *Handbook of North American Indians, Volume 5: Arctic,* ed. D. Damas, 347-58. Washington, DC: Smithsonian Institution Press.

Spaeder, Joseph, and Harvey A. Feit, eds. 2005. *Co-Management and Indigenous Communities: Barriers and Bridges to Decentralized Resource Management.* Special issue of *Anthropologica* 47, 2.

Taylor, Amy, and Marlo Raynolds. 2006. *Thinking Like an Owner: Overhauling the Royalty and Tax Treatment of Alberta's Oil Sands.* Edmonton: Pembina Institute.

Thompson, Janna. 2002. *Taking Responsibility for the Past: Reparation and Historical Justice.* Cambridge: Polity.

Tuhiwai-Smith, Linda. 1999. *Decolonizing Methodologies: Research and Indigenous Peoples.* London: Zed Books.

Tully, James. 1995. *Strange Multiplicity: Constitutionalism in an Age of Diversity.* Cambridge: Cambridge University Press.

–. 2000. "A Just Relationship between Aboriginal and Non-Aboriginal Peoples of Canada." In *Aboriginal Rights and Self-Government,* ed. Curtis Cook and Juan Lindau, 39-71. Montreal: McGill-Queen's University Press.

Turner, Dale. 2004. "Oral Traditions and the Politics of (Mis)Recognition." In *American*

*Indian Thought: Philosophical Essays,* ed. Anne Waters, 229-38. Oxford: Blackwell Publishing.

–. 2006. *This Is Not a Peace Pipe: Towards a Critical Indigenous Philosophy.* Toronto: University of Toronto Press.

"Uranium Exposure Insufficient to Cause Cancer in Délîné Workers." 2005. CBC.ca. http://www.cbc.ca/north (accessed August 12, 2005).

Usher, Peter J. 2003. "Environment, Race, and Nation Reconsidered: Reflections on Aboriginal Land Claims in Canada." *Canadian Geographer* 47, 4: 365-82.

Van Camp, Rosa. 1989. "Bishop Paul Piche." *Arctic* 42, 2: 168-70.

Van Dijk, Teun. 1985. *Handbook of Discourse Analysis.* 4 Vols. London: Academic Press.

Venne, Sharon. 1998. *Our Elders Understand Our Rights.* Vancouver: Theytus Books.

Waldron, Jeremy. 1992. "Superseding Historic Injustice." *Ethics* 103, 1: 4-28.

Warry, Wayne. 1998. *Unfinished Dreams: Community Healing and the Reality of Aboriginal Self-Government.* Toronto: University of Toronto Press.

Waters, Anne, ed. 2004. *American Indian Thought: Philosophical Essays.* Oxford: Blackwell.

Watkins, Mel. 1977. *Dene Nation: The Colony Within.* Toronto: University of Toronto Press.

Weaver, Sally. 1984. "Indian Self-Government: A Concept in Need of a Definition." In *Pathways to Self-Determination: Canadian Indians and the Canadian State,* ed. L. Little Bear, M. Boldt, and J.A. Long, 65-68. Toronto: University of Toronto Press.

Wesley-Esquimaux, Cynthia. 2007. "The Intergenerational Transmission of Historic Trauma and Grief." In *Indigenous Affairs: Social Suffering,* ed. Jack Hicks and Sille Stidsen, 6-11. Copenhagen: International Working Group on Indigenous Affairs.

Wilkinson, Iain. 2001. "Thinking with Suffering." *Cultural Values* 5: 421-44.

–. 2005. *Suffering: A Sociological Introduction.* Cambridge: Polity.

–. 2006. "Editorial: Social Suffering and Health Risk." *Social Suffering and Health Risk.* Special issue of *Health Risk and Society* 8, 1: 1-8.

Wilson, Waziyatawin Angela, and Michael Yellow Bird, eds. 2005. *For Indigenous Eyes Only: A Decolonization Handbook.* Santa Fe: School of American Research.

Woolford, Andrew. 2005. *Between Justice and Certainty: Treaty Making in British Columbia.* Vancouver: UBC Press.

Young, Marion Iris. 2000. *Inclusion and Democracy.* New York: Oxford University Press.

Yellow Horse Brave Heart, Maria, and Lemyra DeBruyn. 1998. "The American Indian Holocaust: Healing Historical Unresolved Grief." *Journal of the National Center* 8: 60-79.

# Index

Note: "(f)" after a page number indicates a figure. "(m)" after a page number indicates a map.

Set in Stone by Kroeger Enterprises

Printed and bound in Canada by Friesens

Copy editor: Dallas Harrison

Proofreader: Sarah Munro

Indexer: Dianne Tiefensee

Cartographer: Eric Leinberger